Leading Extreme Projects

Leading Extreme Projects explores the challenges, obstacles and techniques associated with running large projects in some of the most challenging environments and economies in the world. From an oil and gas program in the Amazon with a background of drug trafficking, delicate indigenous communities and some of the most challenging logistics; to a mining project in West Africa involving a consortium of state and private contractors plus a global supply chain. From a shipping efficiency project involving two joint venture programs with stakeholders from the European, North and South American and Asian continents; to a hostile gold project stakeholder management process in Central America involving substantial cultural differences between the north and the south.

The authors' insights and advice will help the reader understand the global context of leadership in these extreme projects as well as the nature of the structures and teams required to create, design, operate and transfer global capital programs. In particular, they provide perspectives on the issues of leading cross-cultural teams, working amongst sensitive indigenous people and transferring knowledge to build local capacity.

This is an important reference text for senior executives involved in both the strategy and the delivery side of extreme projects, as well as for those researching and studying the field.

Alejandro Arroyo has more than 30 years experience as operator and consultant in global project logistics, stakeholder management, environmental management, and strategic contextual assessment with respect to mining, oil and gas, hydropower, nuclear power and alternative energy projects. Alejandro has worked for and cooperated with a long list of well-known companies in both the natural resources and global transportation industries, such as Pan American Silver; Silver Standard; Aura Minerals; Talisman Energy; Talon Metals; AECL-CANDU; ABB; Alstom; FMC Lithium; ZIM Israel Navigation; and many others.

Thomas Grisham has 40 years of project management and PMO experience gained on projects across a variety of business models and sectors, including medical, infrastructure, transportation, commercial, communications, finance, consulting, utilities, manufacturing, business development and more. Thomas has gained this experience in 73 countries, with expat assignments in Turkey, Saudi Arabia, Thailand, Japan, Korea, China and Hong Kong, and has experience with over 400 companies globally from Abbott Labs to ZTE.

Leading Extreme Projects

Strategy, Risk and Resilience in Practice

Alejandro Arroyo and Thomas Grisham

Routledge
Taylor & Francis Group

LONDON AND NEW YORK

First published in paperback 2024

First published 2017
by Routledge
4 Park Square, Milton Park, Abingdon, Oxon OX14 4RN

and by Routledge
605 Third Avenue, New York, NY 10158

Routledge is an imprint of the Taylor & Francis Group, an informa business

Publisher's Note
The publisher has gone to great lengths to ensure the quality of this reprint but
points out that some imperfections in the original copies may be apparent.

British Library Cataloguing-in-Publication Data
A catalogue record for this book is available from the British Library

Library of Congress Cataloging-in-Publication Data
A catalog record for this book is available from the Library of Congress

ISBN: 978-1-4724-6312-8 (hbk)
ISBN: 978-1-03-283728-4 (pbk)
ISBN: 978-1-315-59182-7 (ebk)

DOI: 10.4324/9781315591827

Typeset in Bembo
by codeMantra

Contents

List of figures   vi

1   Introduction: how extreme conditions challenge traditional project methodology in the oil and gas industry   1

2   Mining and extreme transport: why stakeholders should look twice before committing   36

3   Mining and extreme infrastructure: what shareholders, directors, and management should look at twice before committing   60

4   Mining operations in uncertain environments: what executives and investors should take good care of well in advance   84

5   Mining and regional infrastructure operations in volatile contexts: what operations executives should first consider when deploying resources   107

6   Ocean and river logistics in emerging contexts: variables PMs should pay special attention to in order to accomplish a sustainable operation   127

7   Mining operations in emerging Asia and Oceania: variables beyond the ordinary PMs should render a special look before committing technology and financial resources   148

8   Mining operations in emerging eastern and western Africa: where to keep a sharp eye on the operations and how to balance global context variables with those of a project in extreme settings   163

9   Suggestions for practice   178

Index   191

List of figures

1.1	CPE structure.	3
1.2	CPE for global projects.	4
1.3	Average level Morona River.	6
1.4	Fast boat on Morona River.	7
1.5	Load factor in fast boats.	8
1.6	Level changes Morona River.	10
1.7	Iquitos refinery floating berth at low tide.	11
1.8	Total helicopter efficiency.	15
1.9	Peruvian map and distances to base camp 1.	17
1.10	CPE structure.	21
1.11	Material import circuit.	22
1.12	A global internet.	27
2.1	Argentina's NW region and Chile's region II.	37
2.2	Situational leadership.	39
2.3	San Juan River and ports of entry.	46
2.4	Sources of risk.	47
2.5	Northern Canada's Mackenzie River.	51
2.6	Hay River Port and railway facilities.	52
2.7	Modular homes carried on a flat-type barge.	54
2.8	Multi-barge configuration on Hudson Bay.	55
2.9	Northwest passage routing.	57
3.1	Map of Brazil.	61
3.2	Infrastructure in Pará State.	63
3.3	Vila do Conde Port Terminal 1.	63
3.4	Gross occupation rates.	64
3.5	Barge operations at VDC Port Terminal, Pará.	65
3.6	Brazilian indigenous communities.	65
3.7	Piers 1, 2, 3 Ponta da Madeira and Itaqui Port facilities.	66
3.8	Intended dune area for dry bulk operations.	67
3.9	Pecem Port layout on existing and future facilities.	68
3.10	Suape's Cocaia Island future dry bulk terminal and expansion areas on the sides.	69
3.11	Espadarte Port layout.	70
3.12	Interisland bridge linking the mainland with Espadarte Terminal.	70
3.13	Amapá State – Port of Santana.	78
3.14	Aerial view of Pecem Port facilities.	79

3.15   LNG re-gasification operation at Pecem Port.   80
4.1   Location.   85
4.2   Port locations.   87
4.3   River crossing.   88
4.4   Projects infrastructure, preliminary layout 1.   100
4.5   Projects infrastructure, preliminary layout 2.   101
4.6   Typical global CPE.   105
5.1   Jama border passage facilities on the Argentine side.   111
5.2   View of the existing topography around Paso de Jama border passage.   113
5.3   Land-bridge layout.   115
5.4   Hofstede and GLOBE comparison.   118
5.5   Cultures.   125
6.1   Ship owners clearing curves, quarters 1–3, 2000.   129
6.2   Proposal.   138
6.3   Joint venture showing critical primary players and instrumental
       secondary players.   138
7.1   Stakeholder management model.   150
7.2   Project types – procurement.   154
7.3   Drilling vessel off coast of Papua New Guinea.   158
8.1   Total road extension from port of entry to the job-site.   164
8.2   Bridge over Fiherenana River, 7 KM away from Toliara.   165
8.3   View of dirt roads near the job site.   167
8.4   View of houses by the road.   167
8.5   Structural restrictions.   168
8.6   Cameroon and Gabon's inland deposits and planned railway line.   172
8.7   New deep-water port location and main railway line and its
       extension stretch into DRC.   173

1 Introduction

How extreme conditions challenge
traditional project methodology
in the oil and gas industry

We will use case studies to demonstrate the existing gap between the way decision making is taken at the higher layers of an organization and how those decisions actually work on the job-site. Such a gap encompasses a number of fields or challenges that can be framed within operations management, cross-cultural management, stakeholder management, environmental management, and communications management. By connecting the various dimensions that are broken down in the upcoming case studies, we'll also provide a set of suggestions for avoiding or at least diminishing the impact on future projects. We have explained and developed the structure of each case study in detail, but the names of the participants have been changed.

These case studies describe projects that included construction of two significant hydrocarbon projects in the Americas which involved Canadians and South American nationals from Peru, Bolivia, and Argentina, and included both Americans and Europeans. The first case study concerns a Canadian oil and gas organization that ran heavily overbudget while planning the development of its second rig in the Peruvian Amazon rainforest. Construction related to a new exploration site which included inland ports, barge operations, fast boats, rotor-craft operations (helicopters), ground transportation, warehousing management, and rainforest corridors.

The program generated significant challenges for the participating teams such as:

- tricky suppliers (a cartel of a small number of suppliers),
- autocratic leadership style (on the part of some critical suppliers),
- lack of infrastructure,
- unpredictable operational windows,
- lack of reliable river draught variation data,
- internal management malpractice,
- lack of operational monitoring and financial control,
- poor communicational strategy,
- contracting failures in aerial operations,
- accelerating environmental hazards and restrictions,
- and many other management issues which we will analyze in detail as we move on to the next section.

Substantial cross-cultural gaps also became apparent amongst the project participants both at the headquarters in Canada and their branch offices in Peru, as well as between individuals who were posted in the field deep in the Peruvian jungle. All these variables challenge what theory suggests as good project management practices. Consequently, such practices are highly influenced by the overall contextual circumstances of a given project, particularly in relation to operations, culture, financial arrangements, and infrastructure.

The second case study describes comparable operational challenges in the Peruvian rainforest, though the focus in this case was the project's sustainability profile and the hazards the organization faced as a consequence of the way operations were managed. The role of indigenous communities in project sustainability, along with the challenge of complex environmental management, forms part of a series of topics that are intended to complement the first case study.

A. Case study: oil exploration operations in the Peruvian rainforest

1. *Background to the case*

A Canada-based oil and gas organization (we will call it Stallion Enterprises), with a number of existing operations and explorations, mostly across the developed world, decided to extend its ongoing exploration activities in Peru. For the new project, it depended on its staff based in Lima to manage an operating rig that needed to be dismantled and moved to a location nearby within northern Peru's Loreto department close to the Ecuadorian border. For the project to succeed, the entire facility had to be moved from one exploration site to another.

The proximity of the new job site to the Ecuadorian border may be considered by the unskilled observer (usually a Corporate Operational Officer [COO] comfortably seated in his 36-story skyscraper in Canada) as an advantage. However, it could also represent a risk depending on the political and contextual circumstances at a given point in time – Peru and Ecuador in this particular case. Contextual analysis may also be more challenging when the province or state where the project is located follows a different political line from that of the federal government, either for better or worse. Latin American countries are often dominated by a 10-year cycle of growth or decline involving drastic change in political power and economic models. This alone can affect the project's sustainability if we consider that a hydrocarbon, mining, or energy project may easily require at least 10 years for construction and start operations.

Contextual analysis is a tough business in Latin America, no matter how reasonable or organized a given country, region, or administration. The picture can vary wildly at any given point in time because of the previously mentioned cycles, which may repeat themselves with greater or lesser intensity. Our first practical suggestion here is to leave the analysis to the experts: Latin Americans with field experience and residing in the region, not in Washington, New York, London, Toronto, or Sydney. Professionals in these ex-patriate locations tend towards theoretical or stereotypical perspectives on a region rather than focus on the way the problems on the ground should be tackled in practice. No extrapolation of visions, cultures, idiosyncrasies, or ethics count here. All that counts are the experience and common sense of locals, commodities that cannot be stored and reused of when needed.

Given the location of the project, Ecuador might seem a better option than Peru in terms of access or infrastructure of ocean terminals, roads, and inland terminals. However, the existing regulations on the transit of goods bound for a third world country, along with an indigenous community that held no ties with those on the Peruvian side, would have benefitted from separate analysis for which projects rarely have the time to invest.

Had the project involved two European countries, for example, Sweden and Norway, then any cross-border difficulties might have been easily modeled in terms of costs and time. South America as a whole is a different type of animal that demands not only separate assessments but also repetitive analysis given the constant shifts along a given cycle. Nature, facilities, communities, interests, systems, politics are and should be regarded as ever evolving, for better or for worse. Many areas of the globe, such as Africa, the Middle East, Central Asia, and Asia, share a similar level of unpredictability.

2. Program in detail

The branch office in Lima had budgeted some CAD240 million (Canadian dollars) to carry out dismantling, classifying parts and pieces on the ground, and loading them onto barges and/or rotor-crafts at both the base camp 1 and drilling station 1. The second stage of the operation was planned to involve discharging and handling on the ground all the material and equipment at base camp 2, followed by helicopter transport and final assembly at the second drilling site located a further 36 kilometers away. The Canadian headquarters staff regarded the budget as too high or suspiciously inflated, given their experience in other parts of the world with both onshore and offshore oil and gas operations. The company then decided to hire an operational auditing team to look into the way the plans were designed and eventually executed (the authors being part of this team).

The structure of the program included two projects as shown in Figure 1.1.

Global projects are composed of teams, colocated and virtual, from different organizations, in different countries, brought together to provide a service and a product, like that shown in Figure 1.1. Each organization has its own key performance indicators (KPIs), which hopefully are connected to strategy and success criteria. We think of a Collaborative Project Enterprise (CPE) as a business enterprise (Grisham 2009), and the Collaborative Project Enterprise lead (CPEL) is the CEO. The organizations come together for a time and then go their separate ways.

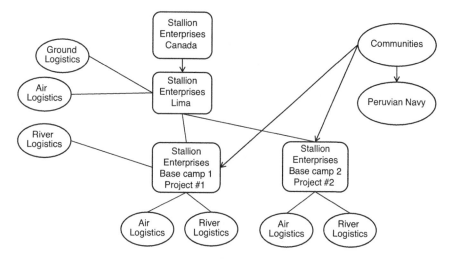

Figure 1.1 CPE structure.

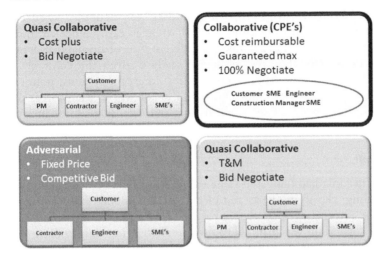

Figure 1.2 CPE for global projects.

One definition of collaborate is to cooperate with or willingly assist an enemy – economically speaking. Another definition is to cooperate with an organization or group with which one is not immediately connected. For enterprise, a definition is a project or an undertaking that is especially difficult, complicated, or risky. And a second definition is a unit of economic organization or activity, especially a business organization. So the challenge for a CPEL is to make the group of organizations feel like a single entity, with an overarching purpose or goal. She or he must create a CPE culture, then articulate it, and practice it consistently. Simply put, leadership and the desire to follow are essential.

Project structures matter as well and are often doomed from the beginning. Have a look at Figure 1.3. At one extreme is the conventional approach used frequently by most organizations – competitive bidding. Of course, the techniques for this technique vary greatly, but in general a group of sellers submit bids for a project with no discussions. There are sometimes bidder conferences to answer questions, but conversations are normally prohibited between the buyer and seller. Then, normally, the low bid wins in a purely transactional relationship. Many organizations utilize a version of this approach but most often for smaller more simple transactions. As we will see in this case study, most of the agreements tended in this direction.

At the opposite extreme is the CPE approach. This option is wide ranging from negotiated agreements with multiple organizations to design-build, design-build-operate-transfer, and to public private partnerships (PPPs). Each of these options may indeed include multiple contract structures depending upon the risk and the appetite of the owner/user to shoulder some of it. In such structures, the importance of recognizing one person as the leader of the CPE is critical. In this way, the owner/user can eliminate contract barriers to open communications.

Operational challenges turned out to be of a different nature and severity given the remoteness of the rigging stations as well as its inaccessibility for both cargo and personnel as well as the heavy-lift and overdimensional pieces of equipment and machinery. It was the auditing team's expert eye, from multiple-site experience, that detected the smallest details apparent through body language, attitudes, and gestures that would not have been noticed. Gestures, expressions, and postures duly mixed with unclear responses and evasive attitudes on the part of the Lima-based staff brought about lots of red flags in a rather short period of time. But cultural gaps and responses to ethical dilemmas, compliance policies, concepts of loyalty, belongingness, risk aversion, uncertainty avoidance, or power distance dimensions tend to be quite different issues.

The common denominator that reduces inhibitions, preconceptions, and postures towards religion or race challenges is money. Recruiters should be vigilant to avoid letting home-based management be paid too much money, leaving operational staff, located far-way with a too modest share of the pie. Naturally, this may lead to a long discussion on what is right or wrong, convenient, or unadvisable as a compensation strategy. But again, this is not a Scandinavian-based project where the gap is minimal and frustrations are manageable. This is South America where not only the nationals, but also the expats too often tend to think that a project of this sort may become their life opportunity to accrue wealth, as if they were Incas facing the Spanish explorers.

This is too often a mistake that is repeated when a foreign-based firm develops a project in an isolated location where there is a lack of control and poor leadership. People are not that much different around the world when it comes to compensation and commitment, on what they may regard as fair or sensible. We no longer live in a world where the internet and global communications are incipient, almost unavailable, or accessible to just a few. Those companies that decide to overlook the existing compensation gaps between executives based abroad in the developed world and executives in the field or towns across the emerging world (even major cities) are by far more likely to face ethical imbalances.

Leaders should make the best effort to anticipate such issues in order to reduce their impact on costs and time and to avoid the potential damage this could exert on the project in terms of sustainability, should these events become public at home. It is unavoidable that sooner or later these mishaps will show up, and so it is essential to have a Plan B in place – risk planning is important. Money works as a lubricant across countries and cultures, and therefore deserves a second thought within the human resources Project Management (PM) dimension. It is actually up to the project developer to think of it prior to committing knowledge and capital. It should never be done during the execution or construction phase. On a US$3 billion project in India, money came from six banks, the Japanese Government, and a number of private US conglomerates, and involved the government of India as well. When the accusation of unfair economic advantage came to light in the international press, it required a public relations (PR) fire-drill to stamp out the blaze, despite the fact that the accusations were proven to be unfounded.

The existing base camp and the new one were located northwest of Iquitos in the Peruvian rainforest where access was restricted to river barges, and only rotor-crafts were able to reach the respective rigging stations deep in the jungle by the Ecuadorian border. There were no roads or even tiny rivers, just pure jungle. The existing distance between base camp 2 on Morona River and rigging station #1 was 36 KM by air, whereas only 21 KM by air separated base camp 2 on the Pastaza River from rigging station #2. However, connecting two base camps by barge in order to carry out an entire river-based operation and later carry on from base camp 2 up to its rigging station by air meant 565 KM of navigation. Moreover, the river transit time meant 10 days, depending on the existing draught and operational windows on both rivers throughout the year. This made the entire operation tricky as no reasonable planning was feasible. To make things even worse, the two rivers did not share the same tide patterns affecting the whole barging operation.

You may wonder at this point why a proper plan could not be carried out and why river draught data was not readily available when needed. In areas where services are cartelized and/or mostly controlled by a dominant player, it is fairly common to observe such interferences along the way when it comes to planning. Data does exist and became to a certain extent available in this particular case. However, its quality left much to be desired and gave the river barge suppliers a lot of discretion on whether to undertake a certain round trip, if it would be better to wait for the tide to rise before committing monies, floating stock, and personnel. Naturally, the project developers were always in a rush, as is the case on almost every project, struggling against delays and increasing costs. And they were held responsible for whatever extra costs might arise out of any act of nature. Figure 1.3 clearly exhibits what the operational restrictions were with respect to river transportation during the year. Both base camps and rigging stations had to be supplied with gas oil and fuel for the generators, equipment, and aircrafts to keep operational, whereas the entire facilities needed foodstuff, medicines and water supply on a 24/7 hour basis.

The sailing windows turned out to be rather limited as the available floating stock was made up of pusher boats, self-propelled barges, and conventional barges which ranged from 5 to 8 feet deep; Whereas the optimal depth to maximize the operational window turned out to be from 5- to 6-feet deep. Once in the jungle any operations manager must make the best use of what is readily available. In most of the cases, neither time nor budget is available either to undertake naval construction that would fit the optimal use of the river throughout the year or to adjust the schedule. Naturally, an oil and gas project that counts on plenty of time for planning and thinking is one thing. One may allocate resources for light naval construction, berths, roads, bridges, communications, energy supply, and further facilities to make operations more efficient and dependence weak. It is something else for a project where the opportunity window is short and therefore calls for rapid decision making. Decisions can be made either in isolation on the job site owing to urgencies or jointly by the PM and the headquarters. Either way, PMs in the field hold an enormous power to persuade headquarters to make decisions that are often in their own rather than in the projects' best interests.

Our experience as auditors here, as well as on many other projects, clearly indicates that quick decision making is not a good approach for PM best practices. Actually, it is the best recipe for a project to degrade sustainability and eventually fade away. Also,

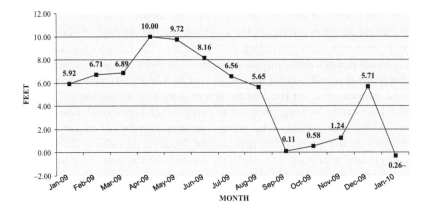

Figure 1.3 Average level Morona River.

multitasking is often erroneously regarded as a valuable skill when it comes to making tough decisions in a short period of time. It may be so in finance or marketing, but definitely not in remote operations. An individual's decisional autonomy on a manufacturing line is often considered critical to quality, as demonstrated by Ford or Toyota. Though we tend to agree in principle, the least advisable strategy for remote projects is to grant a logistics or operations manager in the field decisional autonomy when it comes to hydrocarbon projects in emerging markets.

Logistic operations and quality, though undoubtedly intertwined, must run on different roads, as otherwise it may mean a free ticket towards corruption in its many forms (e.g., double invoicing, overcharging, ghost invoicing, or suppliers' discrimination). Operations monitoring and control is as critical as operations planning and execution in that those carrying out these functions should by all means be knowledgeable – which does not mean acquiring knowledge as they work. However, most expats in South America tend to be generalists, and they bring with them a background that may turn out to be suitable or even reasonably solid in other fields and geographical contexts. The Board of Directors (BOD) should pay much more attention about who they hire to develop a project. Again, Scandinavia is one thing and Peru something very different, no matter the angle one uses to analyze it.

Continuing on the river operations, there was also a very lucrative business, though in a smaller scale. In jungle logistic operations across South America, this is called "fast boats," as shown in Figure 1.4. This modality involved a rather regular and even increasingly repetitive utilization of these boats on an "emergency" basis in order to supply the base camps with last-minute orders that could not be carried on a chopper or light aircraft owing to space or weight restrictions, or could not withstand the relatively longer transit time of a barge. Typically, the cargoes in high last-minute demand were medicines, beverages, foodstuffs, or a specific spare part required by the operations manager at the drilling station. Surprisingly, the auditing team discovered that these fast boats were hired too often. The rates were too high compared to the value of the fast boat or the goods they carried. Moreover, the staff justified these and other kinds of last-minute orders by alleging that the drilling stations CAD250,000 daily running cost could be badly impacted if it had to stop operating as a result.

Figure 1.4 Fast boat on Morona River.

The fast boats belonged to the indigenous communities living around Iquitos on the Marañon River, who made their living on this type of operation under the supervision of the Peruvian navy – all of which made the auditors assume that there was a broader perspective to consider. The Peruvian navy was at all times supportive of the fast boat operations and organization, which clearly indicated to the president that the authority should always be kept happy – in other words, let us make use of a piece of common sense. Always, having an appreciation of how things work locally, without judgment, is essential. As with culture, the key is for a project leader to adapt to the local circumstances, yet maintain their values. He or she must use the local approach rather than trying to impose his or her own ways.

Surprisingly, the fast boat load factors as a measure of productivity were fairly low, as shown in Figure 1.5.

Personnel transportation from Peru's hub city of Iquitos up to the base camps was carried out by light aircraft capable of transporting between 10 and 18 passengers per trip. Occasionally, larger aircrafts were shared with an Argentine oil organization, which happened to be fairly active in the area, and found themselves in the same situation of having to look for innovative ways to lower their operating costs in the area. Helicopters did play a decisive role in carrying both cargo and personnel between the base camps and their respective drilling stations deep in the jungle. Three foreign organizations operating different types of rotor-crafts signed long-term contracts to conduct operations over a six-year period.

An external operational audit team was quickly gathered, hired, and sent out to the scene to look into the entire operation in order to identify the issues and to learn why such a drain of capital resources was occurring. The auditing team was integrated by two Canadian passport holders of Latin American origin, so any purposeful cultural screens imposed in Lima could be lifted. At this point, it is important to highlight that by the time the audit was undertaken this organization had other physical assets deployed mostly across Canada, the USA, the North Atlantic, and minor operations in Southeast Asia – but nothing around South America.

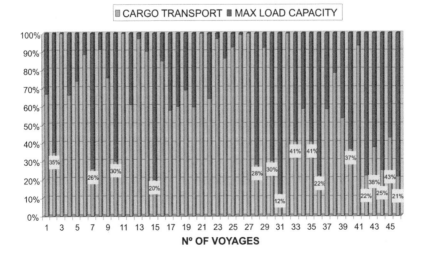

Figure 1.5 Load factor in fast boats.

3. *Audit findings*

Contrary to what a technical auditor would normally expect to see once at the job-site, it was the body language and evasive attitudes of the Lima-based staff that provided the auditing team with an unexpected and extraordinary number of issues or red flags that needed to be addressed. Some examples are worth mentioning and described below.

The contract manager supplied the auditing team with a huge quantity of contracts for us to look into without any kind of explanation or classification of their type, condition, origin, objective, and so forth, right after which he excused himself for an "important" meeting he must attend. The auditing team had a strong impression that the contract manager intended to overwhelm them with tons of papers and countless folders in a disorganized manner in order to confuse, disorient, and pressure, given the short period of time available to survey the contracts.

The auditing team was then led to the logistic manager's office for an introduction. This manager was busy at the phone for at least 20 minutes. The auditing team left the office without even a greeting from the manager. We returned to the office later to witness the logistic manager suddenly pick up the phone and engage in another long chat. By then, we had only had eye contact with the manager – predator and prey perhaps?

The auditors intended to join the general manager for lunch, as he was alone at the restaurant, but he avoided the situation by alleging that he had a key meeting in a few minutes and must end his lunch immediately. It was both surprising and funny to compare the relative speed of his lunch when we arrived, and when he departed – a full meal had suddenly become a light snack.

We finally met with the Lima-based general manager, of Canadian origin, in a small office, other than his, after waiting for more than one hour. He looked nervous and anxious, and seemed to want to leave the room as soon as possible. Then, he systematically highlighted the need to keep the rigs duly supplied 24/7 given its daily running cost of CAD250,000. He was evasive on some concrete questions the auditors raised about contracts, bids, and suppliers while keeping eye contact only with the Canadian executive and justifying any potential overutilization of assets as necessary to keep the rig working. "Urgency" was the word he most used during our short meeting.

The auditors and the logistic manager eventually flew from Lima to Iquitos without having been introduced, and with no handshake or exchange of greetings whatsoever. We were seated a few meters away, yet the manager did not even turn back to say hello – all the while trying to avoid any eye contact. A similar evasive attitude was noticed when he left the plane in a hurry and was not seen until the next day when we were supposed to share breakfast. Obviously, not a great strategist.

The combination of these elementary variables led the auditing team to find the following solutions that might be perfectly applicable in a comparable setting either around South America or any other jungle environment – given that aside from cultural particulars a jungle environment has much the same features all over the world. The operational window on the Morona River ran from mid-January to mid-July and therefore constituted a major barrier in order to build the necessary stocks of consumables and equipment at the base camp 1.

4. *Audit recommendations*

Various issues that required improvement were identified and highlighted as part of the audit. The utilization of lower draught, wider barges and longer convoys (instead of narrower and bigger draught convoys) would improve the total cargo tonnage and volume actually carried per trip using 6-foot draught during the regular window. The number of convoys needed to complete a given stock could be reduced by two-thirds, and the associated barging and port costs could be drastically reduced. More round trips were to be allowed within the regular or high-tide window, and the safety margins within that window would tend to widen. The higher the load factor, the lower the overall costs.

The utilization of 5-foot draught barges and self-propelled units during two narrow additional windows, ranging from mid-July to mid-August and mid-December to mid-January, helped replenish stocks, getting close to minimum levels at the base camps. The regular window operation became the barge owners' sole responsibility for the completion of the trip, and the latter case was the oil organization's full responsibility, given the low-tide period of the year and the risks involved.

By optimizing river supply operations, the barge organization was discouraged from profiting in sending convoys along the low season in order to go aground on purpose. Low-season operations almost always generated demurrage and penalties as the departures were only decided by the oil organization, instead of the barging company which had nothing to lose when facing a low-raught scenario. On the contrary, such a practice enabled the barge operator to keep the floating stock duly contracted and/or safely aground while charging for the services on a consecutive basis. Figure 1.6 shows a typical draught variation during a short period of time.

Independent barging organizations operating single barges with little versatility and capacity were occasionally hired at lower rates, with dual goals of completing the needs at the base camps and avoiding price escalation on the part of the main cartelized barge suppliers. A bigger share was assigned to independent operators as a way of controlling and limiting any rate escalation during the year and discouraging malpractices.

Liquid bulk was carried on single-product barges, either gas, oil or JP1 (aviation fuel designed for use in aircraft), which led to a heavy underutilization when consumables were not available to fill out the barge at the oil refinery's floating berth. Counting on separated tanks to carry both products may help improve the load factor when the

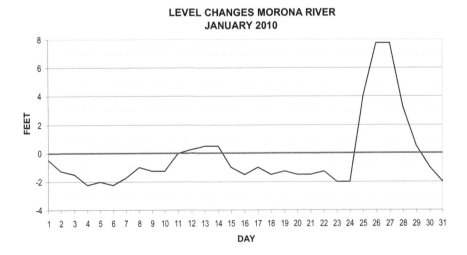

Figure 1.6 Level changes Morona River.

refinery is running low, and the base camps' stock may get replenished in a shorter time period. Naturally, counting on enough time for the planning cycle would be ideal in order to build a small tailor-made fleet of double-hull dual function barges. However, too often one has to work with what is readily available and adjust.

Liquid bulk barges used to be sent to a nearby oil refinery's floating berth. The berth was designed to supply consumables without considering the tide trend or the operational draught at a given point in time, at the entire expense and risk of the charterer. Barges used to wait not only for the tide to rise, but also had to face the accrued waiting time congestion often produces. The decision making as to when to dispatch the barges to the refinery in order to fill out its tanks no longer belonged to the barging organization. Rather, the decision was left to the charterer, who by doing this avoided incurring huge extra expenses in the form of demurrage charges and further penalties induced by the barging organization. Naturally, keeping good timing requires internalization, as decision making relied more on experience than data. Figure 1.7 shows the low-tide situation of a number of barges alongside the refinery's floating berth.

By improving the load factor, shortening round trips, and increasing the number of floating units per trip, the cartelized barging organizations were discouraged from carrying on with their induced demurrage malpractices in collusion with Lima-based staff. In addition, outsourcing of lower cost/price units was also discouraged and, no longer accepted by the charterer. Low-productivity trips in the form of low-load factors were drastically diminished, leading to a substantially higher degree of optimization. Small independent suppliers were called for on a spot basis to keep the predators away.

River transport negotiation strategies included dealing with a sort of cartelized service scheme led by a dominant player whose rates and the operational contractual terms turned out to be one of the most significant cost components of the entire logistic budget – an aspect that tends to repeat itself in jungle environments and that can be offset by supporting outsiders through a supplier development program. This is not easy, but possible if skilled people are standing at the helm.

There were a number of barge organizations whose floating stock and structure could be compared to The Al Pacino, a white Panama hat, of the Amazon – we will call him the Godfather, the main contracting barging organization. However, these other

Figure 1.7 Iquitos refinery floating berth at low tide.

organizations played an important role when the Godfather ran short of barges or did not meet a given specification concerning width or draught by making their units ready under the Godfather's umbrella to sail upon short notice to meet a peak in demand. Sometimes the Godfather's units turned out to be too large or inadequate, and therefore unnecessarily expensive – a very convenient situation for those others in need of extra cash. Typically, a wider or smaller barge may help overcome draught restrictions during low-tide season. Also, a smaller pusher boat may be more adequate to overcome shallow waters, while improving the load factor and reducing the overall cost impact.

The Peruvian river market can be regarded as highly informal and governed more by trade uses and customs and less by maritime law or international practices. It became both advisable and necessary to renegotiate some clauses in the Godfather's contract along the lines of internationally accepted standards embodying liability and cost sharing.

From a nautical point of view, a berth is considered "safe" if a vessel can safely reach it. During her stay at the berth, the vessel must always lie safely afloat without touching the bottom at low tide. Sometimes the words "always afloat" are deleted in a charter party in cases where it can be shown to be customary and safe to load or discharge aground. Either base camp's berths can be considered safe ports every time they can be accessed to and guarantee the barges to carry out a regular operation, even if aground. Consequently, charterers should at this point agree with the Godfather and clearly differentiate the high- and low-tide seasons, and assign a lump-sum voyage trip to each season without hidden costs of any kind. Should a convoy get stranded during high tide, all costs resulting thereof are to be borne by the barge operator. Should a convoy get stranded during low-tide season, all costs are to be borne by the shipper or the charterer.

In both international ocean shipping and Latin American river transportation (Parana-Paraguay Waterways, Brazilian Amazon, Orinoco River, Uruguay River, Magdalena River) going aground does not entitle the ship owner to charge the shipper all the costs arising from this misfortune. The operator is to bear the operational costs, whereas the shipper is to bear the operational or financial loss of not counting on the goods as planned. This is considered "Force Majeure" all over the world and fits well into what is internationally defined as "Perils, Dangers, and Accidents of the Sea or other Navigable Waters." Should this situation arise between two ocean ports, then the shipper could take legal action against the ship owner for the potential incurred losses arising out of not counting on their goods on time and as planned to be sold in the marketplace, or for instance a given equipment to carry on the operations (drilling or exploring). This does not seem to fit in the Peruvian case unless predictability of navigation can be established. This predictability is a given for the high-tide season, and charterers should insist on it and have it clearly defined in the contract based on a reasonable lump-sum voyage trip rate, without subsidies or hidden costs of any kind.

Under the Hague Rules and later the Hamburg Rules (Giles 1986), which are incorporated in the British and American Carriage of Goods by Sea Act, the carriers are bound to exercise due diligence to: (1) make the ship seaworthy, (2) properly man, equip, and supply the ship, and (3) make the holds, refrigerated and cool chambers, and all other parts of the ship in which goods are carried, fit and safe for their reception, carriage, and preservation.

It is the crew who possesses detailed knowledge accrued over the years spent sailing. This entails a key concept that is known as "traditional knowledge," which is precisely the reason why charterers are paying a premium. The barge owner should be liable for the service he is rendering because of two reasons. First, he holds the equipment to initiate the "maritime adventure" (or river trip in this case), and second, he holds the traditional knowledge of river navigation. The Godfather's organization is in a much better position to predict these events than the oil and gas organization whose core business is not river transportation but oil and gas activities.

The Godfather's organization grants the oil organization free days to complete its loading and unloading operations. Even though barge owners in Peru do not issue a Bill of Lading like most river operators do worldwide, the above-mentioned free days are nothing other than a LAYDAY. A LAYDAY is the period of time which the shipper or charterer has at his disposal for loading; any time beyond this period is prima facie his liability. For oceangoing vessels, this is the number of days permitted for the loading and unloading of a ship without payment of demurrage.

To avoid incurring demurrage at either the loading or discharge port, rainy days should be exempted from demurrage, with other operational causes of delay remaining on the shipper's account. A clause on demurrage should bring clarity to the responsibilities of the parties. Should the barge owner reject this concept, charterers should press the Godfather's organization on a "dispatch," charge which is exactly the opposite of demurrage. It is a daily or pro-rata compensation the owner has to pay the charterer for a quicker than allowed loading or unloading operation. Typically, containerization may help charterers offset their losses on demurrage. It might work as a strong motivation factor toward improving productivity further to grant the operations staff a rather wide authority to design and establish a number of KPIs – instead of always focusing on making some extra cash out of evident inefficiencies.

A "General Strike Clause" should be discussed and negotiated. It is internationally accepted to work on the following agreement:

> Neither charterers nor owners shall be responsible for the consequences of any strikes or lock-outs preventing or delaying the fulfillment of any obligation. If there is a strike or lock-out affecting the loading of cargo, or any part of it, charterers are usually requested to reckon the LAYDAYS as if there were no strike or lock-out.

This clause suggests a kind of cooperation on the part of the charterers every time the owners show a positive attitude toward not making the other party responsible for whatever may happen. It may build a sort of trust that can be the foundation for more cooperation. Should a convoy get trapped by a labor lock-out during navigation, each party should bear half of what may be defined as stand-by costs. Naturally, these issues should be brought up when developing potential suppliers, and not later.

The contract allowed the Godfather's organization to escalate their rates according to the oil price level. It is advisable for the charterers to know the percentage diesel oil input plays in the Godfather's organization cost structure prior to engaging in any kind of adjustment formula. Actually, it is always better to know what the cost structure of a main supplier is prior to signing a contract of this type. This is possible if the oil organization counts on enough volume to demand that the potential supplier disclose such a sensitive piece of data. This actually happened to be the case. The issue of transparency is one that plagues projects around the globe. It is dangerous to expose information and dangerous not to. The key is to strike a balance. We suggest that a project leader should expose him- or herself to the maximum extent possible and set the tone.

Fast boats utilization turned out to be excessive and nonsense in most of the surveyed cases, in addition to very low load factors. This service turned out to be heavily overpriced. It needed a deep reengineering without overlooking the role played by the indigenous communities and their links to the Peruvian navy – a delicate situation even for a skilled diplomat. Notwithstanding, a win–win situation was brought to the table and accepted. New fast boats would be designed and built in a nearby shipyard, whereas its operation and ownership would be ceded to the indigenous communities under the supervision of the Peruvian navy as far as health and safety issues were concerned.

Tariff rates were agreed upon by both the Peruvian navy and the oil organization in coordination with the heads of the communities, who felt grateful for the new buildings and the certainty of a long-lasting business relationship. The oil company would be given service priority, and the communities could operate their fast boats to render services to third parties at whatever rate they consider most appropriate. In other words, they could no longer suck the project's blood, should they feel like vampires in the market.

It had been reported by the oil organization that every time a fast boat service was needed, before the mentioned agreement had been reached, a limited number of contenders were consulted (two or three), and the cheapest available was then hired. Even though this system seemed fair, certain variables should be taken into account prior to calling for a tender. The oil and gas business is known in the logistic market as an "opportunity sector" to profit from, owing to its operational urgencies. The expression "the more urgent the more expensive" is even more so in geographical areas of difficult access, where the supply side gets limited to a few operators. Cartelization practices with minimal price differentials were identified and dismantled, so that competition could be kept alive.

Even though the nature of an oil rig construction often involves heavy cargo and not so many voluminous pieces, it would be more accurate to consider the cargo dimensions with respect to the helicopter volume carrying capacity, so as to have a more realistic efficiency ratio. By counting on data on both cargo weights and dimensions, it could be able to make better use of a specific type of helicopter for a specific type of cargo. Volume-based efficiency ratios may show substantial variations when compared to weight-based efficiency ratios. The utilization of both indicators could help better assess the performance in a given time period for each type of helicopter – a means of transport of indisputable importance in a jungle environment.

Three foreign organizations operating differentiated types of rotor-craft signed long-term contracts to conduct operations over a period of six years. Included, was an American-built Chinook-type helicopter capable of carrying up to 12 tons of cargo and overdimensional pieces of cargo combined with up to 44 passengers in a single trip. This helicopter has been designed to carry war equipment in any type of environment, and it is why it turns out to be very suitable to operate in the jungle to carry both cargo and personnel.

A Russian-built MI-17 type helicopter (comparable to the Chinook but smaller in scale) capable of carrying up to five tons of cargo, under special aerial conditions, combined with up to 22 people, was also used. Along with a modern and much smaller Bell 412 capable of undertaking sanitary search and rescue operations and carrying some critical cargoes and personnel on a spot basis. Typically, helicopters have to be brought from abroad, and flying and maintenance crews have to be available at the jobsite. This probably makes helicopter operation costs the highest of all.

It is critical to assess the way these costly capital-intensive assets are utilized in each project and to design a tight and proper way to measure their cargo-carrying performance, especially when considering the duration of the project, the existing weather constraints, and the ergonomics. The latter concept gives the user the chance to improve aerial operations by optimizing what type of cargo fits better into what helicopter aiming at improving the overall productivity.

There is always an opportunity cost point at which one type of rotor-craft turns out to be better than another when it comes to comparing cargo and personnel carrying capacity. Naturally, it depends on the weight and dimensions of every piece of cargo as well as the personnel shifts to be made at both the base camps and drilling stations. Furthermore, indigenous communities often imposed a number of critical restrictions to straight flight plans between spot A and spot B by demanding a zigzag flight plan to avoid any kind of environmental impact over the areas in which they live, hunt, fish, plant, and harvest.

These spatial restrictions often bring about unfair practices on the part of the flight operators who may take advantage by making excessively long zigzags or unnecessary circles in order to increase its equipment's hourly utilization. Inconsistencies were found in the existing contracts, and a number of amendments were enacted in order to reduce the cost impact. Moreover, data and information delivered to the auditing team turned out to be incomplete, tendentious, and misleading.

Figure 1.8 shows a useful and simple way to measure productivity. Surpassing 85% utilization is considered very good, as it will never get to 100% owing to both cargo configuration and inner spatial restrictions of the aircraft. The objective should be to produce graphs and data that are easy to interpret and take action on, by both the specialist and those with no previous experience in aerial project operations.

As mobilization costs represented a substantial amount of money, it was advisable to first check out the helicopter base, instead of taking the operators' words for granted, with respect to where the helicopter is physically based. It is customary to inflate mobilization charges built on aspects that are assumed. It is not the same in Houston, Luanda, London, or Jakarta. Considering contracting and the personnel assigned to it, it is advisable to have a dispersed multidisciplinary team of professionals who at the end of the day can cross-check views and opinions on both technicalities and pricing. Obviously, this is not the way this was done on this project. Again, the issue of transparency

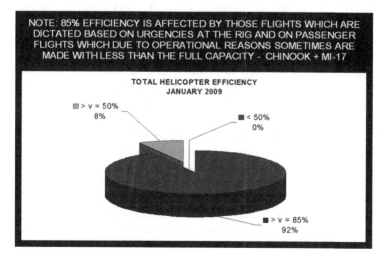

Figure 1.8 Total helicopter efficiency.

comes in. As we noted, what a project leader needs is information from all the players so that the most efficient approach may be employed.

It is advisable that the hourly helicopter rates should commence when the wheels or skids leave the ground and terminate when the wheels or skids are back on the ground. This is the case for both the Chinook and Bell but was not observed in the MI-17 contract. A net flight time should be considered in order to deduct the turn-on/turn-off times from the overall costs incurred. About 20 minutes per hour were spent on warming up and turning the engines off, leading to 20 minutes of increased cost for each flight. This aspect should be discussed and its impact reduced. Do you think there were any hidden agendas here?

Rates should be based on a minimum hourly utilization a month, rather than a monthly fixed rate covering a certain number of flight hours, regardless of whether or not they are used or not. This may depend on the existing balance between demand and supply at a given point in time. However, lump–sum agreements should by all means be avoided, for the operations costs should reflect the hours actually operated, as weather constraints and intangibles represent numerous risks. And utilized flight hours beyond the minimum should be less expensive than the ones in a normal window.

For ground transportation and warehousing, a number of inconsistencies were also identified. The following suggestions or recommendations were made to the oil firm to reduce the loss of capital due to a lack of professional planning and control, as follows:

- Effective satellite monitoring of trucks is not only important, but nowadays essential to coordinate the arrival of the cargo with the barges estimated time of arrival (ETA) at a given inland port. It was noticed that the trucking organization used only a mobile phone-based tracking system, which are not very effective in mountainous or jungle zones, and should be regarded as outdated for capital-intensive operations. This might be solved either by making the trucking organization improve their Global Positioning System (GPS), or by having the oil organization install mobile GPS devices on the equipment. A planned arrival at the inland port of loading along with an efficient transfer and barge loading operation will minimize waiting time and penalties when the river draught is optimal. Here again, we saw indifference, a lack of professionalism and motivation, and hidden agendas. Whatever caused the problem, it demanded a much closer follow-up on the part of the headquarters staff as inefficiencies, the cost of money, and time seriously threatened the project's sustainability.
- Trucking organizations often have large economies of scale, and therefore find themselves in better position to negotiate with warehousing operators. This was an aspect the Lima-based staff failed to understand, and they intended to have negotiations directly with the warehousing provider, with no critical mass behind them. A trucking organization that provides regular traffic between Lima and Pucallpa is likely to have enough economies of scale to provide warehouse services at both ends at substantially lower costs than any smaller scale operator. Whether the trucking firm is willing to share a given gross operational income with a customer much depends on what the latter means in terms of potential business. But, it also depends on the way Stallion's staff manages to sell the corporate image and the future. PMs in the field are often technicians, that fail either to delegate this type of task or just do the opposite and appoint somebody to do the best they can. Either way leads to inefficiencies that may become a

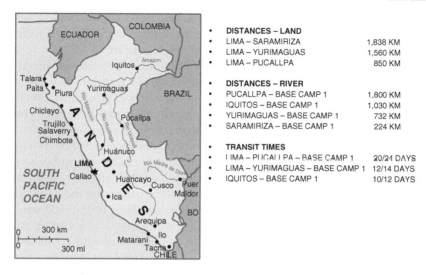

DISTANCES – LAND

LIMA – SARAMIRIZA	1,838 KM
LIMA – YURIMAGUAS	1,560 KM
LIMA – PUCALLPA	850 KM

DISTANCES – RIVER

PUCALLPA – BASE CAMP 1	1,800 KM
IQUITOS – BASE CAMP 1	1,030 KM
YURIMAGUAS – BASE CAMP 1	732 KM
SARAMIRIZA – BASE CAMP 1	224 KM

TRANSIT TIMES

LIMA – PUCALLPA – BASE CAMP 1	20/24 DAYS
LIMA – YURIMAGUAS – BASE CAMP 1	12/14 DAYS
IQUITOS – BASE CAMP 1	10/12 DAYS

Figure 1.9 Peruvian map and distances to base camp 1.

heavy ballast for the project to carry when reaching the execution stage. More-over, the inter-phases deserved a closer look on the part of the oil organization in order to avoid costs escalation resulting from a lack of coordination among the logistic phases.

- Pucallpa, Yurimaguas, and Iquitos warehouses were independent facilities owned by three different operators that the oil organization was dealing with. The oil organization did not even consider grouping its total volume to better negoti-ate storage rates, handling, security, insurance, and other conditions for harm-less and hazardous cargo. This practice resulted in a significant extra cost given the low inventory turnover rate, and the immobilized capital that impacted the overall ground logistic operation. Hidden costs, and above market rates, turned out to be common practice. Figure 1.9 exhibits an overall idea of the existing distances and transit times to operate with base camp 1 in northern Peru.

5. Challenges and suggestions

The challenges that can be taken from this case study turn out to be comparable to those of many other programs and projects that the auditors have experienced. If project best practices and overall transparency are sought, the considerations described above should be studied for extreme projects challenging environments. The following are a few of the lessons learned and our suggestions for extreme projects:

a. Contracting

Excessive itemization either in the oil organization's tenders or in some suppliers' services, should by all means be avoided. Enough detail is necessary to properly lead a program or project, but it must not distract from the larger view as too many things change in this type of environment. The goal is to be prepared and ready for change. Operational trans-parency and conceptual simplicity should be sought in all contracted services. It is typical across South America to try making what should actually be easy and straight forward look difficult, as a way to show upper management in an organization how valuable and resourceful those designing the bids, contracts, and procedures are.

Expats should stay alert at the early stages of a program or project and should take steps to avoid complexity, given that when execution begins it may snowball and create unnecessary interdependencies across organizations. A matrix-type organization is said to be the most efficient when it comes to resource allocation and budgetary control. Yet, the complexity and geographical isolation recommend a bit less interference from the headquarters-based functional managers with no experience in South America or with Lima-based staff. A knowledgeable CCO might fit perfectly into such a scenario by controlling, monitoring and reporting to both ends of the continent, while at the same time expediting the operational process between the origin and the destination.

Market segmentation should be based on both the suppliers' operational structure and geographical specialization, with all the other technical variables being part of the process. Special attention should be paid to the suppliers' core business and relative market strength. Local suppliers first, and regional operators later, may be called to participate in a bid – not larger structure companies with their core businesses far away from the area of the project.

Direct negotiations should be conducted with key suppliers. In addition to tailor-made market segmentation, the focus should be kept on holding negotiations with those service providers that could be hired directly by the oil organization as a way to avoid mark-ups of any kind from brokers or intermediaries. This requires a specialist whose main task should be that of continuous improvement of practices and cost optimization, while developing a set of suppliers fully compliant with the oil organization's values. If such a skill or functional knowledge is not available within the organization, it is always better to sign on a specialist than to add a broker. Specialists will tend to increase the overall contracting expense and make control more difficult and time consuming.

Increasing the contract duration for suppliers would encourage them to become more competitive and transparent if they see a continuity of business. An open-book policy should be sought in the long term as a way to gain trust, transparency, shareholder approval, and the BOD's blessing. This is not easy in a jungle environment with just a few mobster-style suppliers and where the life of an individual is not of value if measured from a local ethical perspective. This is why an open-book approach should focus on the long-term only, never on the fast or short term. In addition, operations-related clauses (penalties, compensation, bad weather, load speed, outsourcing, tracing, and free time) should be negotiated and added to contracts in order to avoid cost surprises.

As noted at the beginning of this chapter, this case never came close to the idea of a CPE. Independent agents were all working toward their own business or personal goals, games abounded, there was little transparency, no leader appeared, communications were poor or disported, and the results speak for themselves. Imagine if the project had a strong leader who was able to negotiate common goals and objectives.

b. *Operations*

Increased operational optimization is necessary. It is critical to always keep high load factors and engage suppliers in better ship-shore practices by planning operations in advance. Market segmentation and direct outsourcing turn out to be of paramount importance if international standards of efficiency and transparency are to be accomplished. Modified tender layout and cartelization should by all means be avoided by first identifying the best suppliers by segment and their market positioning. Then they should be called for a formal bidding process or direct negotiation, with the participation of various executives from different areas. It is advisable to add intended volumes and simplicity to the tender process.

In our experience, it is critically important to have operations people involved in a project from the beginning. So many long-term issues can be mitigated or even avoided by taking a long-term view. This is especially the case when portions of a facility must come online to support the completion of the project – like potable water or power. Also, items such as maintenance, inventory, camp necessities, and more can be seamlessly integrated. On one camp project in Saudi Arabia, the facilities were maintained and then transferred to the next project. This is a very viable option for sites like these where ongoing operations and new projects are anticipated.

c. *Leadership*

It becomes apparent that there was a lack of proper involvement from headquarters in controlling or supervising the Peruvian operations in a closer and more professional manner. To exert control on a given operation, one needs to be knowledgeable about many aspects of a program or project, such as river operations, negotiation, indigenous communities, contextual assessment, aerial operations, port operations, environmental impact, and culture.

Leadership needs to be put into practice by demonstrating trust, empathy, transformation, good communication skills, and the ability to deal with conflict both fairly and effectively. This will then be legitimized by peers and contractors alike. The importance of leadership is something that foreign-based companies too often fail to comprehend. They prefer to appoint home-based generalists with whom they feel comfortable instead of going to the next level by appointing skilled professionals with a solid track-record that may inspire respect and recognition across the project.

For this case, the headquarters made a strategic mistake in accepting a barging organization-related application of a candidate to fill the post of logistic manager for the Peruvian operations. Never accept a candidate that is not 100% independent from the contractor on a project or this lack of independence will sooner or later have to be addressed. Invisible links always remain very much alive – for better or worse – between former employers and current contractors. River operations in a jungle environment are crucial for the project's success and should therefore hold the number 1 priority during the planning stage. The processes were too complicated and time consuming to prequalify suppliers, suggesting that a small number of suppliers were "preferred" based on the argument that they best matched the organization's standards.

Theoretically, the absence of a matrix type of organization caused communications to be diluted and ineffective, especially on the case. The idea of a CPE is based in part on creating a matrix-type temporary organization. Global projects are composed of teams, co-located and virtual, from different organizations, in different countries, brought together to provide a service and a product. See Figure 1.1 to get the idea. Each organization will have its own KPIs, which hopefully are connected to strategy and success criteria. Some will be transactional, some transformational, some political, some selfish, some societal, some environmental, some short term, some long term, and some undefined.

It becomes apparent that what failed was the participation of skilled people during the planning and execution phases of the project. Technical knowledge and managerial skills become extremely relevant given the isolation of the job-site as well as the complexity of the combined operations. How projects are structured is not really the point here, but rather, how knowledge and control are shared and implemented.

d. Ethics

Obviously, the lack of internal auditing processes to avoid incurring contracting malpractices was a significant issue. There was insufficient and inadequate knowledge of the various operational processes of Lima-based executives in charge of accounting and finance. This lack hindered the organization from distinguishing good invoices from fictitious ones. There was a tendency to unify the decision-making process of most of the tasks in a single person, leading to recurrent malpractice and overpricing. There were relationships that were too close and suspiciously friendly between the procurement and logistic team and the main suppliers.

The low staff turnover rate among those who held key roles in the decision-making process led to entrenched hidden agendas. There was also excessive freedom held by a few people to decide on the bids and suppliers. The absence of control routines and audits was amazing.

A balance needs to be struck on projects in such environments. Local customs may accept such behavior, but that does not mean an organization should adopt these practices. If a Scandinavian company brings its customs and practices to the table, conflict will certainly exist. We do not advocate that such a company adopt corrupt practices or the types of behavior seen on this project. Yet, they must be prepared to consistently monitor and ask probing questions. Ignorance in such cases is not bliss. To lead means to set an example and to be consistent. Yet it also means to be tolerant. The key is to achieve the balance that comes from experience, expertise, and curiosity.

So, what does a CPE leader do in an imperfect world? Imagine you are the CPE leader in a Canadian organization (transparency.org rank of 10), and that your country has laws and guidelines relating to the Sullivan Principles and the Triple Bottom Line (TBL). Your project in Peru (transparency.org rank of 85), has social and environmental laws that are significantly more relaxed than those in Canada. You can follow the local laws in Peru and break or reinterpret the guidelines and laws in Canada, thus, for example, reducing the environmental costs of the project to increase short-term profits. Let's say you decide to take this approach and look the other way on an environmental issue. It would be illegal in Canada, but rationalizing, one might think the damage to the local population was not too bad. Think about the message you would be sending to the CPE. It is a certain way to lose trust, which is the foundation for leadership.

What we can offer is a simple suggestion. Set the bar high with the Sullivan Principles, and accept the fact that not everyone will achieve the goals. One cannot change thousands of years of cultural tendencies on a project, nor should one. One can, however, describe a realistic vision that encourages people to achieve as much as they can. To do this in practice, requires confidence in oneself, commitment to a vision, and willingness to accept failure when people try.

The conclusion for this case study is that the distance and lack of control that Canada-based management had over their people and assets in Peru was remarkable. This case suggests that counting on a Canadian or foreign general manager in charge of the operations does not necessarily lead to achieving a quality stamp on the operations as well as a shield against corruption. On the contrary, the evidence suggests that lack of leadership and control, mixed with ingenuity or too much confidence in individuals instead of globally well-proven project management practices, invariably leads to a gradual erosion of processes, ethics, leadership, brand value, and ultimately both OPEX (Operational Expenses) and CAPEX (Capital Expenses). Naturally, PM good practices cannot be taken linearly all over the globe and for all kinds of projects but should become more industry- and site-specific if sustainable development and project success are expected.

B. Case study: consortia–led integrated gas field project in the Peruvian rainforest

1. *Background to the case*

This program included construction of an energy site in the Americas that involved Peruvians, Argentines, Swedes, and Americans. The project consisted of a huge program in the Peruvian rainforest requiring a complex logistic operation carried out by three different consortia on a tight schedule and in demanding topography. It included new infrastructure, ocean shipping, port operations, ground transportation, and river barging. A view of the general structure of the CPE is shown in Figure 1.10.

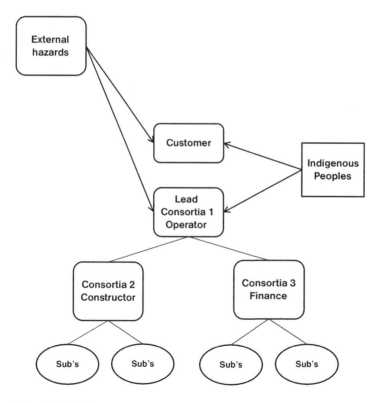

Figure 1.10 CPE structure.

The project also included indigenous communities, politics, drug trafficking exposure, and "Shining Path" events (Shining Path is a brutal Maoist political group in Peru). All of these elements are landmarks of Corporate Social Responsibility (CSR), and they play an important role in all projects – and a crucial role in this case.

People have discussed and debated ethics for thousands of years, as well as the relationship between capitalism and socialism. Needless to say, the debate continues, and there are as many visions of CSR as there are people. The USA has a law, the Foreign Corrupt Practices Act, which forbids anyone from bribing a foreign official – if an organization is found guilty, the CEO goes to jail, in theory. But a criminal offense in the USA is an accounting issue in Germany, where bribes were, at one time a tax deduction. Thus, the rules and application of the rules vary widely.

2. Program in detail

One of the most important stages in this project was represented by logistics and construction operations in view of the time span of the project, the inaccessibility of the various sites, the existing lack of infrastructure, and the climatic hostility which tended to limit the operational life of rivers and roads. River logistics turned out to be crucial for carrying heavy-lift and extradimensional machinery pieces, while air-cargo freighters were normally utilized to avoid incurring construction delays and consequent penalties. Ground logistics worked as a complement for project cargo operations. An overview of the logistics is shown in Figure 1.11.

Ocean carriers normally called at the port of Callao to set up a land-bridge up to the river port terminal of Pucallpa on the Ucayali River. Transportation from Iquitos to Malvinas, where the initial job-site was located, was critical. The main reason for this is that the Urubamba-Ucayali fluvial system is only navigable during four to five months a year, from November to March. During the seven to eight months in which the rivers do have severe draught restrictions, the weather is appropriate for construction – provided that indigenous communities happen to be in a good mood.

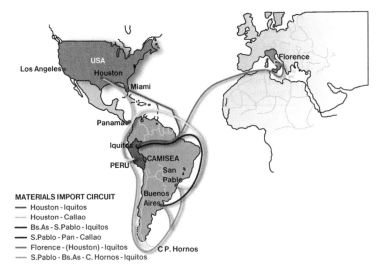

MATERIALS IMPORT CIRCUIT
— Houston - Iquitos
— Houston - Callao
— Bs.As - S.Pablo - Iquitos
— S.Pablo - Pan - Callao
— Florence - (Houston) - Iquitos
— S.Pablo - Bs.As - C. Hornos - Iquitos

Figure 1.11 Material import circuit.

Or put in other words, the procurement, construction, and logistics needed to plan and deploy a perfectly well-coordinated system that will allow works to be completed both on time and under budget. Oceangoing vessels used to call simultaneously at Callao on the Pacific, to further carry on by truck and barge through Pucallpa, and at Iquitos on the Amazon River to transship onto barges in order to proceed to the jobsite, down river in the Malvinas base camp. Heavy-duty helicopters were also deployed in Malvinas to handle and carry machinery and equipment from the Malvinas base camp to each of the drilling locations deep in the jungle.

Again, lack of infrastructure, along with tight operational windows, became apparent as the main challenges to be faced. Intangibles like indigenous communities concerns and expectations gradually became a second- or third-degree challenge that posed no immediate threat to overall project sustainability. The great difference between a tangible and an intangible problem lies precisely in its potential if the intangible is ignored by management. This is especially the case when tangible problems seem to overshadow those challenges posing no evident threats. Intangible barriers tend to evolve or mutate, for better or worse, as time passes and as a project moves to the execution stage. This is precisely the lethal nature of the intangibles and is one of the main reasons why large-scale projects around the world get delayed again and again. The CAPEX component tends to escalate almost endlessly. One does not need to prove this by going to Peru, for it also happens in most all other parts of the world.

A Procurement Management Centre had been set up primarily in Buenos Aires to carry out those negotiations linked to the leading engineering organization, which counted on branches spread all over the Americas and Europe as far as the supply of pipes was concerned. The procurement of machinery, equipment, and spare parts was to be centralized in Lima's Procurement Management Centre, and both offices had to report to the project manager based in Lima.

There is no doubt that growing environmental concerns, coupled with public pressure and stricter regulations, are changing the way organizations do business not only in South America but also around the world. A substantial number of organizations recognize that the implementation of sustainable business strategies can lead to new opportunities and improved results; despite this, it remains unexplored territory for many companies. The fall in the price of most commodities should not serve as a trigger for exploring how to become more competitive by becoming more environmentally proactive.

Perhaps one should regard this issue the other way around, and perhaps the best moment to do it is before one is forced to do so, and thus outperform others. It is easier said than done, but it is a far more sustainable approach – doing the right thing by integrating the various areas of knowledge can pay off. To do this, one needs to count on three basic assets: (1) guts; (2) common sense; and (3) a great communication strategy – assuming of course that knowledge is available within the organization.

The introduction of new environmental regulations, both domestic and international, will force businesses to improve their environmental performance. This becomes apparent with the concept of transboundary litigation whereby national organizations can be legally responsible for their own behaviour overseas and also that of a joint-venture partner, including foreign organizations and state-owned enterprises (Moon and Bonny 2001). We advise organizations to include modified arbitration clauses in their contracts because with more than eight legal systems, litigation is not a prudent approach to resolving disputes. Sharia law and Chinese law are but two examples of how ba⊠ing and arbitrary settlements can be in these venues.

The impact of not complying with new environmental regulations can loom large if one considers that damage can reflect on the corporate or brand reputation, employee recruitment and talent retention, consumer loyalty, risk ratings, or even share prices. Economists still argue about the value of an organizations brand, but recent articles in the *Economist* reveals that there seems to be a general heuristic of 28% of market capitalization. Others say it is 7% or yearly revenue, and of course it is dependent on what market and services the organization provides. If 7% is used and compared to the yearly revenue on a project, that is more likely than the margin. It deserves more attention than it receives.

But compliance often creates unexpected costs that threaten profitability or reduce margins which often make organizations lean towards overlooking those steps which would lead them to anticipate their environmental liabilities. It is often observed in South America and other regions that operating in "compliance" mode, businesses commonly regard environmental protection as an unnecessary burden, a costly undertaking that decreases an organization's competitive position and operational income. However, according to BSD Global (Unknown 2002), "faced with the increasing burden of regulation, some businesses choose to go beyond compliance towards comprehensive environmental programmes and sustainable development," which suggests the existence of a proactive trend towards a new dimension leading to competitive advantage.

Naturally, one may say that a USD100 per barrel oil market situation may enable a company to look after the environment and still make a very good profit, whereas it is something else is to face a market slump where the barrel slides to USD30 or 40 per barrel. Adopting a sustainable environmental strategy in a complex environment that looks far away and exotic to many home-based executives and stakeholders is often too long-term. Often it is seductive to assume that the risk of getting caught is remote. Sooner or later, however, the truth comes out, and the entire project could face serious brand issues globally.

Consumers are demanding that goods and services be produced by socially and environmentally responsible organizations. Many bankers and investors evaluate organizations and make decisions, considering both environmental risks and environmental market opportunities. This was the case on a USD400 million finance facility provided by Japanese banks for a project in India. They wanted a return on their investment, but with emphasis on assuring them that the project was being conducted in a sustainable way with regards to society and the environment.

More organizations are discovering the benefits of going beyond local regulatory compliance, not only toward sustainability, but also looking for market opportunities through such innovation. While sustainable development can be defined as the relationships between environmental, social, and economic benefits, environmental protection is often limited to the impact on nature. Both concepts are tightly linked to the triple bottom-line arguments which to different extents regional organizations tend to overlook for different reasons.

By doing so, these regional organizations are probably reducing expenses, and becoming more competitive today, at the expense of becoming exposed in the future, besides missing the invaluable opportunity of capitalizing on a way to face new regional challenges, and acquiring the experience by doing. One thing seems certain: a remote and isolated job-site is a great temptation for organizations to overlook sustainability practices by prioritizing short-term savings. On this issue, there is no great difference between regional and global companies with respect to the advantages, though they have a different degree of awareness about the consequences should anything go wrong. Environmental hazards do not only apply to construction or manufacturing where the potential impact is well known and can therefore be well defined and anticipated. But in logistic operations, where the risks are high and the probability of occurrence low, leading companies too often take the shortest way and miss the opportunity to outperform others.

Obviously, becoming environmentally friendly means creating and funding contingency plans that reduce margins, invest in R&D, and spend money in educating the stakeholders so that they know everything the company is doing to protect the socio-economic environments across the emerging world. Becoming sustainable and making it known across the world pays off, perhaps not in the short run but definitely in the medium to long run, including other regions. This should be the next step for global companies that expect to expand across the global natural resources market, with the support of global stakeholders. This is called sustainability and should be considered as a competitive tool, and not a cost center.

It is also true that in certain circumstances an organization may be compelled to face field situations that are far from desirable, let alone TBL or CSR oriented, yet predictable. This was the case for an entire convoy of trucks carrying pipe layers, trenchers, and road-making machinery when crossing the Andes from Lima bound to Pucallpa on the Ucayali River. The cargo was supposed to be oﬄoaded in Pucallpa to await a barge convoy that would load and carry the whole cargo up to the base camp within a rather tight operational window.

The convoy was escorted by well-equipped Peruvian police special forces aimed at preventing any potential attack from terrorists, activists, drug traffickers, or just environmentalists along the 850 KM of dirt roads. The convoy stopped in the middle of the night as a group of white-dressed men known as "Ronderos" came out of the jungle and blocked the road (local dwellers are hired by drug dealers to patrol the surroundings to keep them safe and clear for their operations). They were armed and demanded the police forces tell them where the convoy was heading, what were they doing there, as well as what was the nature of the cargo.

After a considerable delay of time and the payment of an informal toll, the convoy was allowed to proceed, and no further incidents occurred during the 18-hour journey. Such a toll was already included on the trucking cost, and the police forces were also given a sort of gratuity as was customary. It may be argued that sustainability may adopt many different faces as long as violence and conflicts of any sort are avoided. However, this may demand two things from a project developer: the capacity to overlook what is going on in the surroundings and an almost blind confidence in the organizations the project hires to conduct the operations. These aspects are of paramount importance and must be addressed on many, if not all, projects. Naturally, it is one thing to develop the capacity to turn the head and look somewhere else as a way to ease a given situation and something else to become blind in purpose by making such behavior an accepted approach. Facilitating corruption goes against sustainability, no matter how many codes a company has signed and officially approved (UN Global Compact, or Sullivan Principles, etc.).

Child labour is abhorrent, but it is absolutely customary to engage in these practices in the Peruvian rainforest. Otherwise, the communities will not render any assistance in the field, and the project will invariably be delayed. Is this enough to justify the hiring of children to carry out a given job? Would this be acceptable if necessary to deliver the project on time and on budget? Obviously not; but what is the alternative?

Changing their habits while introducing Western values or PM best practices? Get them convinced that children should be at school instead of at work? The reality is that child labour is very well regarded by the indigenous communities as children provide income and support for an entire community. School?... what school? There is no school? Would this be acceptable then? Of course not.

Again, where does all this lead us? A simple suggestion: hire children just for simple administrative tasks, with no heavy duties involved, and leave construction and logistic work for adults; get this policy openly communicated to the world as a way to gain acceptance – and critics – from the surgical perspective of the developed world. Also, try providing some schooling and medical assistance in cooperation with the federal authorities – even in remote areas. If children are treated well and adults are there to take care of them, there should not be any problem. This is social innovation. What happens in the real world is that child labor brings about all type of abuses, whereas the tribal chiefs tend to accept these malpractices in order to prosper and take advantage of a job that may be available today but not for too long. No matter whether the executives come from Scandinavia, the USA, or South America, the tyranny of deadlines too often prevails.

The Business Council on Sustainable Development (BCSD) located in Geneva maintains that communities have strong views on what takes place within their region; cultural groups such as aboriginal tribes have rights and attitudes towards sustainable development which need to be respected; and consumers, sometimes situated a continent away, now pay much attention to the origin, production processes, and disposal of goods (Hanson 1994). This is absolutely true.

With the advent of information technology (IT), in facilities at the regional level and even at remote spots in the Amazonian rainforest, organizations have to face a new global data disclosure phenomenon by which consumers come to know project details, with the potential to negatively impact on their brand reputation and, most importantly, the way of practicing project management on the field. IT regional advancement is not only linked to brand value and corporate reputation, but also to access to capital from both banking and insurance standpoints. Another dimension that is clearly looming large as a result of the Internet, is the ethical framework into which organizations have to evolve as a way to successfully tackle stakeholders and gain competitive advantage, even in the Peruvian rainforest job-site far away from the hand of the Lord. Figure 1.12 exhibits what IT can do to encourage organizations to comply with TBL and CSR precepts, even in remote and complex settings for their own project sustainability broadly speaking.

One of the main operators of the consortia was involved (unintentionally) in the sinking of a barge and associated oil pollution in the Marañon River nearby Iquitos. This event, further to not having been the first in the area, had a significant impact at the local level as it made water undrinkable, produced a high rate of fish mortality, and a wide array of then unknown diseases among the local dwellers. The oil spill was widely reported by many Peruvian non-governmental organizations (NGOs), given that some 20,000 indigenous people were deemed to be affected.

The local priest stated that the organization had never shown any interest in alleviating the situation for the people, while the organization had stated that a barge containing 141 tonnes of drinking water had been promptly dispatched to the scene (is this contingency or emergency? There is a world of a difference). Whatever the case, corporate damage and project delays were already there. The Peruvian organization

Figure 1.12 A global internet.

in charge of habitat surveillance, Organismo Supervisor de la Inversion en Energia (OSINERG), proceeded to fine the oil organization and made it public in the local media. For the consortia this was deemed collateral damage.

Surprisingly, a much larger global and experienced organization like the American firm had left in the hands of its regional-based partners – one of whom turned out to be the head of the consortia – not only the handling of the environmental contingency plans, but also the liability of management before third parties, either state or private entities. On the one hand, it may be reasonable to assume that the environmental standards for an American organization turns out to be higher than that of a South American organization, at least in most cases. On the other hand, it is also reasonable to suspect that the regionally based consortia leader was ceded the CPEL ship by the American organization, as the former was culturally adapted and better trained to deal with the uncertainties a project of this type might bring about.

However, the American organization's mission statement reads: "to be a growth-oriented industry leader respected throughout the world for the quality and competency of its people, the efficiency and scope of its operations, and its rich heritage of honesty and integrity." Naturally, this mission statement refers to efficient operations, though it does not use the word "environment" in a type of activity that is simply crucial, which suggests that the environment was not really in this organization's agenda. But even more surprising is the case of the main contractor and head of one of the contracting consortia in charge of EPC (Engineering, Procurement, Construction) functions.

This is the case of a Swedish global engineering organization that through its structure in Buenos Aires, Argentina, led a consortia made up of Swedes, Peruvians, and Argentine executives while presenting the following mission statement: "to develop, build and maintain the physical environment for living, working, and travelling." Its code of conduct stated:

It is the organization's key responsibility to develop and maintain an economically sound and prosperous business. Our organization as a business with a long history and future assumes its responsibilities. These include our responsibilities toward the countries, communities and environments in which we operate, toward our employees and business partners and toward society in general.

Despite the above statements and despite counting on proved and sound higher environmental standards, the Swedish organization left all the environmental responsibility in the hands of its Argentine partners. Was it part of a strategy? Was it fear to the unknown? Was it ignorance? Was it indifference? Was it arrogance? It is difficult to affirm but not that complicated to imagine.

It becomes apparent that the consortia operator had adopted a green corporate image where IT played in their favor, at least in the short run, while the available evidence suggests a different perspective. Direct observation of the procurement and logistic team to which the authors belonged has revealed that at isolated spots well within the Peruvian jungle, both child labor and indigenous people show very different living standards than those of the white workers. Food and water were dramatically rationed, and clothing and tents were simply not available for them. This should not cause any surprise: say 30 years ago when CSR concepts and environmental concerns did not rank as high as nowadays when the Internet, TV documentaries, and magazines love addressing these issues every time they can.

Furthermore, many of the indigenous communities were managed by a tribal chief whom the white workers team boss used to conduct negotiations and fix terms and conditions which always fell into the wrong hands. Such was the case of those trained as welders for the flow-line on whom stressful and hard working conditions were exerted; unlike indigenous people, white people did not resist long periods of time on the field in the open air. As Colonel Alfredo Seminario of the Peruvian air force put it:

> During my years along the exploration phase of the project where I used to fly helicopters 14 hours a day, I have never seen anybody better physically outfitted than the indigenous worker for carrying out long-stay jobs in the jungle; they have developed amazing skills not only for working but also for feeding themselves and surviving in such a hostile environment without any assistance.

Organizations that refuse to accept any responsibility for the practices of their suppliers or partners run the risk of damaging their brand and thereby undermining the value of their business. In an age of expanding mass communication, overseas project malpractice can have a devastating impact on a brand's reputation. Brand value and reputations theory sustains the notion that public perception of an organization includes its products and brands, the personal reputation of the organization manager/owner as well as the brand value of the organization, all of which may affect a number of functions, notably access to capital, ability to attract business partners, ability to hire and retain talented employees, ability to obtain global licenses to operate, and reputation that can be quantified by customer satisfaction surveys, ranking in lists, perception in public opinion polls, and formal valuation of the organization's overall brand (Elkington 1998).

It seems appropriate to cite the words of Britain's largest power organization chairman (National Power) and of the World Energy Council with respect to this governance dimension:

> We need to start moving beyond simple environmental literacy towards a much more strategic capability for understanding the long-term implications of business

processes and practices for the physical and social environment in which we operate. This is where the real debate on stakeholders should be, rather than where it currently is, stuck with a sterile argument on the supremacy of shareholder versus other stakeholder interests.

It would be interesting to see what would have been this gentleman's policy for developing, say, a hydropower facility in the Peruvian rainforest. Environmental management in the middle of nowhere requires as much leadership as the construction itself. It is a matter of competitive strategy as well as awareness on the part of the highest level in the organization on its power to outperform any project a firm comes across. Like anything else, it is a matter of know-how.

Multinationals have had very different approaches to their oil and gas projects in South America with respect to corporate brand value, and practically none has realistically assessed the potential IT may have in discrediting the way projects are completed on the field. Occidental Petroleum in Colombia and Ecuador, Arco and Burlington Resources in Ecuador, and Placer Dome in Venezuela's gold mines add a similar perspective; Petrobras and El Paso Energy International in Brazil, Enron, Total and British Gas in Bolivia, Agip Oil, Alberta Energy, Repsol-YPF, and Techint in Ecuador, have all gone through stressful processes that left open scars which are likely to grow and hit back by impacting the brand value.

Leaving the operations in the hands of regional partners to try eluding the initial exposure a multinational organization may have to face should an event occur is totally unadvisable in today's intertwined world where the entire globe seems to become smaller and smaller and project good practices may become enablers to gain both reputation and market share. Lack of control at the job-site or deployment of poor corporate practices in this particular case entailed a deeper organizational problem that may be reflected first in the way procurement was split into two different cities and second the lack of professional controlling practices on the part of the global foreign organizations. There is little doubt that these types of projects narrow even further the chance for upcoming projects to obtain their social license to operate, owing to circumstances that are not actually related to them, neither conceptually or operationally.

At the end of the day and given the impact of the spill on the river, fishing, health, strong odor, consumable water, and so forth, it was the attitude of the communities that got stiffer and stiffer on all the projects that came right after. Ironically this project got commissioned and built, while others that came later had to struggle twice or became stagnant owing to the distrust of the communities which in some cases reacted with violence and in complicity with Shining Path, drug traffickers, Ronderos (peasants who live in the jungle working for landlords and drug dealers), or whoever wanted to take advantage of the situation.

In conclusion, CSR concepts should not be taken as well-meaning terms for organizations to state on their vision and mission statements only. Either in the short or long run, these concepts may become a boomerang, exert a negative impact on the brand value, and produce a long list of associated corporate misfortunes such as:

- Bad corporate image.
- Fall in share value.
- Higher insurance premiums.
- Stiffer financial terms or lack of them.

- Inability to get a social license to operate.
- Limited expansion areas for exploring and developing.
- Disability to retain talent.
- Withdrawal of key suppliers.
- Difficulty in getting strategic alliances.
- Unwanted delays, and ultimately.
- A straight impact on both CAPEX and OPEX, to just name a few aspects.

3. Lessons learned

Unlike the previous case study and even though both projects hold many areas where operational similarities can be identified, project sustainability plays a crucial role upon which the following recommendations based on a number of lessons learned on the field can be set forth:

- No matter how isolated and hidden a project setting may look; IT will reach you and uncover whatever malpractices are being unfolded. It is a matter of time, and projects take time to develop.
- Be smart; be innovative; be humane; make extensive use of your common sense when dealing with indigenous communities and stakeholders in general; take your time to listen and communicate; do not take the shortcut; and be as careful with a tribal chief as you would possibly be with the head of a union at home – most likely you would like the chief better at the end of the day.
- Do not jump to the job-site without having first assessed the existing socioeconomic needs, expectations, and overall standing. Do not trust what others tell you about the way to accomplish a given task without consulting first with the communities.
- Monitor to exhaustion the fulfillment of logistic operations as regards health and safety, environmental hazards, as well as the perils inherent to the operation. Have a contingency plan ready at hand and let everybody know of its existence and applicability.
- Inform management and make sure they inform the world about your hiring practices in the jungle, along with the cultural patterns your team is willing to work along and respect in every sense.
- Do not try to inculcate or indoctrinate accepted Western values to the communities, but try to adapt the best way possible to what they regard as good practices according to their values, norms, and vision of the world – possibly not PM good practices.
- Be aware that adopting the cover of a reputable consortia global leader to carry out questionable operations is a risky business for a project's sustainability. Best practice would be to make use of that brand to upgrade the regional brand by adopting higher operational standards on the field; communications in this regard may play a crucial role to gain credibility and stakeholder support at home and abroad.
- Design and put into place aerial operations; barging operations; trucking operations; port operations; and even warehousing only after a public consultation has been made. Not only the environmental and construction topics should be addressed but also the way logistic and construction-related aspects are going to be developed as a way to gain operational support and understanding. It should also work as a way for stakeholders to visualize future working opportunities.

- Provide training for locals and communities as much as possible; generate expectations and get them measured as a way of plotting the acceptance degree the operations may get at a given point in time.
- Do not promise what you cannot fulfill. The truth may become somehow unpleasant in the short run but will never become a boomerang in the long run but rather a solid basis to build on.

4. Challenges and suggestions

Some of the critical components PMs must pay attention to both at home and on the field are represented by the way logistic operations are carried out given their context in these two particular case studies. Contracting protocols, transparency or the lack thereof, ethical pressure, malpractice, compliance, probability of corruption occurrence, contingency, monitoring procedures, reporting, communications, and the like are all intertwined variables that should be first identified and lead to design an engulfing strategy upon the scoping of a project rather than during the execution. Corporate knowledge is also a fundamental component of sustainability, as it is the corporate vision in regard to sustainability, community engagement, CSR practices, and operations strategy. Are these variables enough to reach a general conclusion on the way project operations should be planned and executed? Definitely not; however, these are the first steps that, once combined with the findings of the upcoming case studies, will gradually let the reader shape a constructive picture on the way projects may become competitive and much more successful in the future.

Imagine you are doing work in Kazakhstan, and a border official is holding up a shipment until a gratuity is provided. The guard has a family of five and has not been paid in a month because the government is short of cash. Is it unethical to pay? The point is that there are no universally accepted ethical standards, and circumstances often should perhaps trump them even if there were. The Chinese call this situational ethics and practice it regularly.

Transparency.org interviews businesspeople in 174 countries and asks them their opinion of how big a problem corruption is when doing business. It provides a good relative ranking of what an organization can expect as far as the general tendencies within a country are concerned. In 2014, Denmark was ranked as the least corrupt country, and Somalia as the most corrupt. We can attest to the fact that the relative rankings are quite often accurate.

Consider how some governments and societies treat their own citizens with regard to women's rights, ethnicity, religion, age, color, language, caste, economic standing, and such. Imagine an organization from Sweden is doing a project in Saudi Arabia, and the CPEL is a woman. Does one set about changing thousands of years of culture, or does one adjust oneself. Think about a CPEL from the south of Nigeria doing a project in the north. Or consider a team in Japan, where touching women in public is not frowned upon, but the organization does not tolerate sexual harassment in any form.

This is also the consideration in this and most of the case studies, where short-term profits harm the indigenous people in any number of ways ranging from disease to technology to death. Or think about long-term environmental impacts that can lead to generations of health problems – as in Bhopal, India, or the upper reaches of the Amazon. What are the responsibilities of a CPE like that shown in Figure 1.10? And what should the leader (CPEL) set as the standard? In fact, should the project be done at all, and should a CPEL place her/himself in jeopardy of losing her and his job to stand up for a principle? This is the case in a number of case studies where environmental issues suggest caution.

There are projects where the CSR guidelines are well taken care of when planning the operations and others that, despite considering the same guidelines and following strict procedures or processes, do fail and produce a negative impact on either nature or people. This may or may not be done in purpose. These case studies show different perspectives on the way CSR principles may be breached either accidentally as the project finds challenges it cannot successfully overcome or when they are simply ignored to take advantage of a given situation.

An oil spill from a barge that affects water, fish, and consuming habits of indigenous communities in the Peruvian rainforest may be regarded as an unwanted result of a duly planned operation – accidental or not. In these case studies, both nature and communities suffered, whereas project developers and contractors risked their respective corporate image around the world. However, child labor practices in rainforests and social discrimination do constitute a clear TBL breach leading to an ethical issue, as is been exposed. Manipulating operational information in order to favor new suppliers at the expense of traditional suppliers leading to cost escalation and higher operational inefficiency may also be regarded as a typical maneuver that headquarters tend to oversee or complacently accept from their job-site personnel to keep the operations running.

Sad to say, corruption is more than often accepted and kept hidden from shareholders and BODs as long as the intended outcomes are accomplished. This clearly contradicts good CPEL and CSR practices when it comes to economic considerations like in the last case study. Other projects may fall into a thin line between guilty and innocent when it comes to project stakeholder management (PSM) issues. A project that was developed by the book but was put on hold owing to minor omissions as to its environmental impact assessment in Costa Rica is the perfect example. Were they actually minor omissions or purposeful? It is difficult to know. However, serious mistakes by excluding some of the stakeholders in the consultation process during the PSM program looks more like incompetence than breach of CSR precepts and CPEL sound practices, as in this and the previous case study.

Hundreds of guidelines have been promulgated by major organizations and businesses, each with its own outlook. We prefer a simple and direct set of standards that are uncomplicated and straightforward. The one we prefer was created in 1977 by Reverend Leon Sullivan who developed a set of CSR principles to apply economic pressure during apartheid. At the time, he sat on the Board for General Motors, which was the largest employer in South Africa. Then in 1999 Kofi Annan and Reverend Sullivan introduced them jointly at the United Nations. The Global Sullivan Principles are as follows

- Express our support for universal human rights and, particularly, those of our employees, the communities within which we operate, and parties with whom we do business.
- Promote equal opportunity for our employees at all levels of the company with respect to issues such as color, race, gender, age, ethnicity or religious beliefs, and operate without unacceptable worker treatment such as the exploitation of children, physical punishment, female abuse, involuntary servitude, or other forms of abuse.
- Respect our employees' voluntary freedom of association.

- Compensate our employees to enable them to meet at least their basic needs and provide the opportunity to improve their skill and capability in order to raise their social and economic opportunities.
- Provide a safe and healthy workplace; protect human health and the environment; and promote sustainable development.
- Promote fair competition, including respect for intellectual and other property rights, and do not offer, pay, or accept bribes.
- Work with government and communities with whom we do business to improve the quality of life in those communities – their educational, cultural, economic, and social well-being – and seek to provide training and opportunities for workers from disadvantaged backgrounds.
- Promote the application of these principles by those with whom we do business.
- Be transparent in our implementation of these principles and provide information that demonstrates publicly our commitment to them.
- Be profitable – NOT part of the original principles, but essential if one runs a business.

To keep it simple: be good to your employees and the societies in which one works, be good to the environment, be transparent and promote the standards, and make a profit. Treat people like you would want to be treated when they enter your home. This is a foundational ethical principle for all major religions and one that still works as noted (Harris, Pritchard and Rabins 2000).

- Muslim – No man is a true believer unless he desires for his brother that which he desires for himself (Hadith, Muslim, imam 71–72).
- Christian – Treat others as you would like them to treat you (Luke 6:31, New English Bible).
- Hindu – Let not any man do unto another any act that he wisheth not done to himself by others, knowing it to be painful to himself (Mahabharata, Shanti Parva, cclx.21).
- Confucian – Do not do to others what you would not want them to do to you (Analects, Book xii, #2).
- Buddhist – Hurt not others with that which pains yourself (Udanavarga, v. 18).
- Jewish – What is hateful to yourself do not do to your fellow man. That is the whole of the Torah (Babylonian Talmud, Shabbath 31a).

We firmly believe that this serves as a solid foundation for global business. After reading through the case studies, it is relatively easy to see that short-term profits are often, if not always, the overriding focus for 21st-century businesses and that this often leads to disastrous results. Look at the case studies and imagine how it would have gone had the CPEL followed this simple idea.

Jeff Immelt, the Chairman of the Board for General Electric, made the decision to turn away from the quarterly feeding frenzy for metrics and focus on the long-term strategy for the company. Wall Street did not take this well, nor did the 18 presidents of the individual groups in the company. He stuck with it though and has proven it is a viable way to do business. There have been hundreds of studies on the relationship between CSR and profitability, and one led by Gregory (Gregory, Tharyan and Whittaker 2014) that tested a number of existing models found that "[t]aken as a whole, our results show that markets positively value most aspects of CSR, and do so because in the long run, measured across most dimensions, high CSR firms have a higher expected growth rate in their abnormal earnings."

Perhaps the most appalling fact is that many organizations profess their allegiance to high ethical principles and their commitment to CSR, while acting the opposite. The Costa Rica Mining project is one example.

So, what does a CPEL do in an imperfect world? Imagine you are the CPEL in a Canadian organization (transparency.org rank of 10), and that your country has laws and guidelines relating to the Sullivan Principles and CSR. You have a project in the Peruvian rainforest (transparency.org rank of 85), whose social and environmental laws are significantly more relaxed than those in Canada. You can follow the local laws in Peru and break or reinterpret the guidelines and laws in Canada, thus reducing, for example, the environmental costs of the project to increase short-term profits. Let's say you decide to take this approach and look the other way on an environmental issue. It would be illegal in Canada, but rationalizing, one might think the damage to the local population is not too bad. You have a Swedish organization on the project (transparency.org rank of 4) who is observing your actions. Think about the message you would be sending to the CPE. It is a certain way to lose trust, which is the foundation for leadership.

We can offer a simple suggestion. Set the bar high with the Sullivan Principles, and accept the fact that not everyone will achieve the goals. One cannot change thousands of years of cultural tendencies on a project, nor should one. One can, however, describe a realistic vision that encourages people to achieve as much as they can. To do this in practice requires confidence in oneself, commitment to a vision, and the willingness to accept failure when people try. So now let us see how CSR was applied in this case study.

It is an unfortunate reality that organizations engaged in oil and gas exploration and exploitation operate under an ethic of production deadlines, not fulfillment of indigenous peoples' rights. Even though one cannot realistically expect corporations to place indigenous communities on the top of their stakeholder management planning, it should be reasonable to assume they are part of the process, actually an important link of the chain in order to accomplished the much desired Social License to Operate (SLO) – a landmark that too often faces incredible delays owing to having misjudged this very part of the stakeholder management. Indeed, often communities' rights are handled as negotiating points rather than as entitlements.

It is a fact, too, that organizations and governments are increasingly offering services (e.g., educational and medical assistance) as part of the package deal, as if they were bargaining chips for the oil industry to utilize rather than acquired rights. Any stakeholder would expect that rights are there to be respected, not only as a way to overcome an ethical conflict or dilemma, but also and principally for reducing corporate risk exposure, gaining knowledge on a new dimension, ensuring proper and sound financial and insurance back-up, and gaining competitive advantage to be utilized in projects to come.

Actually, this concept relates more to theory than to practice, as the truth is that on the field PMs do what they feel is the shortest way to accomplish what they have been pursuing for so long. PMs actually do not count on the necessary time, patience, or piece of mind in order to find the best possible strategy to overcome operational drawbacks and unpleasant surprises that indigenous communities too often come up with. Even though this is in fact a subject that should have been addressed in a timely way by headquarters-based management along with their contracted field consultants, the reality is that management does not pay too much attention to the field consultants' findings and recommendations. Management tends to be more focused on or concerned with all the technical matters that encompass the permitting process of a project as well as the scoping and appointment of contractors. Community consultants relate more to remaining politically correct on the part of the project developer rather than result-oriented, this being a serious error that too often costs much money and tends to delay the execution stage of a project. Nevertheless, PMs should be acquainted with the community-related variables or at least give this area the relevance it holds for the project's development sake.

The ethical dimension may actually bring about an entire new world of opportunities for project managers and organizations to learn from, capture knowledge, and find ways to disseminate it across the organization, despite the contextual limitations and related timing pressures. It is precisely the complexity of the context that makes organizational learning and its associated by-products a fundamental element to assimilate when seeking for better project management practices leading to the achievement of competitive advantage. In fact, it is up to the organization to adopt them and try gaining a competitive profile for both the ongoing and upcoming projects in hostile contexts.

References

Elkington, J., *Cannibals with Forks: The Triple Bottom Line of 21st Century Business*. 1998, Oxford, UK: Oxford University Press.

Giles, O., *Shipping Law*. 1986, London: Pitman.

Gregory, A., R. Tharyan, and J. Whittaker, Corporate Social Responsibility and Firm Value: Disaggregating the Effects on Cash Flow, Risk and Growth. *Journal of Business Ethics,* 2014. 124(4): 633–657.

Grisham, T., *International Project Management: Leadership in Complex Environments*. 2009, Hoboken, NJ: Wiley, 403.

Hanson, A.J., *Sustainability and Competitiveness*. 1994, International Institute on Sustainable Development.

Harris, C., Pritchard, M., and Rabins, M., *Engineering Ethics: Concepts and Cases*. 2000, Wadsworth.

Moon, C., and Bonny, C., *Business Ethics: Facing up to the Issues*. 2001, London: Profile Books.

Unknown, *Business and Sustainable Development*. 2002; Available from: www.bsglobal.com.

2 Mining and extreme transport

Why stakeholders should look twice before committing

We will use three well-differentiated case studies to demonstrate different angles on the way project-related barriers may be overcome well beyond the known traditional project management guidelines. The scenarios where the case studies unfold range from the tip of South America to Central America, as well as the Canadian Arctic. Operations management, procurement and ethics, operations structure and strategy, and cross-cultural management are the main topics to be discussed, always within a stakeholder management perspective. Stakeholders addressed in the case studies engulf a wide variety of actors for whom diverse strategies are proposed.

A. Case study: silver mine in remote northwest Argentina

1. Background to the case

This project included construction of a new mining site located in northwest Argentina, near the Bolivian border, that involved Argentines, Chileans, and Canadians. A Canadian mining organization was developing silver, zinc, and lead mines in northern Argentina which required that a complex inbound and outbound logistic operation be carried out across the Andes through a number of Chilean port options. Technical matters on logistic and negotiation issues with both Chilean and Argentine suppliers, and authorities, meant hidden agendas and rivalry on the political side and changes from innovation from a managerial perspective.

This project included two well-differentiated phases. The first was construction and the second operations. The first phase was awarded to a well-known Buenos Aires-based engineering organization with modest experience in mining but a significant record on large infrastructure and energy projects around the world. It had solid political connections within both the state and federal governments. It was this organization that launched a logistic Request for Quotation (RFQ) as the appointed EPCM (Engineering, Procurement, Construction, Maintenance), in order to bring the necessary capital goods from diverse origins up to the job-site located at around 4,500 meters above sea level.

Brand-new capital goods such as ball mills, crushers, OHT (OHT refers to Caterpillar off-highway trucks capable of carrying up to 150 tons of mineral concentrates per trip), generators, and transformers had to be sourced and carried from the USA and Canada. Second-hand equipment such as conveyor belts, along with an entire truck shop, was sourced in remote places such as Indonesia, the Philippines, and northern Australia where they had been utilized in the recent past. Some other pieces of equipment were manufactured locally.

The project lies some 800 KM from Antofagasta on the Pacific and 1,500 KM from Buenos Aires on the Atlantic. The Chilean logistic alternative turned out to be shorter in principle, but it actually ran across the Andes Mountains, whereas the Atlantic option turned out to be longer but it ran across flat terrain, making back and forth traffic easier, more reliable, less risky, and possibly faster and more competitive despite the distance. A more benign 12-month weather window on the Atlantic was also a factor, especially when considering that a heavy penalty system was in place should the EPCM get delayed in commissioning the plant. However, the decision to operate through the Antofagasta, Angamos, Mejillones, and Iquique port complex in Chile was taken, given the heavy-lift and overdimensional nature of the cargo to be carried, which made it advisable to cross the Andes through the Paso de Jama border passage.

Unlike Buenos Aires and its upriver satellite ports, this passage turned out to be ideal as it did not show any major physical restrictions in terms of port operations, handling, and ground transport on the low-boy type of truckloads. Paso de Jama had a 10-month working window that gave the project plenty of time for planning inbound operations and effectively crossing the Andes without climatic surprises. However, a presumably good 10 months could suddenly shorten due to extreme weather conditions, and this was regarded as an acceptable risk. Figure 2.1 exhibits the existing relative distances between Argentina's northwest region and the most direct ports in Chile.

The possibility of social unrest on the Argentine side remained low given the remoteness of the border passage, which provided the project with a nearly perfect opportunity to conduct overdimensional cargo operations that otherwise would have possibly resulted in stakeholder protests along the way. The Chilean side remained neutral as the cargo was regarded as cargo in transit and therefore unworthy as a potential target. Even though the Antofagasta port was regarded as far from ideal to handle project cargo, owing to a certain degree of congestion for the cargo to reach the outskirts of the city, other nearby cost-competitive ports were also available and eager to compete for their piece of the project.

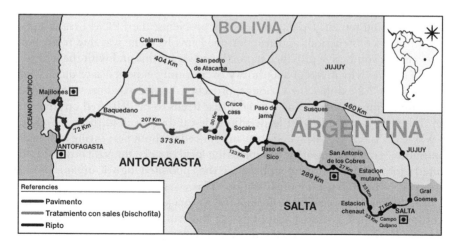

Figure 2.1 Argentina's NW region and Chile's region II.

2. Program in detail?

Like the EPCM, construction-related logistics were awarded to an Argentine organization holding good connections in Canada. This provided a global and unified network of American associates with offices across the critical sourcing places, as mentioned earlier, as well as on a global basis. The Buenos Aires-based EPCM was awarded the construction contract by Vancouver-based management; however, this very same EPCM had chosen to operate with the Argentine logistic organization. It was likely influenced by their awareness of the existing links between the logistic organization and the mining organization's head office in Canada. At that time, the Canadian organization was well aware of the importance of working with local organizations as long as they proved to be efficient and competitive. Their policy was to favor local organizations as much as possible, provided that they were cost-competitive, and could deliver political back-up should a conflict with stakeholders arise. One may assume from a PM standpoint that this may generally be regarded as a good strategy inasmuch as it renders suitable cover from potential social risks at the project site.

Once construction works ended and the mine was eventually commissioned, it was the EPCM that sought to expand its influence and run the logistic operations as well, given the business potential it imagined. However, it was the logistic organization that also pretended to remain active in the export process for the upcoming concentrates. This was based on their strengths and knowledge of the mine, topography, roads, border passages, ports, shipping, and further operational variables they had managed to optimize for the project's benefit. Canada's head office management was well aware of the EPCM's limitations in carrying out export logistic operations, as it was not its core business. Various meetings and discussions with the existing logistic organization were held in Vancouver with respect to planning the exports several months before commissioning occurred.

The EPCM leadership style was regarded as autocratic, close to arrogant at times, and to further complicate the environment, the quality of construction was not up to the miners' expectations. The EPCM's leadership style is well known across Latin America as comparable to Hernán Cortes or the Spanish "conquistador" (or conqueror) who had no mercy for the Aztecs. Cortes's famous strategy, which is actually studied in leadership books and papers, burned his own fleet in order to wipe out any possibility that his men would retreat. Despite the quality problems, the EPCM firm did manage to complete the construction, and its continued involvement was due to its political connections in a conflictive province in northwest Argentina and with the federal government. This was why it was given priority over mining experience or quality of construction. Figure 2.2 exhibits the various approaches a leader may take when addressing project team members concerning a project that needs to be delivered on time and on budget. It is clear that the EPCM leadership style can be placed to the right end of the graph where decisions are taken and then announced without permitting any feedback.

Continuing with their rationale of supporting local players, the Vancouver-based staff promoted a joint-venture agreement between the appointed logistic organization and a large provincial-based trucking organization. This was designed to jointly plan and execute an ambitious exporting plan through the Antofagasta port aimed at delivering the concentrates to a smelter located near Lima city in Peru. The owner of this organization happened to be the son of a national senator and future provincial governor. His family managed a local newspaper, a TV program, a civil construction organization, a hospital,

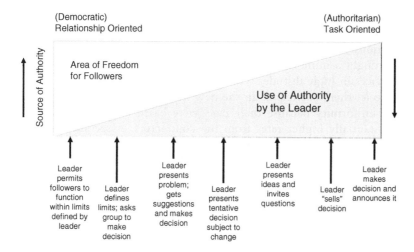

Figure 2.2 Situational leadership.

a tourism complex, a foodstuff distribution organization, and other businesses in town. The second most important trucking organization, a longtime rival and competitor, also edited a daily newspaper that coincidentally competed for the same audience and whose owner also managed a number of other businesses in town. It was not difficult to envision an emerging conflict of interest, just around the corner.

The initial exports during the first few months meant just a few containers a week that allowed the logistic operator to smoothly coordinate the ship-shore interface with no major interference, while gaining knowledge of the conditions along the way. By then, the mine had set up a number of processes aimed at optimizing the processing of concentrates and defining the grade for silver and other minerals. As the weeks passed and problems were worked out, the number of containers increased from 8 to 25 or 30 per week, with peaks of 50 containers per week. But in some of the following weeks no trucks at all were needed, so the processes varied from high peaks to deep valleys, mostly on short notice.

This type of operation was needed to fulfill what the Peruvian smelter organization ordered; otherwise the purchases of materials and equipment would switch to other organizations. Production proved to be running well, but the logistic side was struggling. This resulted in a lack of equipment, and operational bottlenecks recurrently turned up at various spots. Inappropriate truckloads of equipment were the rule rather than the exception, along with inadequate communications on a number of stretches across the Andes. Satellite tracing of the units became too expensive and unreliable because of the existing topography. This coupled with icy roads during winter time, heavy rains in the wet season, a wide array of natural perils, and operational drawbacks, made logistics a key component for the ongoing operations.

Operational peaks and valleys continued ranging from 200 trucks a week to just 20 to 30 containers in the following week. This situation brought about equipment imbalances leading to lack of chassis and containers, operational bottlenecks, congestion along the chain, extra customs clearance expenses, higher ocean freight due to lack of carrying capacity, higher port costs, and demurrages arising out of accrued delays. But, it also opened the door for other suppliers that were previously not selected to provide services to offset whatever service became needed in a peak time. An excess of demand made ground transportation, port, shipping, and customs clearance rates and expenses spike, while margins for the mine became narrower because concentrate grades did not meet the expectations of the feasibility study. The perfect storm was closing in.

The EPCM brought a number of different and unqualified provincial truckers to provide their services in high altitudes while exerting a great deal of pressure on the Vancouver staff to let them participate in the new matrix. The new suppliers did not commit to tariff uniformity because their rates were based on supply and demand, which led to substantially higher rates from the contractors. A second trucking organization, and ever-rival of who was by then the main trucking supplier, offered its fleet to support the operation, provided it paid a 30% premium. Other larger Buenos Aires-based organizations that had to position their units from the south to northern Argentina also offered their units either directly to the project or under the umbrella of any of the other mentioned players, leading to the formation of a sort of ground transportation services cartel.

Some large Chilean organizations also contributed to the general confusion by offering their Antofagasta-based trucking units. In addition, the indigenous communities, which had been quiet and did not object to the convoys passing through their lands, suddenly demanded the payment of tolls or sharing of profits for their communities. In the meantime, shareholders also exerted a tremendous amount of pressure on management to optimize the ongoing operations by matching the purchasing orders coming from Lima with both production and logistics in an effort to operate under a lean operation philosophy.

As a result, various general managers, COOs, and higher executives who were sent down from Canada to Buenos Aires and then to northern Argentina, saw themselves at the helm for a short period of time and then removed in just a matter of months – owing to an apparent lack of ability to overcome the challenges. A port strike throughout Chile burst into the middle of the peak season, making things even more chaotic for both the management and suppliers. This led to heavy congestion along the supply chain and resulted in all sorts of monetary claims.

The locally based Argentine staff saw a great opportunity to gain influence with Vancouver's head office, as the locals were actually where the action was taking place and where effective short-term solutions were badly needed – the war was raging and there was little time to take decisions. The locals made promises to management to quickly provide responses by appointing those suppliers who, in their experience and professional opinion, turned out to be the most qualified and duly certified to carry out the operations in an orderly manner. Probably correct if only looking at the certificates, stamps, and quality programs, they attended and received certifications. But the results turned out to be the following:

- Little by little, a number of third-party truckers were engaged under the umbrella of a couple of large Buenos Aires-based organizations. A few units were still hired from the original contractor, as a way to show some gradualness in their new procurement strategy, while hiding their actual intentions.
- Rates were substantially higher, casualties occurred along icy roads due to inadequate truckloads, and unskilled or drunk drivers as well as a lack of proper training became more than evident.
- Truckload and unload demurrage charges became an invoicing industry, rarely neglected by the site-based management, and ever justified by alleging weather

constraints, unexpected customs clearance processes, or short notice to prepare the supply chain.

- Demand was never matched as requested from the Peruvian smelter.
- Contingency planning became an opportunity for site-based staff to hire auxiliary services, such as the positioning and operation of crane-trucks to repair an engine or structural breakdown of outdated equipment, whose breakdown was often attributed to severe weather conditions.
- Extraordinary customs clearance expenses too often arose out of overtime charges at the job-site, due to the truckloads not being ready to be inspected and cleared when requested.
- Newcomers were paid at once, whereas original suppliers were paid only after 90 to 120 days. This led to holding everlasting and eroding discussions on the applied rate of exchange under an inflationary context between management and the original suppliers.
- Too often, the original trucking organization was requested to position its units a week before the cargo was ready. In fact, the mining management tended to neglect the waiting time-related demurrage. Or if paid, badly renegotiated it. It became clear that management's intention was to gradually erode and get rid of the original suppliers on the grounds of their "apparent inability" to adapt or adjust to the operational requirements at a given point in time.
- The new suppliers only incurred demurrage in less visible places, such as at the border or in Chile, while their invoices were never reviewed or renegotiated but were paid at once. Discretion turned out to be the unwritten procurement policy at the expense of the project's objectives of lean manufacturing, and efficiency along the chain.

Even though it is difficult to understand why the decision-making power was gradually left to the Argentine staff, given that their decisions had a negative impact on the mine's operations cost, one may only assume that Vancouver-based management let the locals play their own game in exchange for meeting the sales deadlines. In other words, keeping unskilled and ineffective foreign staff in South America is like throwing beef to a herd of lions in Africa. Local staff can smell unfit personnel (beef) from a distance and have no doubt they will act accordingly (lions). The authors have witnessed this phenomenon on numerous occasions across the emerging world, and foreign-based organizations seem not to learn from it. In this case, and all others, knowledge of the local languages, cultures, and business models is essential. If one is to gamble, one must know the rules.

3. Lessons learned

a. Culture

The high turnover rate of the Canadian executives, along with the gradualism on the part of the headquarters, eliminated the ability to narrow the gap between shareholders, Canadian executives, and Argentine managers. These societal, corporate, and project cultures require trust, empathy, and a sharing of goals. They require leadership that is inclusive rather than exclusive. Canada-based executives clearly failed in anticipating the Argentine executives' methodology. In leading global multicultural teams, it is important to understand local custom and culture, not to buy into it carte blanch, and not walk away from one's ethics and values. Looking the other way is never a prudent strategy.

In providing leadership, where local practice is questionable, it is mandatory that the parent organization have even more participation in a project. This is often done in a few different ways. One is to hire a local and move it to the home office for a rigorous training program, then watch it closely. Another way is to send a home office person to the local environment and have him or her trained by locals in the way business is conducted. The home office needs to trust the person running the local operation and should be comfortable that he or she will not expose the project or the home office to unnecessary risks.

As one example, we were in need of a person to work in India. We hired an Indian national and sent him to Thailand for training. We then sent him to Korea, China, and back to India. Now we had what we needed: an Indian national with global goggles. We were extremely successful, as an Indian conglomerate hired him away within a very short time.

b. Sustainability

An excessive fear of dealing with stakeholder-based protests hindered the mining organization from setting up a higher quality integrated engineering scheme that could have been adopted foreign and domestic organizations. As noted above, the key to sustainability is to understand exactly what is happening on a project. Once the initial planning is completed, it is essential to have regular reviews of all aspects on a project, including CSR, stakeholders, communications, scope, risk, time, quality, time, politics, and indigenous needs and wants. If there is mutual trust and respect, this is not an impossible task. In the absence of trust and respect, this is impossible and leads to the results of this case.

c. Operations

Arrogance, a lack of vision, a lack of knowledge of the available capacity, or the dynamics of the region could well have been the reasons why Vancouver-based management did not design a contingency plan to avoid interruptions due to the Chilean port strike. This event happens systematically every three years. How come nobody in Chile or Argentina made Vancouver-based management aware of this? Domestic roguery is an expensive industry to ignore across Latin America, if it is not dealt with by skilled executives with combat experience in mining operations. Great financiers or strategists are not likely to make great operational minds in conflictive territories.

What we have found in numerous global organizations is that they tend to ignore local environments, regardless of the continent. Most organizations have marketing or sales teams made up of business analysts, whose job it is to create relationships with potential customers. Frequently, their pay packages are designed to motivate finding new business, and not necessarily to give assurance that they have considered the new business risks in their efforts. This is especially the case when the new project involves design, construction, and operations. The simple reason is that organizations do not maintain all of this expertise, but rather outsources portions. Outsourcing leaves gaps in leadership, responsibilities, knowledge, and operations.

George Washington, the first president of the USA, is known to have said: "give me six hours to chop down a tree and I will spend the first four sharpening the axe." We have often attempted to lead our customers to this way of strategic thinking, and that avoidance is by far the most effective approach on global projects. Unfortunately, most customers do not listen, which is good for consultants like ourselves but bad for the local governments, citizens, and businesses. As we have indicated above, often projects turn out to be lose-lose propositions for all concerned. Short-term wins for corruption are long-term losses.

d. Leadership

The concepts of gradualism and relativism on the part of the site-based management reflects the headquarter's transactional leadership approach. This results in a negative message to the original suppliers, who do their utmost to overcome challenges as they arise. Exposing them to pressures and demands from other suppliers, not originally selected, clearly exhibits a lack of leadership and of the necessary ability to make decisions under pressure in order to dismantle issues that can escalate. Leaving decision making in the hands of the site-based management, exerting no control, and hiding vital information from the shareholders on the way operations were conducted were hallmarks of this project, and it often is the rule and not the exception. A lack of leadership, coupled with a lack of skills and ignorance with respect to the market demands, creates fertile ground for problems to escalate with almost no limits.

e. Communication

The permanent rotation of Argentina-based foreign executives suggests a poor and inefficient communication effort leading to the gradual empowerment of local management to take over the running of operations, while at the same time displacing expatriates. Again, operations can be run well or poorly, and most likely the project will move on regardless. However, poor operating results will drag down profitability, especially during a slump in prices or a crisis.

It is essential that a reliable communications plan be established at the beginning of a project and be kept up to date as it progresses. As we have seen in the case studies, organizations change, people change, and stakeholders change. In a global environment, a CPE lead must establish a list of key stakeholders and establish dependable communication methods and timing. Assuming that the CPE lead has built trust, the communication plan will enable key stakeholders to be contacted directly and off hours. Trust must be present, and caution needs to be exercised so that the privilege is not abused. When unanticipated changes happen or when a strike can be anticipated, timing is critical.

f. Contracting and ethics

Hiring whatever supplier was available at whatever rate proved to be a huge mistake, with deep implications in terms of liabilities and associated costs. This encouraged corruption in the site-based management, late payments, and tendentious negotiations of trucking demurrage charges. It also increased the quota of unqualified suppliers, decreasing the share of experienced and more competitive qualified suppliers. It contributed to overpricing practices, murky contracting practices, based on false technical variables, and higher OPEX figures and noncompliance with commercial targets.

The rule of law is especially important in such circumstances, for without it there are no standards that can be used to keep order. The CPE lead must strive to apply a legal framework for the project and consistently push back on behavior that breaks the rules. Selecting a governing law is not an easy task, and one that should consider the maturity and dependability of the local system(s). Contracts should be crafted to fit within the national system, they should be fair to both parties, and they should be negotiated, and not just a competitively bid fixed price.

4. Challenges and suggestions

The following are some suggestions regarding how challenges may be dealt with from this case study:

- Corporate Complacency. Every time a difficult operational project located in the emerging world combines with very well-paid expatriates, and even better paid foreign-based managers who happen to travel regularly to the site, it is likely to bring about corporate complacency. The former ones tend to take advantage of the lack of knowledge and commitment of the latter ones, who too often are more interested in getting results the soonest possible. However, if one presents oneself as a juicy rich mark, the result is more than obvious. The repellent is hiring knowledgeable executives with strong personalities that may inspire followers with respect and perhaps a bit of admiration as well. Avoiding corporate complacency turns out to be critical.

- Corporate Inefficiency. Too often headquartered-based management and BODs are regarded, by both peers and media, as outstanding individuals with remarkable knowledge and strategic understanding capable of directing project investment across the globe. It has been the experience of the authors that most often a gap exists that tends to widen between the foreign-based management and the project site-based executives. PM practice tries to deal with this gap through the PM areas of knowledge by stating a number of steps and guidelines to follow on this or that situation. The reality is that inefficiencies tend to be hidden, changed, covered, and kicked out, to be ultimately accepted as the only way out to carry out the desired operations in a given setting. Inefficiencies should be avoided by making good use of knowledge sharing and transfer techniques that are well known in large retail corporations and many global oil and gas firms. This has little to do with calling for open bids with multiple contenders; it entails a much broader and pragmatic approach to PM practice. A firm does not need to become global to set up a knowledge repository from which their executives can profit. In doing so, the firm can make their projects more efficient and less dependent on hidden traps along the value chain. Field practice combined with corporate knowledge sharing and transfer strategy may become a powerful tool for any company that wants to be successful on both the financial and operations side of their operations worldwide.

- Operational Uncertainty. Always, trucking companies and suppliers of services for a remotely located project (e.g., cranes, catering, medical aid, mechanical assistance, and accounting) should first be locally sourced. If the local organizations are not fully suited to the task, an alliance or joint service with a regionally based firm should be encouraged and supported. Only if not available should it be sourced first at the regional level, and then at the federal level as the very last option. Loyalty and transparency are intertwined concepts that are the pillars of a successful operations strategy, on the part of both the suppliers and employees, provided that the geographical gradualism is duly observed and monitored. Keeping a sort of dual communication channel (e.g., headquarters and project site) with the suppliers may also serve as an incentive to avoid deviations and abuses of all kinds. The bigger the distance, the greater the OPEX becomes.

- Negative Leadership: This may become a contagious virus along the supply chain of a project procurement team if not timely identified and stopped. Suppliers tend to possess the rare ability to smell a negative orientation or behavior at a distance much earlier than globally experienced executives do. A negative leadership profile may prove expensive to a project, as too often the best suppliers tend to keep away from malpractices to reorient their sales efforts to more transparent and honest undertakings. A consultation process attempts to identify and separate positive leaders from the negative ones within a given community of stakeholders, and the CPE lead should be ready and able to do so for the procurement and logistic team in order to send clear signals to the market. When global organizations enter remote markets, the locals seek to understand how business is really to be done. Will it be the local way, the national way, the Western way, the Asian way, and so on. We recommend transparency, fairness, and a culture of CSR in all dealings. Your reputation will follow and often quickly.

B. Case study: a gold mine trapped between politics and environmental hazards in Costa Rica

1. Background to the case

This case study is about a well-funded Canadian gold mining organization developing its program in Costa Rica. Suddenly, and against all the odds, the program was interrupted due to allegations from a number of stakeholders that they had felled ancient trees. In doing so, agricultural and grazing lands were invaded and became unavailable for the communities. The felling of trees, occupation of the lands, and many other environmental-related variables had been approved by the government in an Environmental Impact Assessment (EIA) report that was submitted in a timely manner. Consultation, negotiation, and political issues, not logistic issues, took center stage in this case study.

2. Program in detail

This was a relatively small USD120 million CAPEX open-pit gold mining project to be developed in a country where mining was not a traditional industry and where a substantial part of Costa Rica's national income remains based on ecotourism. The project was located on the San Juan River by the Nicaraguan border where a number of communities made their living. The project had fulfilled all the necessary legal steps with respect to the permitting process and had successfully submitted and approved the EIA. Furthermore, it had also successfully completed the Feasibility Study (FS) by following strict rules set forth per Canadian standards. Even though the organization counted on official FS approval, there was a growing current of opinion that turned out to be contrary to the conceptual development of mining in Costa Rica and certainly very opposed to open-pit mining.

Despite this contrary opinion, the mining organization started to place purchase orders in 2007 across both coasts of the USA and Canada, Australia, and South Africa, intending to cope with long lead times for capital mining goods. Suppliers were located from New York State to Washington State, as well as all over Canada from the Maritimes and Quebec to British Columbia. Such a dispersion of suppliers led the project to channel its cargoes through three different entry ports in two countries to reach the job-site, despite its small relative size and nearness to the job-site. Costa Rica's Puerto Limon on the Caribbean Sea and Puerto Caldera on the Pacific as well as Nicaragua's Corinto port were the typical ports of call for project cargo-carrying vessels.

Figure 2.3 shows the locations of the two main ports of entry, along with the San Juan River on the border. Both global logistics operations and domestic ex-port to site meant a substantial share of the CAPEX, and payment had to be advanced to secure the manufacturing of the equipment given the existing long lead times. Moreover, transit time ex-works up to the job-site tended to be longer than usual despite the relative geographical proximity of Central America to the USA, Canada, and South Africa. This was due to the need to transship in one or two ports and to poor frequency of sailings bound to any of the entry ports.

Inbound construction-related logistics, along with earth removal and early civil works, had already begun, despite an increasing movement of activists on both sides of the border. The project developer turned a deaf ear, given that it was clear by then that a community movement against the project was very much alive, growing strong, and expanding across the country. Communities that made their livings on the San Juan River in both countries joined forces with a number of groups with political influence in Costa Rica's capital San José. There the leaders were stiff opponents to the ruling party's position that supported open-pit mining. Both the communities and the political activists were against any type of mining activity, especially open pit, given its potential to harm the environment. Such issues usually demand a decisive stakeholder management counteraction strategy to limit or neutralize potential risks that may ultimately become an unstoppable snowball.

Thirty-two communities had raised concerns with respect to this project's potential impact on both the environment and economic activities on the San Juan River such as artisanal fishing, ecotourism, sport fishing, bird watching, aesthetic value, and coastal fish farming. To make things worse, the political activists used the potential political tensions this project brought up between Costa Rica and Nicaragua, especially when considering the Nicaragua's contemporary background of civil war and violence. It is amazing to notice how different two neighboring countries may become in terms of culture, values, and way of life, despite sharing comparable topography, weather,

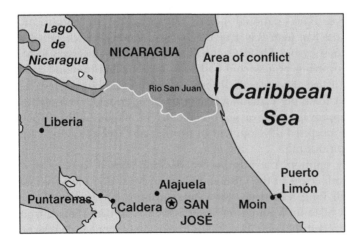

Figure 2.3 San Juan River and ports of entry.

history, music, culture, and even food customs. Identifying these aspects is of utmost importance during the planning phase of any project.

As a consequence of the evolving events, and considering that presidential elections would soon bring about a different set of considerations, the project reduced its drilling and future processing operational physical area from 126 to only 50 hectares in an attempt to avoid a still unlikely escalation of social unrest to levels that could endanger the project. Good will and transparency were regarded as credible signals as well as a considerable move by the Canadian management. Yet, one should never try to extrapolate home values and behaviors to a foreign setting without first giving it careful consideration. It becomes clear at this point that needs and expectations could not be more different in Canada and Costa Rica, and one does not need to be a strategist to visualize the upcoming set of problems should these issues remain unaddressed – unaddressed from the local level, not the Canadian level.

A right of way had to be cleared in order to start field operations, which quickly became the perfect opportunity for activists to deploy ever stiffer protests, which were shielded by the proximity to the presidential elections. A new president won the election and eventually gave in to the pressure exerted by both activists and communities to halt the project in 2009. Costa Rica's Supreme Court is at present dealing with the mining organization's lawsuit, and the country is facing the potential risk of having to compensate the investors for USD1 billion. Compare that to what would have been a capital-intensive project of USD120 million in a developing country full of social needs. It is easy to see who wins and who loses in terms of future capital disbursements. However, one can also allege that beyond the monies to be collected in future, the Canadian prospectors lost a lot of their corporate reputation in being unable to work out a solution for a small-scaled project in a low-profile country. This would translate into restricted capital for future undertakings, higher insurance rates, and higher collateral coverage, just to name a few impacts.

Figure 2.4 shows some of the many risks such a project must consider. Manageable risks encompass those of a technical and operational nature, environmental, social, and economic. However, hard-to-manage risks are more closely related to legal issues,

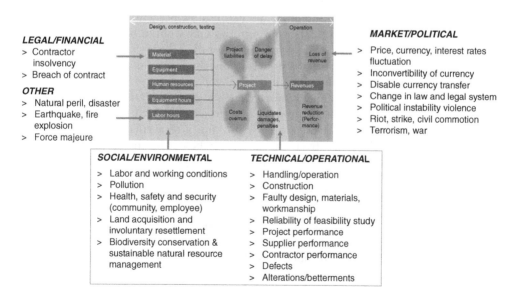

LEGAL/FINANCIAL
> Contractor insolvency
> Breach of contract

OTHER
> Natural peril, disaster
> Earthquake, fire explosion
> Force majeure

MARKET/POLITICAL
> Price, currency, interest rates fluctuation
> Inconvertibility of currency
> Disable currency transfer
> Change in law and legal system
> Political instability violence
> Riot, strike, civil commotion
> Terrorism, war

SOCIAL/ENVIRONMENTAL
> Labor and working conditions
> Pollution
> Health, safety and security (community, employee)
> Land acquisition and involuntary resettlement
> Biodiversity conservation & sustainable natural resource management

TECHNICAL/OPERATIONAL
> Handling/operation
> Construction
> Faulty design, materials, workmanship
> Reliability of feasibility study
> Project performance
> Supplier performance
> Contractor performance
> Defects
> Alterations/betterments

Figure 2.4 Sources of risk.

market conditions, and politics, which are sometimes considered to be force majeure, depending upon the contract. Other risks such as those of a cross-cultural nature are not so easy to identify and manage, especially in a project where two countries are involved, which, despite being neighbors, have deep attitudinal differences.

3. Challenges and conclusions

This case study provides a number of lessons through its focus on some of the critically important aspects of planning our such an endeavor:

- Stakeholder Identification. It should be apparent that the project stakeholder management (PSM) process turned out be totally unsuitable and counterproductive in identifying the real issues. More attention should have been paid to identifying the negative, positive, and indifferent stakeholders. The plan should then have suggested how to neutralize the negative and have the positive aligned and to help them spread their voices across the community. In doing so for the positive stakeholders, those showing indifference could be recruited to support the project. Those who were environmentally concerned and those showing interest in potential training and employment should have been recruited as allies to support the positive side. All this should have been methodically or professionally planned and executed prior to commencing the civil works and purchasing capital goods not as it had actually been done once capital endowments had been committed and announced through press releases. This is clear evidence of mismanagement at the consultation stage, which should have been formulated and put into practice by trained specialists who could identify issues and work out solutions in the shortest possible time.
- Stakeholder Management. Underestimation of conflicts occurs more often than suspected, especially when stakeholders do not feel inclined to speak out and clearly say what they think or how they feel; or when hidden interests lie concealed behind their words and cause the project team to receive misleading signals. PSM is a crucial part of a project's planning phase, no matter how peaceful a given setting may initially look or how friendly the communities may seem to be. As one often says in Latin America, "think bad, and you will most likely be right." Try it by yourself as it never fails. Once a project is in execution, the team must identify and repair stakeholder oversights in the planning.
- Stakeholder Suggestions. The authors were successful in creating a stakeholder management plan on another project. The project involved the construction of a new power generation facility in close proximity to a village of powerful and wealthy individuals. Aside from the normal stakeholders for a project, like the customer and sponsors, we determined that a small group of rather noisy residents could inflict significant damage on the project. One of the local neighbors was the daughter of a presidential hopeful. In this case, the neighbors had no formal association, so we created one to ensure that communications were effective and complete. We then created a series of regular public discussions in order to learn, educate, and include the residents in the planning process. Although there were still problems and conflicts, as the operations did not go well, we had created a reservoir of trust that could be drawn upon to mitigate the complaints.
- Politics Gone Wrong. Carrying out an open-pit mining project in a country with no tradition in the activity should have been a red flag for the Canadian mining

organization, regardless of how solid its political contacts or promises were. It is common across Latin American countries that a rather wide gap exists between executive power and that of the people, especially when politicians give a project the green light believing their reelection is highly likely. Or even when they rely upon constitutional amendments to make their stay in power the longest possible or even everlasting. It should also be noted that the independence of the state in Latin America is very weak, and as such the executive branch exerts influences of all types over the legislature. This variable is one that foreign-based companies often believe they may identify and comprehend through the vision of their embassies or by holding meetings and making commitments with the on-going politicians in office. This is a tricky business given the ever-dynamic political process of the region, which includes each nation's personality and the way a country's political shift may force changes to take place beyond its borders. This is a trend, which if not detected and adequately dealt early on, may deal a fatal blow to the project, as was the case here.

- Politics Alternative. Before Hong Kong reverted to China, the authors were consulting for an organization that had keen interests in the Chinese market. Hong Kong is an excellent base for operations in mainland China, and so we set about finding our representative for mainland China. Our selection came from the political elite, and we studied his connections (guanxi) in detail. Ideally, one wishes to find an individual who is powerful but in a nonpublic way that shares to some extent the values of the organization; who is a national; and who speaks a few languages. When Hong Kong was returned to China, the first president of the city state was that person. This requires long-term strategy, planning, and building a solid foundation for the future. For this case study, it would have helped the organization and two countries.

- Involvement and Education. Underestimating the impact of modestly educated stakeholders on public opinion and politicians proved to be another serious mistake. Contrary to previous case studies, this impact turns is more common than what one may expect. Those who attend a consultation process during a PSM program are often individuals who live near the project, with little formal education and limited access to the Internet or the outside world. This was a gold mining project located far from the main cities in Costa Rica by the border of Nicaragua: featuring jungle, rivers, lots of rain, small settlements, and limited infrastructure. A typical mistake lies in delegating the face-to-face process to lower ranking people when in fact what the stakeholders expect, despite their limited education, is to bring their concerns to the highest level. What happens most often is that the PM participates in the initial stage of the PMS process and then transfers the responsibility to members of the team. Stakeholders expect and demand that the CPE lead not only introduce and explain the project in detail, but also continue to receive their concerns, respond, and talk to them face to face without intermediaries and ambiguities of any kind. There is nothing stronger or more solid than a handshake, a straight look, and an honest response on what can or cannot be done. But it must be consistent throughout the project and must seem to come from the person who can take action.

- The CPE Lead. In this particular case, the PM kept busy travelling back and forth to the capital and the project site, and further abroad as he placed more importance on monitoring the suppliers than on the key stakeholders. Project management theory highlights the importance of stakeholders but from the internal rather than the external view. Where should the CPE lead have focused its attention? The answer is to all the key stakeholders, starting with the public, political class and then to the organizations that are implementing the project. In this case it was backwards. The fact is that a lead CPE must prioritize his or her time and simply must reserve time to hold the necessary meetings, and perform handshakes with all the key stakeholders.

- Culture. Culture played a key role here, as communities on both sides of the river shared a common interest in defending their rights to make use of the available resources. However, their values, backgrounds, history, and realities should have been assessed in greater detail before beginning execution of the project. As we noted, this proved to be a fatal error in the PSM process, as there are huge cultural differences between Canadians and Costa Ricans. Then there are the Nicaraguans with a tragic past who are much more decisive as a people than their southern neighbors.

- Culture of Costa Rica. Considering the Hofstede dimension of uncertainty avoidance, Canada is generally more accepting of change. Costa Rica is the opposite. The same is the case when it comes to individualism, with Costa Rica being very collectivistic. Central America was heavily influenced by the Spanish and wrenching changes they brought, for good and bad, and as a result the people are less willing to subject themselves to change. Given these tendencies, and not just stereotypes, it is extremely important to provide a sense of stability and trust, especially in those seen to have power. As we suggested above, it is very important that those in power are the ones providing the education and assurances.

- Culture of Nicaragua. Nicaragua and Costa Rica were a single autonomous province at one time, and so their cultural backgrounds are similar but not the same. Nicaragua is more subject to hurricanes and earthquakes, and as a result the people are strong, proud, resilient, and more prone to accept change than their colleagues to the south. Hofstede never measured the Nicaraguans on his scale, so there is no direct comparison numerically. Much similarity exists on the dimension of collectivism from our experience, but less on uncertainty. So while Nicaraguans may be more resilient to change than their Costa Rican neighbors, they are less so than the Canadians. If you are going to a knife fight, perhaps take a colleague from Nicaragua rather than Costa Rica.

C. Case study: a globalization strategy in the Canadian Arctic

1. Background to the case

This case describes a vertically integrated leading marine operator that intended to shift from a seasonal operation (June to October) to a year-round operation. This organization operates from coast to coast in northern Canada and along the Mackenzie River, serving local populations, defense installations, mining facilities, and oil rigs both onshore and offshore. The case focuses on what this organization should do to enlarge its operational window and move to continuous operation.

This organization, which will be referred to as Western Arctic Navigation (WAN), is the main transportation link for the movement of bulk petroleum products and dry cargo to communities, defense installations, and exploration sites across much of Canada's far northern territories. It counts on seasonal terminal facilities in many communities across Canada, which are strategically located to deliver dry and liquid bulk cargo in a cost competitive way throughout its extensive northern network.

With a floating stock of over 100 vessels and barges, it offers cargo delivery services from coast to coast from its operations in Richmond, British Columbia; Halifax, Nova Scotia; Churchill, Manitoba; and along the Mackenzie River in the Northwest Territories from the Port of Hay River. Figure 2.5 shows how the Mackenzie River runs across Canada's Northwest Territories, linking the Beaufort Sea with inland locations. Figure 2.6 exhibits the way Mackenzie River stretches its long arm connecting to the oil and gas province of Alberta through Hay River port and railway facilities.

The organization employs over 250 people during the peak season and is the founding subsidiary of a Canadian investment and management organization. This organization is jointly owned and integrated by Inuit communities from the Western Arctic and Nunavut regions, which this case study refers to as the Northern Territories Organization (NTO). With more than a 75-year history and a unique position in its market, this organization has a sense of safety and business continuity based on two solid pillars: Canada's long-term economic stability and the natural high-entry barriers such a harsh environment represents. However, the time had come for management to provide the strategic direction and future vision for the organization as it entered a new era of increased competition and new approaches to northern shipping routes.

2. Program in detail

Previously focused entirely on Arctic seasonal activity, the organization's shareholders decided to pursue a strategy of diversifying its scope to year-round operations, as noted. Management was aware that strengthening customer relationships and developing

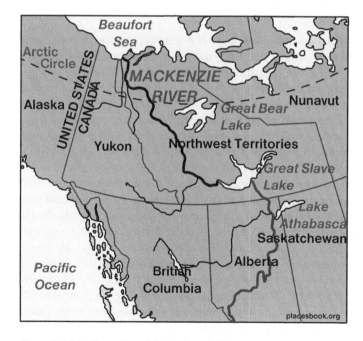

Figure 2.5 Northern Canada's Mackenzie River.

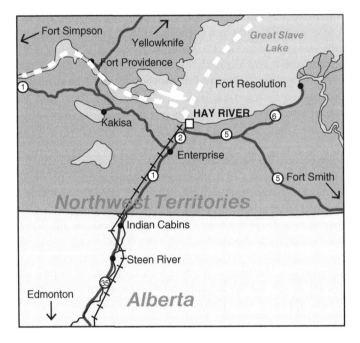

Figure 2.6 Hay River Port and railway facilities.

potential new markets would be early areas of focus, as well as providing strong leadership to a team in a transitioning environment. Given the upcoming competitive environment and the organization's new targets, the following challenges can be identified:

• Customer Focus. Management at any level communicates with the organization's current customer base to ensure that their needs are being met and that opportunities are identified where the organization may be able to enhance its offerings. A big part of connecting with northern customers was going to be demonstrating the organization's commitment to be responsive to its customers by meeting "on their turf." As the organization had recently refocused on its core operations, ensuring that its core customer base was being well served was vital. Such a strategy suggests a rather defensive approach by trying to improve upon what was apparently already being done well. It entailed no innovation, and there were no metrics available to measure some project competitive dimensions from a customer's perspective, given the complete absence of competition. KPIs should be designed and put into practice.

• Strategy. Increased competition from the Eastern Arctic has been gradually changing the marine shipping landscape in the North. That is why the organization needed to explore and evaluate commercial opportunities beyond its core community supply contracts. Opportunities included potential big industry contracts (mostly in mining and oil and gas), off-season activities, partnering opportunities, and the bundling of services. WANs management, with the support of the NTO executive team, needed to lead the development of a renewed corporate vision and a strategic plan that charted the organization's future direction and how it fit into the new competitive marketplace. This organization had been operating as a sole capital-intensive operator in a harsh environment where technology, as well as knowledge sharing and transfer seem to have played a key role in preparing them to face a new competitive context.

- Leadership. Reenergizing its team was a challenge for WAN. It had experienced competition in some of its markets for the first time, which cost the organization some customers, leading to a modest downsizing. At the same time, the level of industrial activity in Canada's north has continued to grow, and with it significant commercial opportunities for all modes of transportation. A new corporate vision that is clearly articulated and balances optimism with realism should provide a good stimulus to reinvigorate the team that is still transitioning from its crown organization roots to a competitive enterprise. The adjustment to a more competitive market was an easier adjustment for some. However, others on the WAN team needed mentoring, coaching, and encouragement to help good people work through the changes. Additionally, some areas of the organization were predetermined to benefit from bringing in new talent, skills, and perspectives, especially those who could provide the operations with innovation and efficiency.

- Operations. WAN had previously never needed to become a low-cost operator to ensure success, suggesting that historically business discipline and metrics never became necessary within the organization. However, due to increased competition from the eastern Arctic, market dynamics had changed. Driving costs down, optimizing operations, improving marketing effectiveness, and enhancing business development were required to ensure that future contracts started to be analyzed from a profitability perspective. Headquartered in Edmonton, Alberta, the NTO shareholders are aboriginal birthright development organizations, whose mandates are to maximize profits, develop economic opportunities, and create training and employment opportunities for beneficiaries, all of which suggests cohesion on the part of the stakeholders.

The NTO story begins with WAN's more than 80 years of uninterrupted operations as the marine service lifeline to the Mackenzie River watershed. Since then, it has grown to become Canada's only pan-Arctic marine organization. It is a foundation piece of the transportation infrastructure in the North and the cornerstone of the NTO group of organizations, purchased by the Inuit communities from the federal government in the early 1980s.

During the 1990s, NTO grew, using sound business principles, to become one of Canada's top 500 organizations. Building with corporate profits and private-sector financing, the organization diversified into southern Canada and then expanded its role as a major provider of northern infrastructure by acquiring a strategic airline covering a wide northern strip. Conducting solid business and making strategic investments established this organization as a leader in the Arctic, but also as a major conduit to the southern business world for the people of the north. This organization is divided into four business units that contribute to the overall revenue and profitability of operations:

a. Western operations

These operations encompass a full range of marine transportation services for dry cargo and fuel to all the communities of the Western Arctic from Point Barrow, Alaska, to Taloyoak, Nunavut. In addition, marine equipment is chartered to oil and gas and mining customers to provide additional marine support as required. The primary shipping route for dry cargo is based in Richmond, BC. Cargo is containerized and moved north along the West Coast, east along the North Slope of Alaska, and into Canadian waters for delivery to Western Arctic communities, mining, government, and industrial projects.

The organization operates out of a seasonally contracted port in Richmond, relying on the management and logistics capabilities of its sister subsidiary organization to run a customer call center, book cargo, coordinate delivery, log and containerize freight, manage the terminal, and load cargo. It uses owned equipment to provide this service, including Arctic Class II supply tugs and 10,000 to 12,000 tons of ocean-capable barges. Additional, year-over-year cargo demands are managed through the addition of a chartered barge, which is pulled in tandem tow with the existing 10,000- to 12,000-ton barges. Western operations are inclusive of the Hay River-based fleet of tugs and barges running 24/7 in the operating window that is also used for a portion of the distribution of freight arriving from Richmond destined for smaller communities.

Typically, the organization can move up to 350,000 tons of goods annually in the short 4-month shipping season, from July to the end of September, by leaving Hay River in barge trains loaded with 6,000 tons of cargo. A single 4,500 HP tug is often engaged to push six barges down the Mackenzie River in 6 feet of water, which may drop as low as 2–3 feet by the end of the season. This is an aspect that turns out to be surprisingly comparable to the jungle operations described earlier.

The organization had also developed the technology and expertise to successfully transport modular rigs and support buildings that serve oil and gas organizations. Fuel destined for the Western Arctic is provided by third-party fuel providers and arrives by tanker into the Western Arctic, where it is transshipped to its own barges for furtherance to community, mine, and project site delivery. Enlarging operations beyond a modest 4-month window required deepening both vertical and horizontal integration options further and looking beyond the Arctic and Canada. Not even the world's best technology can beat 2-foot draught waters in competitive terms, this being the main reason for this organization to look for strategic alliances to make use of its assets elsewhere during the off-season. Figure 2.7 exhibits a set of on-wheels modular homes getting ready to sail the Mackenzie River on a flat-type barge.

Figure 2.7 Modular homes carried on a flat-type barge.

b. Eastern operations

These operations are managed out of the Edmonton office, and provide dry cargo delivery to the communities around Hudson Bay out of the Port of Churchill, MB. The port operations in Churchill are carried out by combining owned and chartered marine equipment to provide marine services on a short seasonal basis from July to October. Marine support to offshore drilling and exploration projects from Russia is also provided, with the North Sea and Atlantic Canada using a state-of-the art fleet of three ice-class offshore supply vessels.

Providing marine services in such a harsh environment for global foreign oil and gas organizations from Russia, the USA, or China would present a great opportunity. It could lead to discussions of potential joint ventures, partnerships, or alliances to render services to such groups elsewhere during the off-season. Operational expertise and traditional knowledge are project competitive dimensions that become critical if year-round operators are intended. For instance, Figure 2.8 exhibits a multibarge configuration carrying project cargo and supplies on Hudson Bay.

c. Fuel sales

Historically, many customers contracted WAN for both supply and delivery of fuel. For a number of years up to 2009, the organization made arrangements to purchase and resell fuel to these customers. Then, it entered into an arrangement with a third-party fuel provider that would offer fuel sold directly to customers with WAN and any tug and barge delivery component required as a sub-contractor to the fuel provider. Such a strategy suggests a shift by concentrating on the organization's core business and by leaving ancillary businesses or services to those who may prove more competitive. A reduction in liabilities may have also played a role here, though none of these actions probably had an impact on bringing new businesses to enlarge the operating window.

d. Shipyard operations

WAN owns and operates a large shipyard facility that is utilized to repair and maintain its massive fleet of tugs and barges. In Hay River, a Syncro-lift facility and rail transfer system are used to lift and launch equipment, all of which demands counting on

Figure 2.8 Multi-barge configuration on Hudson Bay.

highly skilled maintenance and repair crews in a remote location. It counts on a fully modern high-pressure steel fabrication shop, a large freight-handling facility complete with heavy-lift cranes and International Organization for Standardization (ISO) containers, a fully equipped heavy- and light-duty mechanical services shop, industrial and marine supplies, including spill containment equipment and supplies, equipment rentals and leases, and electronic sales and services. Fixed assets are of course not mobile, so it is the mobile assets that need to be utilized outside the Arctic environment.

e. Geopolitics

NTO's objective is to assist Arctic indigenous beneficiaries in becoming meaningful participants in the economies of the Arctic and Canada as a whole by acquiring and operating the transportation infrastructure that connects beneficiaries with each other and the rest of the world. With infrastructure investments that provide stability, profitability, and a solid base for expansion, its vision is to continue as a major player in Canada's Arctic, demonstrating leadership, physical presence, operational support, business excellence, and growth.

Today, the Northern Territories Organization fully owns five subsidiary organizations:

- Subsidiary A, a key player in northern transportation infrastructure offering passenger, cargo and charter services.
- Subsidiary B, Canada's only pan-Arctic marine transportation organization.
- Subsidiary C, Canada's largest manufacturer of heavy equipment attachments and truck-mounted cranes.
- Subsidiary D, a recent acquisition in the expediting and logistics business.
- Subsidiary E, a network of retail industrial supply stores catering to the forestry, mining, oil and gas, and transportation industries in the north.

The Inuit communities that owned the mentioned organizations are each represented by their own development organizations in the Western Arctic. These organizations began with a vision to create more meaningful participation in the Canadian and trans-Arctic economies for the people they represent. They embody 20 subsidiary enterprises and joint ventures in a number of business sectors: transportation, petroleum services, retail, construction, manufacturing, environmental services, northern services, real estate, tourism and accommodation, and digital communications.

This group of organizations is in a very favorable geopolitical situation to demand from the Canadian government both financial and operational support in order to enlarge their business given the upcoming impact the Northwest Passage may have in the years to come – possibly with a PPP approach. Even though administrative control over the passage, and even its sovereignty, remain the ambition of various countries, it might be advisable for the organization to stay close to the various contenders. Counting on both fixed and mobile assets in such a remote region may provide a tremendous competitive advantage and therefore in this case, a geopolitical advantage. Figure 2.9 shows the routing of the Northwest Passage, which is becoming gradually operational as the ice keeps on melting, as a consequence of the so far unstoppable global warming impact on the poles. This region not only has strategic value in terms of shortening sailing routes and bringing bulk consumption and production closer, but also it encompasses valuable strategic natural resources such as rare earth elements that provide a varied number of applications in the defense, electronic, and automotive industries, to name a few. The

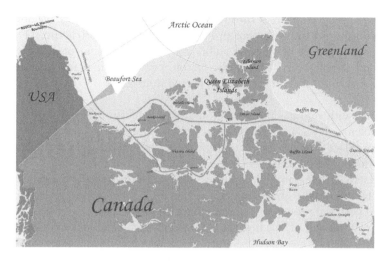

Figure 2.9 Northwest passage routing.

area is apparently full of hydrocarbons, iron ore, precious metals, and even diamonds as well. It promises to be either one of the world's future best examples of multilateral cooperation or the ground for severe sovereignty conflicts and disputes to come.

WAN has served some customers for over 50 years on the Mackenzie River and has developed many long-standing business relationships with territorial governments, Arctic communities, major oil and gas and mining organizations, as well as related service organizations. Therefore, its environmental protection and safety programs become of crucial importance in terms of both equipment and personnel. Strict procedures are prescribed for the handling of hazardous materials and for the loading and discharging of fuel from barges and tankers in order to prevent oil spills from taking place in such a fragile environment.

Given that the eyes of the world will be watching the way operations are conducted in such a delicate environment, it is advisable to keep the highest environmental standards along with CSR practices aimed at adding brand value, not only for the organization, but also for the organizations being served. Such a reputation may also trigger the interest of other organizations, bankers, and insurers to make partnerships to expand the marine and other services beyond Canada during the off-season. Maintaining good environmental practices and making them public may also help enlarge the operational window well beyond the Arctic. Perhaps most importantly, it might help bankers and insurers improve their corporate brands worldwide.

WAN demonstrates both leadership and commitment in all aspects of its operations to its employees and clients, showing consistent attention to health, safety, and environmental considerations. These are the jewels for a banker in need of becoming environmentally friendly. At WAN, meeting quality, health, safety, and environmental standards is the responsibility of each and every employee, across the organization, and includes all satellite operations. Hazard recognition is achieved through a broad variety of tools and techniques, including workplace inspections and the ongoing job hazard analysis completed by employees.

All levels of the organization are required to participate in strategies for preventing and eliminating hazards and spills. In order to sustain the highest levels of conduct in Quality, Health, Safety, and Environment (QHSE), the organization is committed to appropriately equipping employees through training and professional development and to building continuous improvement processes into their infrastructure. This is reflected through the conduct of internal audits and the monitoring of related performance management objectives. Part of the reason for an organization's continued success lies in its concern for it workers and is reflected in its goals:

- Treat all people with dignity and respect and have professional communications regarding problem solving and QHSE improvement strategies.
- Ensure the workplace is safe to enter and to work in, particularly for confined space entry and all fueling operations.
- Take the initiative to preplan jobs to ensure safeguards are in place to protect its people, equipment, and the environment.
- Wear required personal protective equipment for all tasks.
- Work only on equipment or machinery that is deenergized and locked out.

Total Quality Management (TQM) guidelines not only work as an entry barrier to competition in such a harsh environment, but also lead to a clean record and to project sustainability. This project dimension may work not only in favor of the marine organization, but also in support of the so often criticized global hydrocarbon and mining contractors that are increasingly active across the Arctic. Again, an impeccable track record in this respect may help the organization gain overseas contracts off-season and add brand value. It may also provide access to softer interest rates or lower insurance premium costs.

3. Lessons learned

Some important lessons are learned from this uncommon project, notably:

- Environment and Operations. WAN's tugs and barges are its lifeline, and, therefore, the maintenance and modernization of its fleet are of paramount importance. In compliance with ship safety regulations and self-imposed standards of quality, WAN adheres to a rigorous and comprehensive repair and maintenance schedule for all of its marine equipment. Mechanical and electronic components are constantly upgraded and replaced to ensure that only the most modern and effective equipment is at the hands of the ships' crews. This quality distinction should help gain the attention of potential off-season contractors beyond Arctic and Canadian waters. The potential for knowledge sharing and transfer may play a critical role for any investor in search of project differentiation and quality distinction.
- Indigenous Culture. Northern Canada's Inuit communities live and work in hard, depressing, and isolated places where the harsh climate leaves its marks on the people's attitude, vision, codes, norms, and the way they see themselves and the world. Canadian history has also set a mark on their minds, spirits, and hearts. In terms of cross-cultural leadership, this makes it difficult for them to look beyond the Canadian Arctic. Potential alliances or partnerships aimed at optimizing the utilization of their mobile assets overseas during the off-season might require hiring foreign-oriented management with a positive attitude towards globalization, along with a better or wider understanding of available business opportunities. Cross-cultural adjustments may be badly needed here if a company intends to achieve full-year assets operation.

- Other Cultures. As noted, the potential partners and service users might come from the European Union (EU), Russia, the USA, and Asia. As such, the range of business and social behavior varies drastically. The EU has strict regulations regarding the environment, and the rights of indigenous peoples; the USA does not. Russia has little current regard for any such considerations, and Asia is a mixed bag. China's concerns are probably less severe than Russia's, whereas Japan's are more restrictive than the EU's in many cases. Thus, WAN will face challenges. Groups that disrespect the environment and people will be difficult to understand, and so WAN will be forced to educate and lead. They will concurrently be in the position of learning from the other players about the functioning and competition in the global marketplace.

- Strategy. Natural resources globalization is a growing trend, and for the Canadian Arctic-oriented organization, an opportunity to learn from those who are truly global by adopting their best practices and discarding those that do not fit into their context. It is at this point that knowledge sharing and transfer may work as a strategic tool for this organization to gain competitive advantage, provided that the effort is well internalized and applied. Strategic alliances, partnerships, or associations that generate off-season revenues in foreign waters may also help this organization build and consolidate a knowledge database to become more competitive both at home and abroad. The incorporation of a Chief Information Officer (CIO) is highly advisable, given a firm's desire to jump into uncharted waters.

- Learning. As described above, learning about markets, attitudes, politics, technology, cultures, contracts, and more will challenge WAN. As a way to collect and integrate such knowledge, part of the strategy of relationship building should be a knowledge transfer component, regardless of the type of agreement. A partnership agreement should include moving local people to other geographical locations to learn the lessons that will see the organization into the 22nd century. The development banks have funded such endeavors for years, and such funding continues to pay large dividends.

- Entrepreneurship. From a CPE lead standpoint, WAN is in an unsurpassable position to operate its mobile assets in foreign waters based on its existing knowledge in harsh climate operations. Furthermore, WAN could also sell its expertise in the setup and operation of shipyard facilities, along with its ancillary services in complex comparable environments. To do that, shareholders' risk aversion, individualism, power distance, uncertainty avoidance, and long-term orientation should at least be assessed and worked out in order to generate off-season revenues while gaining competitive advantage. Other cultural dimensions such as humane orientation, institutional collectivism, performance orientation, and assertiveness may loom large and deserve an adequate weighing if distant geographies, languages, ethics, and further barriers become apparent along the horizon. As noted above, these can be easily addressed by putting WAN personnel into the countries that may utilize its services.

- Leadership. Based on a number of projects delivered on time and under budget, along with state-of-the-art technology in both fixed and mobile capital-intensive assets, WAN should be able to create global alliances and partnerships – provided of course that cultural barriers and fears to deal with global operations are effectively removed. A solid CPE lead track record, along with knowledge and technology, turn out to be powerful tools to accomplish better utilization of assets outside the Arctic region.

3 Mining and extreme infrastructure

What shareholders, directors, and management should look at twice before committing

In this chapter, we will use three well-differentiated case studies to demonstrate different angles on the way project-related barriers may be overcome.

A. Case study: massive iron ore project in northern Brazil

1. Background to the case

This case study encompasses a port logistic feasibility study, commissioned by a Canada-based mining organization, concerning the potential exports of 35 million tons per annum (MTPA) of iron ore extracted some 900 KM south of VALE's Ponta da Madeira port located in northern Brazil's Maranhão State. VALE is a major mining multinational based in Rio de Janeiro and a global player in the iron ore market, among many other things. Brazil repeatedly faces a significant logistic infrastructure imbalance as demand for transport and handling capacity largely surpasses supply. Consequently, this leads manufacturing firms to face serious operational bottlenecks, not only with respect to the available ports of loading, but also to ground and river transportation options. Even though there are an increasing number of infrastructure projects at any point, given the nature of Brazil's expansive economy, it is apparent that demand for infrastructural facilities tends to grow faster than supply. Narrowing the gap seems to remain a big challenge, no matter who is at the helm of the government.

2. Program in detail

The project site is located in the State of Pará, which together with the states of Maranhão, Amazonas, and Mato Grosso constitute what has been strategically defined as the New Agricultural Frontier. This area should be capable of feeding hundreds of millions of people around the world in the decades to come, as shown in Figure 3.1. Naturally, this requires both time to develop and infrastructure to be built, as well as a lot of capital endowments. The situation causes a great deal of pressure to be exerted from a number of current world-class exporters and importers, who export and import iron ore, copper, concentrates, manganese, construction materials, alumina, potash, fertilizers, steel coils and slabs, bauxite, coal, pitch, aluminum, caustic soda, dry and reefer containers, automobiles, and more. These industries place a strain on the limited carrying capacity that railways and river assets provide, as well as the insufficient road network linking poles of production and consumption with maritime and river terminals across Brazil's huge territory.

Roraima
Amapã
Amazonas
Pará
Maranhão
Ceará
Rio Grande do Norte
Parabia
Piaui
Pernambuco
Acre
Alagoãs
Rondônia
Tocantins
Sérgipe
Mato Grosso
Bahia
Goiás
Distrito Federal
Mato Grosso do Sul
Minas Gerais
Espiroto santo
São Paulo
Rio de Janerio
Paraná
Santa Catarina
Rio Grande do Sul

☐ Região Norte
☐ Região Nordeste
☐ Região Centro-Oeste
☐ Região Sudeste
☐ Região Sul

Figure 3.1 Map of Brazil.

The study concentrated on surveying a number of potential logistic alternatives: (1) the needed operational features a number of ports should possess along the northern and northeastern coast of Brazil in order to cope with the upcoming export volume; (2) the feasibility of utilizing a slurry pipeline leading most cargo volume to a single port of loading, e.g., job-sites; and (3) a combination these two alternatives. The case study points out the mining company's BOD's apparent, and surprising, lack of initial understanding or awareness of the actual critical role of logistic operations, with respect to a massive export operation prior to deciding on a given project investment.

Given the potential export volume, it was impossible to get it all channeled through a single port of export to split it into two nearby ports, or to combine two major and a minor scaled nearby marine terminals. Keeping economies of scale both homogeneous and constant is as important to the manufacturing process as it is to the export logistic operation. There are no existing railways in the area that would allow the design of a truck-rail interface that would reach a given port of export or complex of marine terminals capable of stockpiling and efficiently transferring some 35 MTPAs bound to the export marketplace.

Only a modest river terminal facility was available that might be adapted and converted into a kind of artisanal river port terminal, only after heavy investment and a long permitting process. This was in Marabá city on the Tocantins River, along which a number of barge convoys could alternatively be operated to reach the Port of Vila do Conde, leading to the Atlantic. However, this port terminal showed serious operational restrictions as it could only operate PANAMAX-type vessels capable of loading up to 60,000 tons, given the existing draught restrictions both at the entrance channel and alongside the piers.

What one must consider when designing a massive commodity export or import operation is the efficiency with which the entire chain works. The truck leg and the river leg, along with its respective loading/discharging terminals, must all be in line with the targeted vessels' carrying capacity if economies of scale and high productivity are needed. Iron ore's low relative value can be offset with large export volumes. However, lack of infrastructure and inadequate logistics too often means a death sentence for a project. The ores may be abundant, their extraction relatively easy, the metallurgy results may be encouraging, and the EIA and stakeholder approval may be achievable in a reasonable period of time. None of this is useful, however, if the logistic operations represent a huge bottleneck that can only be worked out by substantially increasing the CAPEX, if feasible from a technical standpoint. The authors have often witnessed how arrogance can blind the judgment of those in charge of deciding whether to continue or withdraw: "there is nothing our engineers cannot overcome." This is a statement we have often heard from the highest layer of various natural resources firms across the Americas.

Typically, the term "PANAMAX" refers to the size limit for ships travelling through the Panama Canal, although the canal is nowadays capable of passing much bigger vessels. But the increased size of the canal will not matter if Brazil's physical restrictions are still in place, and will be for a long time. Again, keeping the entire supply chain duly aligned is simply critical for a project's sustainability.

Even though the draught alongside the berths varied from 14 to 20 M, ships could only operate safely up to the 12-M depth restriction at the Quiriri access channel right outside the breakwater, which was planned to be dredged in the future in order to let larger vessels operate at the new terminal. Moreover, restrictions on the length of the vessels also hindered the port from operating larger vessels. Larger vessels can make their way by entering the port on a 14.5-M high tide, provided they do not exceed other operational restrictions. This aspect tends to increase operational risks and run against project sustainability. Typically, operations time, insurance premiums, labor costs, and even interest rates are likely to rise in such conditions. This marine terminal already had shore space commitments with several strong and influential players in the steel and fertilizer industries, who demanded a significant free surface to stockpile its inbound raw materials and outbound end products.

Figure 3.2 shows the relative locations of Vila do Conde and Marabá terminals, which are linked by the Tocantins River. A number of existing and planned railways can also be seen, but the most critical running from Carajás up to the northern coast turns out to be fully owned and utilized by VALE. One must ask where were the project strategists when the BOD had to decide to invest or withdraw. Is it possible they had omitted surveying such critical variables? How come nobody could anticipate the need of adequate infrastructure to remain competitive in the global marketplace? These are the first questions that we will try to answer as we move on with the case study.

Expansion programs were in place to enlarge Terminal 1 and build Terminal 2 at Vila do Conde, but iron ore was not a priority, as shown in Figure 3.3. Terminal 1's pier allocation clearly defines where the port priorities actually stand, with focus on alumina, manganese, coal, fertilizers, and containers. Figure 3.4 shows the projected gross occupation rates for each berthing position. It is important to highlight that no berth can sustain a gross occupation rate beyond 80% without incurring congestion. The 20%

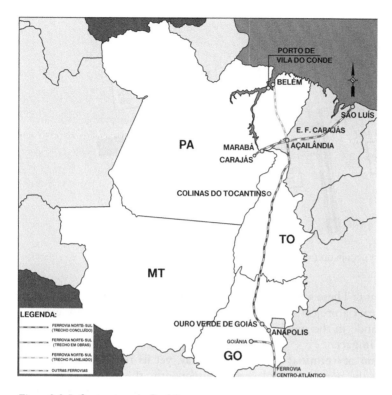

Figure 3.2 Infrastructure in Pará State.

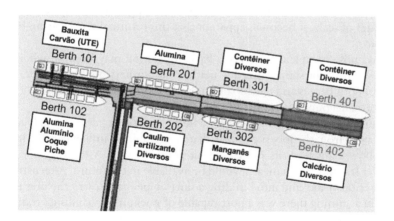

Figure 3.3 Vila do Conde Port Terminal 1.

balance encompasses mooring, unmooring, opening and closing of hatch covers, sanitary paperwork, hull and machinery certificate inspections, and further bureaucratic matters prior to departing.

The greater the balance rate, the less efficient and more costly a terminal becomes. In a massive commodity market, it is simply unachievable. In other words, counting on adequate river and/or marine terminal facilities is critical, though its productivity

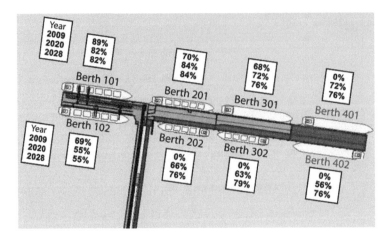

Figure 3.4 Gross occupation rates.

is equally important. These are not independent variables but rather are intertwined. They directly impact a project's very sustainability. Here one may easily envision the importance of a node in the supply chain and how risky it becomes to overlook it or underestimate its impact.

The construction of Terminal 2 is still underway, yet its future piers were already allocated amongst the ports' major players. Consequently, this port provided a minor volume alternative operated by engaging heterogeneous barge convoys to later stockpile pig iron ashore and load PANAMAX vessels by engaging a bucket-loading system. Despite this port's relative nearness to the job-site, and given the impossibility of achieving economies of scale, it becomes apparent that this terminal was far from being an acceptable choice.

Figure 3.5 shows how complex and risky a barge operation may become when the available floating stock is not standardized – neither the pushers nor the barges. The turnaround time of both barges and truckloads makes this type of operation slow, risky, costly, and therefore uneconomic and inadvisable.

Consequently, management decided to survey a number of other port terminals across Brazil and farther away from the job-site's immediate geographical influence zone in order to define into how many ports its annual output should be split. Assuming appropriate ground and river transportation means would be available in the future. Alternatively, management was seriously looking into building a slurry pipeline to carry the ores up to a given port – again assuming there was a port capable of stockpiling, handling, transferring, and loading 35 MTPAs. This option rapidly came to an end when the organization discovered that no port could handle 35 MTPAs – not even 10 million. Moreover, building an 800- to 2,000-KM-long pipeline running across various states in Brazil would invariably be rejected by the environmental agency, dozens of indigenous communities living nearby, and possibly an increasing number of stakeholders of any nature, size, and influence. Figure 3.6 shows an image that is common along the northern Brazilian states every time any type of construction threatens to invade aboriginal territories.

The job-site was in the Carajás area within the northern State of Pará, which is a world-class prolific region for iron ore, manganese, and copper exploration and exploitation. However, the dominant player is VALE which not only operates the world's

Figure 3.5 Barge operations at VDC Port Terminal, Pará.

Figure 3.6 Brazilian indigenous communities.

largest iron ore mine in the Carajás area, but also owns most of the existing and future railways to be constructed across Brazil, along with some of the largest ocean port terminals that serve its cargoes exclusively. At this point, one may wonder if this company had carried out some sort of strategic analysis, trade-off study, or SWOT (Strengths, Weakness, Opportunity, Threats) approach prior to committing to the development of this project as the number and quality of barriers to overcome appear to be gigantic.

Given that demand for infrastructure exceeded supply, VALE had no other option than loading its CAPESIZE (120 to 180,000 deadweight tonnage [DWT]) and VALE-MAX (380,000 DWT) type vessels without any possibility of hiring out any underutilized facility; not even one terminal had the capacity to efficiently operate their vessels. The term "CAPESIZE" refers to those ships that are too large to transit the Suez Canal or the Panama Canal, and so have to pass through either the Cape of Good Hope or Cape Horn to traverse between oceans. The term "VALEMAX" refers to the largest bulk carrier ever constructed and is only comparable to the CHINAMAX-type vessel, both of which are designed to carry iron ore to Asia.

Other marine terminals farther away were then surveyed in an attempt to provide another set of possible solutions, including the following:

- Itaqui Port in the State of Maranhão lies right next to VALE's Ponta da Madeira marine terminal where VALE loads its VALEMAX-type vessels and enables them to achieve world–class shipping economies of scale. This is absolutely key if they want to outperform much closer Australian suppliers to China. Ponta da Madeira was full and unlikely to open to competitors should they have available capacity at a given point in time. Whereas Itaqui could only offer a limited share within their future expansion plans in the range of two to three MTPAs. Comparable to Vila do Conde, Itaqui was already facing congestion and severe draught restrictions, making economies of scale even less likely to be achieved. Figure 3.7 shows an aerial view of Piers 1, 2, and 3 at Ponta da Madeira, as well as Itaqui port facilities right behind.
- The Pecem Port facility in the State of Ceará was designed as an offshore port terminal by considering both the protection of the marine environment and the maximum permissible draught in order to house from PANAMAX to short-range CAPESIZE vessels. This makes it attractive for massive bulk operations. Thus, both a long breakwater and access bridge became critical to keep its environmental-oriented offshore concept alive and make it at the same time safe and competitive by building a number of piers to target different cargo segments. The considerations here were the following:

Figure 3.7 Piers 1, 2, 3 Ponta da Madeira and Itaqui Port facilities.

- The administration took pride in highlighting its environmental commitment by preserving the local fauna and flora. A green belt with 3,000 hectares of dunes and vegetation separates the terminal from the industrial area, which also has an ecological station and two environmental protection areas. However, given the port's necessity to accomplish economies of scale and encourage its potential customers to channel their cargoes through this offshore terminal, they have allocated a large dune area next to the container terminal to operate massive cargoes such as iron ore.
- The demand to operate larger vessels, the need to count on larger yards conveniently located, and the absence of major urban centers near the port suggested a certain flexibility with respect to its environmental mandate. It is an aspect that may become critical when planning a massive iron ore operation. Another aspect to consider is that even though this port was intended to keep an industrial profile, about 43% of the fruits exported by Brazil pass through this terminal. That represents a total of 369,500 tons, including fresh fruit, pulp, and juice, all of which may lead to a new environmental standpoint. Dune areas, fruit exports, and environmentally friendly offshore design are not encouraging signals for planning a massive ore export operation. They represent an unclear impact on the environment. One should take all the necessary steps to safeguard the environment from any possible impact. It is necessary to explain such considerations to the stakeholders, including federal agencies, so there is understanding of the concept when granting final approval.
- This port was also undergoing an ambitious expansion plan that contemplated the construction of three more berths in addition to the two existing ones capable of operating both 120,000 DWT dry bulk carriers and multipurpose vessels. However, the critical aspect lies in the transfer operation, which can be defined as both the reception and stockpile capacity outside the port and the handling system and gear to reach the ships' holds. The port had not yet defined the area where the ores were planned to be discharged, either within the terminal or somewhere outside. Figure 3.8 shows the dune area that might be destined to operate dry bulk cargoes, provided that its EIA is approved.
- The existing railways also had to be considered to determine if a track extension would be built to enter the port or just a transfer station near the terminal. A multiple conveyor belt with a carrying capacity of 1,250 tons per hour might be

Figure 3.8 Intended dune area for dry bulk operations.

operationally acceptable as it could fully load a smaller type CAPESIZE in four to five days. Figure 3.9 presents the port layout with the existing and future facilities and shows the possibility of operating five vessels simultaneously in the existing infrastructure. Even though reception, transfer, operation, and railway operations were yet to be further surveyed, assuming environmental permits were granted, this terminal could handle around eight MTPA, far from the exportable target and too far from the job-site as well.

- The Port of Suape lies in Pernambuco State on the northeastern strip of Brazil. It counts on a 140-KM^2 active industrial hinterland that provides the port with an immense volume of inbound and outbound varieties of industrial cargoes. The master plan for Suape Port foresees the construction of an entire dry bulk terminal over the Cocaia Island right in front of the container terminal, as can be seen in Figure 3.10.

A number of topics need to be considered when surveying a dry bulk terminal:

- The projected terminal not only intends building a 350-M-long berth but also a 21-KM railway access that was being constructed by the Port Authority by the time this survey was conducted, in order to connect the future terminal to the existing railways' main track network.
- The operational draught at Cocaia Island was intended to reach 19- to 20-M, which would enable the operation of CAPESIZE vessels.
- The inner railway network will surround the future dry bulk terminal, meaning that the access to the stockpile yard should be versatile and reachable from various sides.
- The dry bulk terminal has been designed to operate an overall volume of up to 20 million tons, out of which 10 million tons are expected to be iron ore with the balance shared between coke (export) and clinker (import). This suggests that it

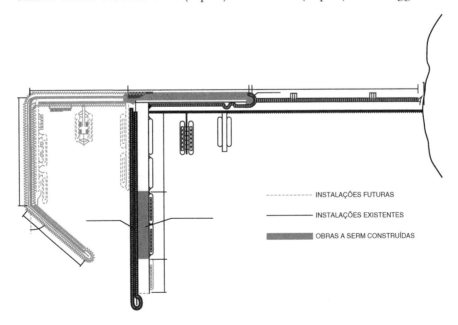

Figure 3.9 Pecem Port layout on existing and future facilities.

Figure 3.10 Suape's Cocaia Island future dry bulk terminal and expansion areas on the sides.

will be hard for the mining organization to be awarded a substantial area where it can stockpile and load. Moreover, many powerful bidders will assuredly demand their share.

- The loading gear and its load speed will have to be specified by the port operator at the time of bidding. However, given the intended volumes, it would have to be efficient enough to at least remain comparable to international standards. This aspect was crucial for the mining company in terms of productivity and cost optimization.
- The upcoming dry bulk terminal lies next to a natural reserve upon which a physical asset expansion is highly unlikely if needed in future. The possibility to expand is always a variable to bear in mind.
- Heavy rains during the wet season as well as strong winds throughout the year may impact negatively on port and shipping operations. These variables should always be taken seriously when figuring out the scale of a shipping operation.

The proposed VALE's Espadarte offshore maritime terminal lies at 00° 33' 17" S, and 47°53' 51" W on the island of Guarás by Curuçás county's northern coast – a very remote and isolated region. It lies 70 KM from the city of Castanhal and 140 KM from Belém. It is interesting to underline that the existing distance between Carajás and Ponta da Maderia's terminal is 892 KM away, where it is only 520 KM from Carajás up to Espadarte Terminal. Such a difference in distance leads to achieving a potentially lower cost per ton-KM (a variable that becomes more and more critical for massive ore volumes searching to gain competitive advantage based on operational efficiencies). China, Japan, and South Korea lie far away from Brazil, which was why it was critical to keep transportation costs low.

The projected terminal of Espadarte with a layout shown in Figure 3.11 was assigned a handling potential of 80 million tons and a 800-M berthing length. Its main commodities were soybeans and by-products, iron ore, manganese ore, pig iron, and copper concentrates, operating on the basis of an inner draught of 16 meters and outer draught

Figure 3.11 Espadarte Port layout.

of 25 meters. Thus, it indicates the possibility of anchoring a 200,000–DWT Floating Storage Transfer Station (FSTS) at the outer port in order to regularly feed CAPESIZE vessels by engaging PANAMAX shuttle vessels back and forth by linking the pier to the FSTS. Not only is iron ore acting as the driveshaft towards larger marine terminals and greater economies of scale, but other commodities that need to lower transportation costs and increase competitiveness include steel, nickel, copper, aluminum, biofuels, timber, cellulose, grain, and so forth. Consequently, there will be a battleground for facilities in northern Brazil once this megaterminal gets built and assigned to its new operators.

However, all facilities share a common, and so far unsurpassable, barrier represented by the huge environmental impact a project this size would have on both people and the environment. Espadarte offshore terminal is planned to be developed on Mãe Grande de Curuçá, a natural reserve that is characterized by large coastal areas of mangrove swamps inhabited by people who make a living along the coast, as shown in Figure 3.12.

Figure 3.12 Interisland bridge linking the mainland with Espadarte Terminal.

Consequently, both the federal and state environmental agencies expect this area to have an impact on both the ecosystem and their inhabitants. These are two aspects VALE is already working on while keeping a low profile.

Not only is VALE interested, but also MMX and Anglo American are some of the organizations that are silently moving forward with their plans to develop massive dry bulk operations on Guarás Island. One can imagine that much of this development might be accelerated should oil and gas be discovered near the entrance of Pará's Amazonian fluvial system, since new infrastructure would be badly needed to support hydrocarbon operations. All of this would require a cycle of high commodity prices to become viable. At the end of the day, all that matters is to forecast the effects that competing commodity prices will have in order to establish iron ore's real chance to get a share of the intended facilities.

3. Suggestions and conclusions

Operational issues were not well considered prior to investing in a project that turned out to be immensely voluminous. Brazil may be regarded as the world's seventh largest economy, but it has many features of a developing or emerging economy. It is of no matter how attractive a given mining project might be in terms of share price or opportunity cost, or how good the metallurgy test of a given ore turns out to be, or even how accessible the extraction of ores is, if there is no physical way to carry them competitively up to the marketplace. Investment will definitely turn away.

Existing or future infrastructure, operations productivity, environmental concerns, social realities and limits, cultural patterns across a huge geography, dominant players, and geopolitical variables are just a few topics within a project operation that should first be systemically surveyed. Surveying just a few project segments without undergoing an integral approach may prove to be the difference between success and failure. A systemic approach considering the project as a whole would have been advisable, especially in such a remote geographical setting where most, if not all, of the project variables are truly intertwined.

In the authors' experience, mining engineers, geologists, and financiers alike tend to believe too often that once a property is secured, there will be a way to provide the project with the required infrastructure. Then they need to work out ancillary aspects such as indigenous communities, environmental impact, cross-cultural features, and physical bottlenecks. This is seldom done.

Should these operation variables become too complex or costly, the organization will try to sell the project to a major mining organization capable of working things out their own way. However, the operational challenges will remain, and the ever-evolving technology is often not a solution but part of the problem. The evidence suggests that no matter the size of a given project, it needs a systemic approach in order to measure and monitor the quality and actual feasibility of its deliverables. In countries where the basic infrastructure does not exist, India for example, organizations must consider building the additional infrastructure as an integral part of the capital outlay. Had this been the case for Brazil, it becomes apparent that this project would have never been a viable option. The volume is there to potentially become a world-class project.

Severe infrastructure and transportation restrictions are not limited to emerging economies, but can also be found in Canada's so-called Maritimes Provinces where demand for iron ore hugely exceeds the capacity of railways and marine terminals. The main difference here is that the various contenders for the limited existing facilities find a way to partially make use of the facilities while keeping minor shareholders and corporate investors duly posted on what it takes to make their projects sustainable, and how long this process would take. Naturally, this process is carried out under rather tight supervision from both the federal and state governments which are well aware of the long life cycle a project this big may have, especially the planning stage where all the drilling results and socioeconomic studies must be completed and aligned. These are questions nobody is able to be certain of in a context like Brazil, where dominant global players own huge extraction mines, but they also use a good part of the existing facilities that are precisely the ones needed to make new projects sustainable.

The lessons learned are that a short-term financial focus for development projects ignores the potential long-term implications. Not all EIPs provide adequate consideration of such implications. The authors contend that they must. It is also important to have the person who will lead the CPE in such an undertaking from the beginning. It will greatly benefit the project and all of the stakeholders if a single individual can see all of the components and the challenges. In the 21st century, the global economy is extremely variable, and basing large investments on futures prices and Asian demand is extremely risky. Likewise, just look at the current political issues in Brazil, and imagine having projected that Dilma Rousseff would have been impeached two years ago. A serious risk assessment is always required for projects that take years to plan and execute. Here, that was missing.

For another organization in Asia, the question was one of infrastructure. The choice was to build manufacturing capacity for global demand in India or China. India has horrible infrastructure, for it is cheaper to ship on a barge around the country from Mumbai to Kolkata than to ship by road or rail. The government is bureaucratic, and the workforce is in need of significant training. Yet, they speak English. In China, the infrastructure is good and people know how to make things, but the government relies on laws that are byzantine and on situational ethics. Moreover, English is not common in China. As with this case study, a long-term perspective is more appropriate and with it a serious risk assessment.

B. Case study: dual mining project in central Brazil

1. Background to the case

This case study involves a Canadian mining corporation that needed to assess the logistic infrastructure concerning the construction of an entire plant and the export of three MTPA iron ore as well as some 300,000 TPA of copper concentrates. Even though the project lies close to the shore and therefore ports, railways, warehouses, roads, customs houses, and further facilities were inadequate to meet the demand; this led the project to face some challenging situations. This situation that is common across the huge Brazilian territory.

VALE is no doubt a dominant player that operates not only mines and steel factories, but also ports and railways all over Brazil (as described in the previous case study). However, there is an ever-expanding natural resources sector making the logistic marketplace a battlefield for slot allocations. Unlike the previous case study in which the job-site was far away in the deep Brazilian rainforest and export volumes turned out to be huge, this project required a limited cargo volume and its location was quite central and therefore more convenient.

Even though the available logistic alternatives were numerous, the carrying capacity demand was much bigger than the available supply. Furthermore, the stakeholders were more numerous and influential, given their proximity to industrial centers and cities. This suggests that a project that lies by the coast and close to export facilities may actually be more challenging, given the strong influence of the stakeholders when compared to projects that are remotely located. It has been the authors' experience that this aspect needs to be surveyed on a case-by-case basis and always needs to be related to a given supply-demand balance at a given point in time. It also requires projecting utilization rates over the years of operation, which is an exercise that requires a survey of a wide array of commodities subject to be carried or handled by a railway line, inland or sea terminal, warehouse, transfer station, and so forth.

Naturally, the influence other stakeholders may exert on the existing and future facilities to be constructed may always be offset or neutralized by entering into a joint venture or partnership of some type with a Brazilian corporation. There will always be Brazil-based corporations in search of expanding their corporate business strategies or in search of a good business opportunity. However, infrastructure and logistics are barriers for investors and project developers and need to be connected with trend commodity prices, economic cycles, politics, the environment, and the other items mentioned in the previous case study. This case study is a good example of the boundaries a project may be compelled to face given the existing infrastructural restrictions.

2. *Program in detail*

The Port of Maceio lies in the State of Alagoas, whereas the job-site was located immediately below the State of Sergipe, as shown on Brazil's map in Figure 3.1. The proximity between a job site and a given marine terminal may mean very little if that port is not fit to operate copper concentrates. It is an aspect often underestimated by investors and corporate executives, despite its strategic relevance. They usually tend to believe a port is by definition suitable to handle any type of cargo, regardless of its nature, volume, and origin. The typical port's trade-off survey should be taken into account when designing an adequate export operation. First, the advantages to consider are as follows:

- Suitable draft to operate HANDYSIZE-type vessels in the range of 12,000 to 16,000 DWT – a size normally utilized to carry copper concentrates in small parcels.
- Short existing distance between the job-site and the port of export, which enables the project to work with a fully dedicated fleet of trucks and drivers who can easily familiarize themselves with both the product and the organization's policies. A short distance is always better for outsourcing a dedicated fleet, as monitoring its roundtrip efficiency turns out to be easier and the operation becomes safer if mechanical or environmental problems occur.
- Medium-term expansion plans for infrastructure means further facilities and therefore more possible options to operate.
- Neither the current congestion rate nor the possibility of escalation in the medium run.
- Easy maritime access and fast berthing operation – two variables that too often tend to negative impact on the OPEX of any project.
- Availability of a weighing scale at the port's entrance – not so common to see in minor marine terminals across Latin America.

- Possibility of bidding for an area next to the grain terminal with direct access to a berth – this might lead the project to plan a greater scale of operation in future and therefore add value to the project.
- Upcoming container feeding liner services – useful to plan for inbound construction-related cargoes via main Brazilian entry ports such as Santos or Rio de Janeiro.

Now let us look at the potential disadvantages that should be considered:

- No specific infrastructure available to operate copper concentrates, which means negotiations should be undertaken prior to initiating construction.
- Unsuitable existing covered depots – only open yards without any clear definition as to which users would be allowed to make use of them and for what type of cargoes.
- Last berthing priority for dry bulk vessels – certainly not a good thing in an area where tourism is king and fruits exports play a big role in such a small state.
- Steady expansion on the container and cruise passenger segments – which can be read as a cargo segment business that is gaining priority over those laggards or holding some sort of environmental impact.
- Overlapping of high season for sugar carriers (September through March) and cruise ships (November through February), which may bring about congestion, which is bad news for both inbound and outbound cargoes as operational windows should by all means be avoided.
- Few berthing alternatives and consequent poor site versatility. Long-lasting bureaucratic permitting procedures and related paperwork on the part of both the environmental agency and marine authority. Not counting on berthing alternatives, coupled with potential congestion, overlapping factor, operational windows, lesser relative importance, and bureaucratic procedures, are all in line with what an efficient operation should avoid.

It becomes apparent that the list of disadvantages encompasses a number of issues that need to be negotiated with primary stakeholders who have a definitive say on the proposals. But it also demands a substantial CAPEX on the part of the port authority that will definitely impact the copper concentrate's final OPEX equation. Given the small size of the port, its tourism-oriented profile, and the type of exported goods, it did not seem to be the appropriate choice.

Iron ore export volume in the ground of three MTPAs entails a different approach as larger marine terminals as well as railway operations will be needed to make it operationally feasible. Consequently, the Port of Aratu in Bahia State had to be surveyed, and we will look at the advantages and disadvantages. First, the advantages:

- Operational draft capable of sheltering HANDYMAX-, PANAMAX-, and POST-PANAMAX-type vessels of up to 70,000 to 80,000 tons – a good thing when it comes to supplying heavy or extradimensional inbound cargoes as well as for achieving greater outbound economies of scale.
- Future possibility to operate vessels of up to 100,000 DWT or even larger – great news if larger economies of scale are required.
- Available space to stockpile iron ore within the port area and open for hire – no doubt an opportunity for the project to commit to and ensure a physical place wherefrom an export ship can be supplied.

- Apparent willingness of the port authority to look into new investment possibilities.
- Available scales for weighing trucks.
- Medium-run expansion plans on infrastructure.

Now, for the disadvantages:

- No direct railway access within the port area, which leads the project to face extra handling, greater OPEX, and a certain percentage of waste throughout the process.
- Existing high rate of berth occupancy – appalling news for a project looking for operational certainty throughout 12 months a year.
- Overall port congestion, which comes as a direct consequence of the previous restriction.
- Modest loading speed through an integrated conveyor belt system of 1,200 tons per hour leading to increased ship laydays and associated costs. Even though the integration of conveyor belts often works as a solution to combine different terminal sites with the existing berths as a way to optimize the gross berth occupancy rate of a terminal, its operation may result in breakdowns and associated delays. Installing direct conveying systems for every available berth would entail a long-lasting permitting process for the terminal management.
- Single-vessel operation at a time in the Dry Bulk Terminal (TGS I) – meaning slow operations and increased port handling and shipping costs.
- Impossibility to utilize an alternative pier for a massive ore operation – no segmentation.
- Time-out arising out of conveyor belts' and accessories' wash-out requirements – this is one of the associated costs mentioned earlier.
- High berth occupancy for fertilizers discharged March through September – conflict of interest and congestion.
- High diversification of users and commodities on TGS I and potential conflict of interest – being a newcomer in Brazil is never a good thing, even if one is powerful and influential.
- Berthing and maneuvering restrictions for ships at TGS I. A wrong maneuver or even a good one that needs completion of a given protocol means the project would face potential delays. A delay may hurt the project's finances, as capital goods may not be readily available when needed for construction, and it may become a heavy burden on the exports as the ores would face additional stockpile costs (assuming space is available) and result in overtime work at the terminal. In addition, the supply leg job-site to the terminal would likely need a reprogramming that would affect both turnaround-time and carrying capacity of the ground transportation units (either truckloads or railways).

Compared to Maceio, this ocean terminal also exhibits a number of disadvantages that are difficult to surmount. It also requires undergoing a delicate negotiation process with a diversified number of stakeholders that come to operate common infrastructure for their own businesses, which would invariably lead to hidden agendas (e.g., fertilizers, concentrates, steel slabs, steel rolls, alumina, chemicals, and containers). Variables such as high berth occupation rates, no direct railway access into the port, interconnected conveyors that require wash-outs before getting ready to operate, overall congestion, and one vessel operation at a time are variables that are strictly operational and would have a direct impact on both the CAPEX and OPEX projects.

A combined railway operation might also become necessary to carry both copper concentrates and the iron ore ex job-site in Sergipe up to Aratu or nearby to VALE's offered Terminal Maritima Inacio Barbosa (TMIB), which is also located in Sergipe. TMIB was by then underutilized and therefore open for negotiations, its operational features being quite modest. TMIB can only operate HANDYMAX vessels and would need substantial investment to become a PANAMAX fit operator upon entrance into an agreement with the project developer.

To move the ores off the job-site, two railways had to combine rolling stock and tracks at a given crossing point as their networks covered different regions of Brazil and even had different gauges. Ferrovia Centro-Atlantico (FCA) was one of VALE's own railways reaching both TMIB and ARATU ocean terminals, whereas Transnordestina, a pioneering railway network in Brazil, was more focused on the northeasterm strip of the country. This could provide transportation up to the Suape marine terminal and other locations further to the northeast. They operated a varied type of rolling stock that was allocated amongst a significant number of users within an industrial central area of the country; this meant facing a potential additional stakeholder management challenge.

Options were either to split the operation into two different terminals by engaging different means of transport and handling or unifying the operations in a single terminal like TMIB. Or it was possible to combine a truck-rail-ship mode of operation that represented a huge challenge. CAPEX and OPEX figures would likely be badly affected long after monies had been poured into this mine. Unlike the previous case study, this one offers almost an excess of logistic options, though all of them seem to require substantial investment and a time-consuming consultation management process associated with an efficient stakeholder identification and neutralization scheme.

3. Suggestions and conclusions

Despite the fact that a more systemic approach seems to be needed here, this is another example of the way operations tend to be overlooked or its potential challenges are minimized by a foreign-based management that prioritizes both geological and financial indicators over operational realities. Existing infrastructure restrictions as well as supply-demand imbalances should be assessed in parallel with any other technical consideration. This may be one of the main reasons why global organizations' large projects CAPEX and OPEX tend to suffer over and over from delays in time and cost differentials throughout the years.

Typically, such delays and cost escalations reflect bad management and project management practices that fall outside the project logistics' (PLs') competitive dimensions and tend not to be limited to emerging economies. Comparable situations may be found in Canada's eastern provinces where huge territories with limited infrastructure and great geology can be found. It is often the case when capital expenditures for assets are separated from the operations. This is sometimes required by tendering rules and sometimes simply overlooked, as noted above. We believe that for projects to be viable for all stakeholders, a long-term view should be taken and not a short-term one. Unfortunately, we live in a short-term environment. There are other reasons for project delays and cost deviations; we will discuss some of these in later case studies.

In conclusion, this is an example of operations issues that should not be overlooked by management and that require careful follow-up and double checking by investors. The nearness of ports, railways, roads, and further infrastructure may be significant factors, and these variables need to be surveyed by an expert eye and included in the project's feasibility study. It is amazing to see how little importance infrastructure and logistics are given in most project feasibility studies across the Americas. One assumes this is because when project developers identify roads, railways, tunnels, bridges, marine and river terminals, railways and customs clearance facilities, energy and pipelines in the USA and Canada, they tend to believe their operations will be planned and begun one way or the other. Normally, they would be correct but not in Latin America. One should never assume that the existence of infrastructure and logistics means that plenty of suppliers can provide realistic options to figure out what is best for a project. Actually, it means almost nothing!

Most interestingly, despite management being advised about the restrictions and challenges faced in Maceio, ARATU, and TMIB marine terminals, they had already decided to focus on Maceio for the inbound construction-related cargo flow and export of copper concentrates. Yet, TMIB was the one that should have been targeted for the export of iron ore. One must wonder if the owner of TMIB, a global player, should find an opportunity other than in Brazil. Or if it would be more advantageous for the owner to make the project fade and acquire it at a later stage at a much lower value. This is what VALE normally does with those projects that cannot be successfully developed owing to physical restrictions.

So what was it? Foolishness, obstinacy, inability to visualize the obstacles, arrogance, a strategic error, a sense of superiority, contempt for operations? There is nothing our engineers cannot work out or possibly develop a mix of them. Regardless, overlooking these variables is unforgivable from a management standpoint. This project faded until infrastructure was built and put into service.

The tougher the world economy becomes, the more difficult it will become for project developers to raise funds if they keep regarding project operations management as a second category function. Operations do matter more than a specific strategic investment opportunity at a given point in time across the emerging world. Infrastructure may be plentiful in the developed world, but it is definitely inadequate or nonexistent across the developing world. Knowing the difference and acting accordingly means leadership at the inception of a project. Underestimating operations often leads projects to face higher exit barriers for those wishing to divest and higher entry barriers for those looking for an opportunity. Stakeholder assessment also is critical prior to deciding on a given project, never afterwards.

C. Case study: global operator committing operational errors of global dimension in remote northern Brazil

1. Background to the case

This case study concerns a London-based organization with mining projects in South America, Australia, Africa, and Central Asia. This organization operates a significant number of assets of their own across Central Asia, including iron ore mines, railways, transfer stations, maritime terminals, and oceangoing vessels. It has a number of explorations across

Brazil, and one single producing mine in northern Brazil's Amapá State. That mine was acquired from one of the major global mining organizations who decided it was no longer a core asset given its small output. It is important to highlight that the major mining organization never managed to achieve economies of scale because of severe logistic restrictions that demanded huge capital endowments to match the mines' output potential. However, the mine was operating by the time it was acquired by the London-based corporation.

Figure 3.13 shows the extreme location of Amapá State bordering French Guiana and Suriname in South America's far north.

The river port of Santana is only capable of loading HANDYMAX vessels of up to 45,000 tons, given its draught restrictions alongside the pier and on the navigation channel. Running an iron ore export business on the basis of HANDYMAX vessels is uneconomical because the ocean freight rate differential compared to larger ships makes it noncompetitive for delivering the product in Asia. However, it could be workable on a domestic basis within Brazilian waters. An alternative lies in surveying different FSTS options that include northern Brazil and Caribbean ports in order to operate CAPESIZE vessels well above 120,000 DWT and achieve greater economies of scale.

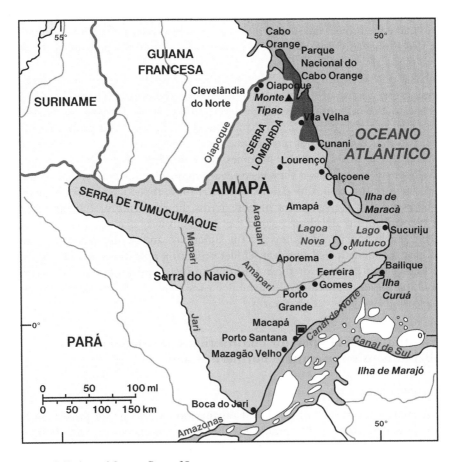

Figure 3.13 Amapá State – Port of Santana.

2. Program in detail

Unlike the two previous case studies in Brazil, this one does not represent a supply-demand imbalance, but rather the impossibility of enlarging the extraction and export of ores given both natural restrictions and environmental hazards. This particular case encompasses a professional global mining organization with a solid understanding of the role infrastructure assets play in making a project economical and sustainable. The organization then sold the project to another global organization with a regional focus in Brazil. Yet, this suggests that both of the organizations had committed the same mistake of underestimating the impact of inadequate infrastructure combined with natural restrictions. Worse yet, they did not realize that the necessary investment to overcome these challenges was far too high.

The challenge here lies in looking for feasible alternatives to enlarge the size of export shipments to gain shipping economies of scale, which would be in line with the organizations' other operating mines around the world. They were serving the very same customers in Asia. After assessing a long list of potential combinations, it was decided to shortlist two alternatives. With regard to the first, given the existing draught restrictions at the available ports within Brazilian inland waters, it was decided to look into Pecem's offshore terminal in the State of Ceará. This port was carrying out an ambitious expansion plan of its facilities and had plenty of water space to alternatively anchor a FSTS in its inner water space right behind the breakwater, and at a distance from the operating piers. The considerations were as follows:

- Such a facility should at least be capable of operating vessels the size of a CAPESIZE in order to permanently transfer at least 120,000 tons to a similar oceangoing vessel. The FSTS would regularly be fed in shorter cycles from Amapá's Santana port by engaging 40,000 to 45,000 DWT HANDYMAX ships, whereas an outbound CAPESIZE vessel mooring alongside the FSTS would transfer the ores on a longer cycle basis.
- Figure 3.14 shows a floating re-gasification vessel permanently moored at pier 2. Figure 3.15 identifies a Liquefied Natural Gas carrier (LNG) operating alongside

Figure 3.14 Aerial view of Pecem Port facilities.

Figure 3.15 LNG re-gasification operation at Pecem Port.

the re-gasification unit to which it is connected. This LNG operation meant running high risks for both the port authority and the mining organization should the FSTS cast off for whatever force majeure reason during a storm, hard currents, or a gale, or even on a regular day owing to human error. Any emergency maneuver by any vessel that might take place within the inner port area might become a potential disaster of regional consequences affecting not only the port assets and stakeholders but also the mining organizations' overall global reputation and operations.

• Risks turned out to be very high. Safety and brand value were also regarded as strong fundamentals to safeguard, which led the organization to discard the idea of using a FSTS facility. Even though Pecem's harbor master requested deepening the existing studies on currents, tides, and prevailing winds, the whole idea did not match what the mines' shareholders and BOD wanted to hear about an innovative way to accomplish greater economies of scale. Safety and project sustainability were undoubtedly connected here.

A second option became worth studying off Brazilian waters. This option would use an offshore spot located somewhere between Venezuela and Trinidad and Tobago, where an even larger 180,000 DWT FSTS was anchored and operated by a Venezuelan organization. The FSTS counted on four MacGregor heavy-duty grab cranes, each holding a capacity of 800 TPH, allowing the FSTS to self-load from conventional gearless bulk carriers such as a HANDYMAX-type carrier. It was also outfitted with a BMH-Nordströms self-unloading system with the ability to discharge iron ore at 6,000 MTPH onto the export oceangoing vessel. This variable was regarded as efficient and promising given the very few existing alternatives to make the project sustainable. Further considerations were as follows:

• Such an operation if carried out nonstop would allow filling out a 120,000 DWT CAPESIZE in less than a day and even operate larger vessels in the range of 120,000 to 160,000 DWT. However, iron ore is regularly shipped from Puerto Ordaz on the Orinoco River by two 90,000 DWT self-discharging shuttle vessels that have priority and were continuously sailing back and forth all year long.

- Although the FSTS showed in principle a pretty efficient transfer operation, it was anchored in a 30-meter draught channel that made it unstable to operate under swell, heavy winds, or rains during a number of unpredictable windows throughout the year. Given that the mining organization would have to engage in long-term contracts with a number of HANDYMAX ships to carry out the shuttle leg, a couple of CAPESIZE vessels would have to be committed and time-chartered on a long-term basis. As a result, the entire operation turned out to be unsustainable. Moreover, the Venezuelan exporters had a long-standing relationship with the FSTS operator who, despite promising to expand operations by bringing a second comparable FSTS facility, did not provide the mining organization with any guarantees as regards available capacity in the long run. This aspect prevented the mining organization from signing any contract with the shipping organizations that demanded a regular schedule on which to work.

The Port of Santana could not be enlarged to operate larger vessels than a HANDYMAX, as the river channel had a sedimentary bottom that would have required a capital-intensive dredging operation all year long and that would have badly impacted the OPEX. Weather conditions were unstable and would have also influenced the dredging, coupled with the risk of producing port congestion and increased laydays. Dredging and building bigger port facilities would also have required an intensive and time-consuming permitting process.

3. Suggestions and conclusions

Unlike the two previous case studies in Brazil, this one refers to a global mining corporation that, despite knowing what the limitations were, decided to proceed with the acquisition. The evidence suggests that management had underestimated the magnitude of the operational challenges they were going to face. Perhaps they relied excessively on their operational skills, given their past experiences in other countries across Central Asia or Africa. Or perhaps thought they could improve the overall shipping logistics by increasing the project OPEX without jeopardizing its CAPEX. However, it is even more surprising that the original developer of the property, from whom this mine was later acquired, did not come to realize what the logistical barriers were in spite of being a top-10 global mining giant with worldwide operations. Central Asia and Africa are not regions that offer state-of-the-art infrastructure that allows operators great economies of scale.

Whatever the reason, it becomes apparent that management overlooked a number of critical aspects that the former owner could not work out and that they underestimated the power of nature and its associated restrictions. Operational challenges do not seem to show a direct connection with the level of knowledge a given organization may have amongst their engineers and operations staff. It seems to do more with the way a real Project Management Office (PMO) should work to avoid making this type of strategic mistake.

All the variables of a project should be surveyed in an orderly manner and be aligned with the corporate objectives, and not based primarily on geology, financial fundamentals, or market opportunities. Operations strategy design in a poor-infrastructure emerging economy should be one of the first priorities to survey right after geology and financing have been figured out. Too many times the authors have witnessed projects that are given financial or geological potential preference over its operational realities. The result often leads to an inability to get financed, the absence of a development partner, and the impossibility of getting the asset sold. All of these factors lead the project to fail. A systemic approach becomes highly advisable and of paramount relevance in emerging economies.

Central Asia as well as Australia and Africa show remarkable logistical asymmetries that might have been realistically dealt with, had this organization had in place a true knowledge sharing and transfer system prior to taking over this project. Knowledge is another tool that global mining companies tend to underestimate, possibly owing to the very same conceptual vision limitation they have with respect to assigning an excessive relevance to geology and finance. These are two very important variables for a project of this kind but may mean little if not duly backed up by operational certainty.

It becomes apparent that mining projects tend to underestimate operations over and over around the world until they come to face the hard reality of their own impossibility to successfully develop their projects. Operational blindness can only be treated and ultimately cured by engaging professional COOs before taking any decision to invest and by avoiding overoptimistic income estimates driven by current commodity prices and opportunity costs that a given metal or mine may have at a given point in time. Operations cannot, and should not, be managed in isolation by corporate development managers, chief financial officers, or CEOs who hold a financial or stock exchange background, no matter how successful they had been in the recent past. Projects tend to fail and fade away too often owing to the nonobservance of this basic rule.

All the described case studies so far have exposed serious operational mistakes that may easily be associated with lack of leadership as well as an elementary misevaluation of the projects' contextual limitations and specific features, which could be social or environmental, ethical or operational. Some may consider this a lack of common sense. How could three large iron ore and copper projects in Brazil end suddenly and be helpless to face and overcome a number of operational challenges when the price of their respective commodities still was on the high side? Had these projects evaluated the mentioned challenges prior to jumping into them, would this have led their BOD and executive teams to avoid any investment in the first place? An incredible lack of leadership and common sense can be regarded as the main causes of failure in creating value for their respective companies and shareholders as well as for both primary and secondary stakeholders.

How to avoid such issues? The answer is simple: hire sound professionals who understand operations, finance, corporate development, mineral economics, communications, and construction-based PMs. Operations encompass ports, roads, rivers, ocean shipping, aerial operations, ground transportation, customs clearance, border passages, the environment, communities, utilities, consumables, energy supply, and many other variables of critical importance that are too often taken for granted.

The three case studies in this chapter suggest that the hard work and high expectations these firms have invested in their projects are most likely to end by having to sell them to Brazil's leading mining company, which has its own exploration and producing assets both within Brazil and worldwide. One does not need to be a strategist to envision that this will end up being an imbalanced game of power between a giant and three separate minor mining organizations having little with which to negotiate. Either they sell to VALE, which utilizes its own railways, truckloads, barges, coastal vessels, and terminals, or they wait for a miracle to happen. Again, a knowledge sharing and transfer system should be in place to avoid committing corporate and operations strategy errors. And operations should be internalized by directors, managers, and shareholders as a key topic for evaluation prior to deciding to invest.

Many organizations rely on business analysts to evaluate potential projects, markets, societies, and political systems with the intention of creating a portfolio that is balanced with some high-risk and some low-risk projects. Often such professionals are incentivized to make projects happen in the short term. This is a risky approach, as we have seen in these case studies. We have frequently seen business analysts recommend projects without consulting with project managers, engineers, operations managers, and other professionals when developing projects. This approach creates a barrier to knowledge, to the detriment of the industry, society, and organization.

Our experience is that organizations prefer to spend large amounts of money on consultants to fix a problem project, rather than hire the expertise up front and avoid the types of issues described in these case studies. Upfront expertise is a very inexpensive alternative to hundreds of millions of US dollars of sunk costs. Yet, it seldom persuades, even when people like us tell these stories.

4 Mining operations in uncertain environments

What executives and investors should take good care of well in advance

In this chapter, we will focus on two case studies located in different countries in South America. Both have rather unique topography and comparable physical limitations demonstrating the way both underestimation of operational variables and omission of cultural profile assessments can negatively impact the planning stages of a project. Although for different reasons, both case studies were in a delicate situation bordering on the impossibility of successfully completing the planning stage, given some critical operational and social omissions. Infrastructure restrictions, coupled with a harsh climate and complicated history of unsolved conflicts, led these projects to delays and cost escalations that could have been neutralized at the planning stage or totally avoided if detected in a timely manner.

A. Case study: gold mine operations in the middle of nowhere – Guyana

1. Background to the case

This case study involves a Canadian- and American-managed USD250 million CAPEX project that unfolds in a country lacking any basic infrastructure. The little infrastructure that does exist is heavily utilized by both traditional and influential contenders: the logging industry and the sugar cane exporters. Shipping to a newly built and yet non-operational port of entry in Guyana (Buckhall) from Houston, Texas, Europe, Asia, and nearby Caribbean nations presents a number of socio-operational challenges. Among these challenges are heavy port congestion, draught restrictions, time-consuming customs clearance procedures, dirt road trucking across the jungle, complex barging operations and aerial support, resistance from loggers and sugar cane producers, and severe weather constraints, including rains, tidal changes, dust, fog, and winds, all converging into a rather tight operational window. It is a real challenge even for a skilled jungle operations specialist.

The mining corporation had changed its operations staff several times due to the lack of agreement on the way operations should be carried out and the way contractors should be hired. The mining firms' institutional presentations at mining conventions before both interested investors and potential technical partners did not manage to dissipate the concerns over operational challenges that a setting this remote would mean. On the contrary, their commercial arguments and technical explanations turned out to be weak and confusing, in part owing to the lack of precision and ambiguity the project developers projected, when responding to a number of critical questions from potential stakeholders. They had some difficulty explaining the way construction supply operations were going to be carried out and providing reasonable or credible responses to very simple questions such as:

- What are your plans to make truckloads run on dirt roads during the rainy season?
- How will you manage to get the social license to operate in such a fluctuating context?
- Will local suppliers cooperate with a gold project and leave aside their regular logging and sugar cane customers? If so, would that be all year long or just during the off-season?
- What is the contingency plan for the rainy season? What is your plan to operate in shallow-water ports?
- What is the Venezuelan government's actual view on a project to be built within a historically disputed territory?

These and many other questions will introduce the reader to the existing socio-operational complexities of this case study. Also, why would a global player not be able to answer such rudimentary questions? And perhaps more importantly, why would a company put its lack of planning on display for potential investors?

2. Program in detail

Figure 4.1 shows the location of the project that lies west of the Essequibo River, in a 159,500-KM² area named and claimed by Venezuela as "The Guayana Esequiba." Even though Venezuela's claim is 100 years old, its potential political consequences should not be overlooked, as the Venezuelan government is not disposed to amicable dialogue. And if they chose to demand sovereignty, it would literally cut Guyana's territory in

Figure 4.1 Location.

half. Territorial disputes, even if thought unlikely to progress and jeopardize the development of a given project, may indeed work as a brake for foreign investors, commercial strategic allies, or technical partners.

Despite the project's weak presentation by their executives, the mining corporation managed to get financed given its low operating cost vis-à-vis gold's potential earnings. One can begin to see why many investors respond to the allure of quick profits and ignore the realities. Once more the evidence suggests that too often the temptation to invest in good promising returns prevails over what common sense would advise, given the existing operational barriers and social complexities. This is an error committed not only by the project developer but also by those who prefer ignoring present and future risks, as if the exit barriers were comparable to the entry barriers. Coming into a project is mostly easy, whereas coming out of a project or getting rid of it is a costly and frustrating process.

The governmental support for Guyana's first gold mine and the interest the project generated amongst investors were evident despite the logistical challenges, which did not seem to trouble anyone. A consortium made up of an Australian and Peruvian EPCM was hired on a lump-sum basis with the mandate to design and carry out the logistic operations in order to meet the construction budget and deadline. These two engineering organizations had no track records in Guyana but presented the lowest offer, this being the reason for their being hired. After all the research and publications, one would think that investors would have learned that the lowest price may not be the best price.

The Australians were deemed as technically knowledgeable, and the Peruvians were recognized as having knowledge in tropical weather construction. This consortium tackled the entire logistic chapter by carrying out a sort of general and elementary transportation budget and cost estimate, from the point of origin up to the port of entry and for ground transport operations from the port of entry up to the job-site. As we will see, it was a serious underestimation, to say the least, given the lack of operational details and little interest they showed concerning the area where they would develop the project.

The mining corporation had previously been provided with a number of guidelines that were listed by three different global logistic organizations they had hired. These guidelines alerted them to a series of issues, which if not taken care of could escalate further and jeopardize the project's timing and OPEX, and negatively impact the CAPEX. After realizing the nature of these challenges, the miners decided to pass the whole logistic responsibility on to the EPCM consortium, along with the previously commissioned preliminary logistic studies. Was it a lack of leadership, lack of knowledge, fear to face the firm's BOD, or too much exposure for the executive team to bear? Whatever their reasons were, one thing is certain: by ceding this part of the operations to the EPCM firm, the OPEX is highly likely to increase. The reason is the miners would have no knowledge or capacity to audit or monitor who the EPCM's contractors would be, or the way they would carry out the operations. This practice happens too often. In other words, it is a matter of passing the risk onto third parties, who were not in a position to manage them or had the experience to do so.

A preliminary operations layout intended to utilize Georgetown as the main point of entry, then later send all inbound cargo by barge up to the Buckhall inland port terminal. Alternatively, there was a layout to make use of Trinidad and Tobago's port facilities as a hub to later engage ocean barges up to Buckhall. Customs clearance and ground transportation up to the mine site would be concentrated at Buckhall, given that there was

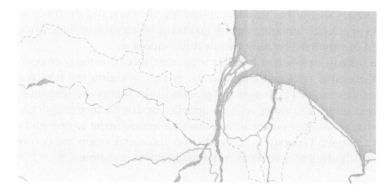

Figure 4.2 Port locations.

an existing dirt road connecting the inland port to the mine site. Figure 4.2 exhibits the relative location of the entry ports with respect to the project site.

A sample description of what a jungle logistic feasibility study looks like for this or other comparable projects should consider the following parameters:

a. Buckhall and Georgetown port facilities

Buckhall was an inland port terminal under construction with an uncertain date of completion by the time this project was being developed. It was intended to operate only low draft barges on the Essequibo River, whereas Georgetown was the only operating marine terminal capable of handling project cargoes and containers, though with severe restrictions. Buckhall was intended to operate 3-meter maximum draft barges, whereas Georgetown's draft turned out to be 12 meters, but it had both severe lifting capacity and berth resistance limitations. These aspects were of critical importance when designing the way operations should be carried out. The following variables should always be surveyed to establish the extent to which a given terminal may be trusted:

- Berth facilities (length + width, resistance per M^2, cranes, back area).
- Existing operational draught at the entrance and alongside the piers.
- Berthing policy (who holds priority over what type of vessels?).
- Shipping access, approaching procedures, access channels, pilotage, tugs.
- Warehousing facilities (location, unpacking, storage, handling, space).
- Third-party users and potential conflict of interest.
- Transfer procedure: ship-shore interphase, handling means, gear; gate-out.
- Complete operational cost breakdown.
- Traffic particulars and seasonality.
- Weather constraints and operational windows.
- Health and safety standards and certifications.
- Environmental protection and certifications.
- Impact of unions and identification of hidden agendas.
- Security context assessment and survey on procedures.

Both the existing inner and outer transfer facilities at the two terminals should have been clearly established. To secure a cost-efficient and safe transfer process out of the two ports, as well as the logistic link between them, the customs clearance process and warehousing procedures should be included. These are the typical grey zones where handling costs tend to escalate without control, especially when most of the services are either monopolized or cartelized by only two or three suppliers.

A country with a small number of projects is another incentive for port operators to both increase their tariff rates and lengthen the processes within the port transfer area in order to double charge. The longer the process is, the higher the revenues. The absence of valid port terminals, along with an appetite by contractors to quickly and conveniently cartelize, is another powerful incentive for management to consider prior to committing to a project. Geographical remoteness and cartelization are two of the most typical variables leading to an ever-increasing CAPEX escalation.

b. *Road survey from Buckhall and Georgetown ports to the job-site*

The following variables should always be audited to avoid unpleasant operational surprises along the way:

- Detailed digital road survey (around 170 KM from Buckhall to site).
- Type of road, topography, bridges, curves, slopes, turning ratios, creeks.
- Weather constraints: rains, floods, winds, seasonality, drainage patterns.
- Maximum road weight limits and oversize cargo regulations, along with uses and customs.
- Indigenous communities and settlements along the road.

This particular survey entailed examining in detail what the road features were along the 170-KM-long road linking Buckhall terminal and the job-site, including the crossing of the Cuyuni River at Tapir as shown in Figure 4.3.

A survey should not only check out the road, to ensure both what its particulars are for containerized and unitized type of cargoes, but also the critical spots to pass through with heavy-lift and oversize cargoes. The entire road was dirt, which meant that weather constraints and existing traffic particulars might definitely work against accomplishing operational optimization and efficiency ratios. A survey should also include the layout of a realistic contingency plan by considering mechanical aid and environmental remediation functions, as well as whatever animosity influential third-party conflictive operators may pose to a new type of industry in a small country.

Figure 4.3 River crossing.

A preliminary approach to the existing trucking companies should also be inclusive and should be done prior to surveying what their operational modalities are. This modality often becomes pretty useful to preidentify hidden agendas. The following variables needed to be considered.

First, ground transportation needs to be considered. A survey of transportation suppliers should have included:

- Survey on their technical capability (number of trucks, age, skills, availability, type of equipment, training guidelines, maintenance, repair shops, etc.).
- Survey of the suppliers' willingness and interest to provide services, and their existing commitments as well as equipment availability.
- Survey of their financial standing, including cost indications, cost simulation analysis, and the rate tariff update system.
- Identification of potential conflicts of interests with logging organizations, sugar cane plantations, main industries, and of course hidden agendas.
- Health and safety and environmental impact assessment.
- The crossing operation at Tapir to cross the Cuyuni River.

Traffic particulars, including traffic density, weather constraints, community support, truckers' cost structure, insurance practices, risk analysis, maximum payload per wheel or axis, and permitting process must also be taken care of if operational unexpected and undesired surprises want to be avoided.

Next, there should be contingency planning for unions and strike patterns, weather, and safety. Included in this category are the following considerations:

- The rainy season runs in two periods from December through February with 250 to 300 MM a month, and May through July with 300 MM a month, with rains farther inland being even more intense from April through September. The topographic particulars of the 170-KM-long road might cause trucking operations to face recurrent delays in these windows and result in a negative impact on the construction schedule at the job-site. All this would further tend to substantially increase the insurance rate on ground transportation as well as the demurrage rate. These two variables often tend to be underestimated or ignored, and they only get a bit of attention towards the final stages of the execution of a project.
- A high and unpredictable rate of interruption in the flow of trucks will definitely have a negative impact on both safety and insurance, and further increase the overall supply cost. These effects will require a consistent drawdown of contingency funds. The combination of dirt roads, heavy rains, dense traffic, dust leading to poor visibility, steep hills, tight-narrow curves, insufficient width, dominant players (logger and sugar cane producers), few suppliers, a river crossing with primitive facilities, communities living by the road, and the government's interest or involvement constitute the perfect storm for the project to be delayed and its budget to overrun.
- Potential driving accidents owing to lack of infrastructure turned out to be one of the major concerns, as it might easily become a direct threat to the project's sustainability once its causes became public knowledge in Canada – the home country for the mining organization. Both the mining organization's executive team and BOD decided to leave this aspect in the hands of the EPCM consortium. The authors

have witnessed this practice on many occasions when operations become either too risky for the executives or too far out of scope. This is well known by large EPCM organizations and often will not let the opportunity pass without heavily charging the customer for such a service. The results are often surprisingly poor, despite the increased cost. A local view of such matters is significantly different from that of the home country.

c. River transportation in Guyana

An alternative way of transport by engaging a hover-barge was also proposed to reach the job-site by river, aiming at being able to function in either the rainy season or the dry season – of course, the trucking suppliers were openly against the idea. Given the existing rain pattern in the project area, along with the pressure shareholders and other primary stakeholders often exerted on both OPEX and CAPEX, it became advisable to look for alternatives to offset both the reigning weather constraints and lack of adequate facilities and means. Typically, the following variables should be considered:

- Barging capability for both containerized and project cargoes further to fuel oil and JP1 (aircraft fuel) between the ports of Georgetown and Buckhall.
- Fast boat operations up to the job-site and community engagement. This would provide a means of transport that proved both efficient and community-oriented, as in the Peruvian rainforest case studies.
- Hover-barge operation feasibility for break-bulk and general cargo supply from the ports of entry up to the job-site. This was a rather innovative way to work out whatever river tide fluctuation or heavy rain one may encounter across a tricky topography.
- Health and safety standards and environmental impact.
- Identification of suppliers and a technical assessment of their capabilities.
- Identification of critical spots along Essequibo and Cuyuni rivers as well as between Georgetown and Buckhall ports. Stranding of barges usually becomes a profitable source of income for independent spot operators during the off-season. Every time the operations window hinders the barge operators from working all year long, it is very likely they feel inclined to speculate by running aground on uncharted spots right before or after such a window.
- Listing of traffic particulars and seasonality impact.
- Full operational cost breakdown.
- Contingency planning.
- SWOT Analysis (Strengths, Weakness, Opportunity, Threats).

Jungle operations always offer the possibility of combining dry and wet seasons with river tidal variations, in order to assess the feasibility of optimizing road and river operations. The latter option encompassed a number of alternatives which it was suggested should be surveyed in greater detail in order to be adopted or discarded in full accordance with the project's priorities and budgetary parameters. Modular 90-ton payload hover-barge operations might bring about practical solutions during the rainy season, whereas fast boat operations may both gain community support and offer rapid responses to urgent supply problems, on a limited scale.

Depending on the technology utilized, a hover-barge operation often produces a significant level of noise that is likely to bring about environmental claims from nearby indigenous communities that live on coastal areas. This aspect may go against the project's sustainability model. Moreover, traditional barging between Georgetown and the Buckhall terminal should be carefully surveyed, as most barges were owned by individuals and not organizations, leading management to have serious concerns on seaworthiness, safety, maintenance, and certification. This further added to transparency-related issues from a corporate viewpoint.

d. *Barging from Trinidad and Tobago to Guyana's ports of entry*

Another barging option was to barge from Trinidad and Tobago to Guyana's ports of entry. The three main ports on the island of Trinidad are located approximately 10 KM from each other: they are Port of Spain, La Brea-Labidco, and Point Lisas-Plipdeco. These ports turned out to be suitable and therefore deserved to be duly surveyed given the islands' vast availability of cranes, barges, tugboats, ship agents, customs brokers, storage facilities, liner services, and regular charter operations – all due to the large and developed oil and gas industry. This option resulted in an offshore possibility that was worth looking into, despite the fact that it might be resisted by Guyana's government as well as barging suppliers, marine surveyors, insurance organizations, port operators, stevedoring organizations, and ancillary services providers with an interest in rendering services in the host country.

It becomes apparent that what may look as a tailor-made, efficient operational solution may cause a project to face issues in other areas and consequently threaten the project's sustainability. This topic is one that large EPCM organizations tend to minimize by relying on their project completion global track record as well as their power or ability to impose their views at a given point in time, either on their clients or the authorities.

It has been the authors' experience that every time an EPCM organization does not interfere in the way logistics should be conducted but accepts the clients' recommendations, it is the client who faces the cost implications, regardless of whatever lump-sum contract had been signed. Even if the EPCM agrees to certain operations, the client ends up paying the bills, especially if there is a huge size difference between the EPCM firms and the customer.

Also, design discrepancies include logistic operations and often lead to extra costs that EPCM firms know how to transfer to their customers, when the entire function is not part of their contract. The design of a project should not only encompass the construction stage, but also its inbound and outbound logistics. Otherwise, controversies over design are likely to show up sooner than later; these are the ideal excuse for EPCM organizations to redo the logistic budget to their advantage or alternatively face a setback in the form of a lawsuit. The following variables should be thoroughly surveyed during the design:

- Existing coastal barging system with technical assessment on both ocean barges and tugboats (seaworthiness, hull and machinery, inspection reports and certificates, insurance policy, project track record.
- Available reception facilities in Trinidad and transfer process from the inland yard up to the port of loading, available loading gear, a complete cost breakdown, and in-transit customs clearance formalities.

- Floating assets availability, existing commitments, priority policy and certainty on its fulfillment, navigational aspects, turnaround time analysis, and allocation restrictions.
- Number of suppliers and cartelization practices, if any.

e. Ocean shipping from Houston or Suriname to Guyana

The procurement team also evaluated alternative supply sources near the Caribbean other than the traditional spots across the USA or Canada. This was why logistics were becoming even more atomized and complex. The project was intending to utilize a 100%-owned fleet of containers because regular shipping lines either did not want their containers handled or lost in Guyana. Or they charged high demurrage fees that, due to the slow turnaround time of the units, meant two or three times the value of a second-hand container. Furthermore, some nearby countries such as Suriname might supply second-hand break-bulk mining equipment encouraged by its early involvement in the industry, though the logistic infrastructure remained very poor in those places as well.

Surveying the infrastructure of Caribbean nations in order to make the best possible use of the available fixed and floating assets demands the ability and propensity to imagine, improvise, change, and certainly innovate. These features might well be found either in a mining organization or an EPCM organization when engineering design and construction tasks are involved. However, dealing with outdated logistic infrastructure or making the best out of a given piece of industrial antique (barge, tugboat, inland berth, or crane), are tasks that fall far beyond the EPCMs' interests or core business. A certain dichotomy exists as both organizations strive to accomplish greater economies of scale on every process they undertake, at the expense of each other.

The miner intends to pass the entire liability on to the EPCM, despite knowing that the EPCM is unable to complete a given process with what is readily available in the market. The miner is only accustomed to deal with the latest technology and plenty of suppliers to choose from. It is a way for the mining executives to get rid of a function that may expose them should anything go wrong, which is in fact what happens most of the time. One could well consider this process as some sort of "collateral damage." This policy grants the engineering organization operational certainty and a sense of confidence to meet the project deadline, even when the OPEX dimension could have been substantially reduced had the mining organization counted on the right knowledge, interest, willingness, and skills to carry out the project. Obviously, the same rationale may be applied to the logistic process, the OPEX and CAPEX projects being the ultimate victims that executive teams fear to face.

Acquiring a fleet of maritime containers is a typical example of those remotely located projects that work out the obstacles by increasing the OPEX, instead of hiring knowledgeable operations staff duly aligned to a COO, with a proven track record of cost and process optimization in harsh environments. Mining corporations tend to adopt this practice when their management is afraid to face their BOD and shareholders to explain the actual challenges. To appoint a well-known international EPCM organization is usually regarded as a quality stamp by the primary stakeholders, although not necessarily by the secondary stakeholders. The results, however, seem always to lead to the same conclusions: longer deadlines and delayed deliverables reflected on extended Gantt graphs, inflated OPEX, greater CAPEX, increased shareholders concerns, BOD members' faster rotation (a signal of alert for stakeholders!), potential social unrest, increased media exposure, and greater concerns about the projects' sustainability.

The following facilities should be subject to a survey prior to deciding on the procurement options for this case study:

* Identification and survey of potential self-sustained vessels or oceangoing barges capable of providing safe and competitive maritime transportation to either Georgetown or Buckhall with or without a prior call at Trinidad.
* Discharge and transfer operations onto truck, barge, and/or hover-barge to further continue to the job-site.
* Frequency, transit time, space availability, service commitment, seasonality, and weather constraints.
* Full operational cost breakdown from port of loading to port of discharge.

f. Customs clearance analysis for import and export operations

Even though there were a number of customs clearance operational alternatives, only those that were realistic and convenient for the projects' benefit from a logistic standpoint were considered. This normally depends on the existing customs regulations in every region or area, ongoing uses and customs of every customs house, the existing rules and regulations for the import process, and the current or future physical capacity of ports, roads, and further logistic facilities and players. Georgetown's customs house was the only operating customs facility in Guyana where the import entries were filed manually. This is the first clear signal of potential discretion and bribe practices on the part of local customs officers. It took around 15 days on average to get the cargoes cleared, which is a time span that was detrimental to meeting construction schedules. In addition, a special permit was in progress to set up a sort of branch office at Buckhall terminal in order to clear customs at a bonded warehouse nearby the river port terminal.

Both the miners and the EPCM regarded this (far from being an obstacle or barrier) as a unique opportunity to add a bit of sustainability by setting up an entire computer-based customs system for Guyana. Customs clearance software is inexpensive, and training for Guyanese officers could easily be provided by a specialized organization hired by the mining organization. The authors have seen this strategy work successfully in a number of countries where the existing IT facilities, inspection yards for truckloads, offices, communications, and further facilities leave much to be desired. Development banks call it "capacity enhancement," whereas we may call it "getting things done on the field."

Investment in these types of endeavors are likely to help considerably in consolidating sustainability, especially when this type of task is not left to the EPCM or other contractors. For these organizations, sustainability is not a long-term value as their commitment is rather based on the short or medium term, depending on the project's size. A gold mining project always commands the attention of all kinds of stakeholders, who reason that providing the current administration with IT and/or other facilities may well be regarded as a defensive or deterrent strategy.

The following aspects should be surveyed on every potential customs clearance facility across the emerging world:

- Available infrastructure and equipment (IT, scanners, verification yards, fences, illumination, security, covered or open warehouses, hazardous cargoes, isolated stowage, and handling gear).
- Modus operandi of the controlling entities within the Customs Primary Zones (ZPA), and possible overlapping controls leading to duplications of fees and excessive time.
- Identification of customs, timing, and malpractices, if any.
- Operational description of the import process by commodity segment (e.g., containers, break-bulk, big-bags, liquid bulk, heavy-lift, oversize, hazardous, reefer cargoes, and so forth).
- Customs rules and regulations for final or temporary import of capital goods and raw materials, and mining or capital goods regimes.
- Custom rules and regulations for the export of minerals.
- Transit-related paperwork on the export operation.
- Job-site customs clearance requisites and associated costs.

g. Crane management

Both ports of entry turned out to be poorly outfitted with just a 60-ton lifting capacity port crane at Georgetown and a discharging speed of 18 containers per hour. Compared to a South American average of 45 units per hour, this was clearly detrimental for whatever ship or barge owner was to operate there. There also was a 90-ton lifting capacity mobile crane owned by a stevedoring organization. Buckhall port did not see why a couple of cranes should be positioned there in order to carry out the discharge and transfer process, in addition to another set of cranes to operate both at Tapir crossing and the job-site.

The authors have witnessed, on numerous occasions, what it means for the host government and local contractors to face the threat of a global engineering organization trying to impose their views on how an efficient operation should be conducted. Even though Guyana's ports were in need of bigger cranes to operate both at the pier and the transfer operation, it was the domestic contractors who opposed losing control over what had been their business for decades. Similarly, the fast boat operation that was handed over to the local communities, under a mutually agreed tariff rate basis in the Peruvian rainforest case study, could be a model that could be explored for cranes.

Undertaking a sort of joint operation such as the BOT (Build, Operate, Transfer) method where the term "build" is replaced by the term "import," given Guyana's limited industrial profile, might lead to mutual gains. Clearly, such an approach encompasses potential support of the local contractors, which should help the project's sustainability. This concept should not be overlooked when outsourcing construction and logistics. Once the mine gets commissioned the cranes can always be ceded to the port operators in a sort of leasing or eventually sold out and reexported as a way to generate cash. This can also help shape the relationship amongst the various stakeholders at a given point in time. Variables that need to be surveyed for cranes include:

- Identification of types of cranes to be utilized at every process.
- Crane operation at port, Tapir crossing site, base camp by Cuyuni River, and the job-site.

- Crane supply costs and mobilization expenses.
- Contractual requirements and the BOT method.

3. Suggestions and conclusions

Various aspects can be taken from this case study as an example of what should not be done if sustainability is sought. These aspects have to do more with the survival of the project's executive team, who too often make decisions in their best personal interest rather than that of the project. It may also include the lack of knowledge that share-holders, BOD, and key primary stakeholders often have in the way operations should be dealt with for the project's best interest. Lessons learned from this case study include the following:

- Mining organizations' executive teams often prefer global EPCM firms, given their global market reach, reputation, structure, size, and expertise. This is the case even if the final lump sum turns out to be higher than their regional, smaller, and more focused competitors. It is common to see small to medium-size projects hiring a large and global EPCM organization that pays little attention to the design of the assigned project. Actually, it is not worthwhile for their engineers to spend too much time on small projects, as they tend to be simpler and have less revenue. Also, completing a small project on time and on budget offers little for the reputation the EPCM may achieve.
- The topographic complexity and harsh socioeconomic conditions of a project do not add prestige to an EPCM. The CAPEX magnitude is what projects look at, erroneously, and adds global exposure in terms of relative weight and importance. Further, knowledge of a particular country or specific region, not matching the relative size of the EPCM with that of the project, may easily lead to operational inefficiencies where operations management plays a key role.
- Larger projects always monopolize the best available talent given the EPCM's matrix-type organization, where a team member may work for various projects simultaneously according to size and projected image (perceived reputation), though not with similar intensity. The preference will always be given to those projects of higher relative significance, in terms of either CAPEX or country image. What usually happens in these situations is that junior and less experienced engineers get assigned and later, when back to the head office, search for the necessary technical back-up and overall guidance. Often, this choice is the mining executives' fear of larger potential failures; yet it can leave them defenseless or speechless before the shareholders and BOD. Often they have little idea about how to work out issues.
- If an "AAA"-rated EPCM makes a mistake, the implications for the executive team are different than if a lower rated EPCM with only regional coverage and reputation for less quality commits the very same mistake. One may also assume that a higher rated, experienced EPCM organization provides the project with a better risk/reward ratio exposure for financial markets and stakeholders. However, most of the time project financing depends on the momentum for a given market segment where liquidity and commodity prices do play a role (e.g., gold, silver, copper, iron ore, coal, lead, lithium, potash, uranium, or rare earth minerals). However, mining executives tend to rely almost blindly on the EPCM brand value without really looking into the final project CAPEX or into the way OPEX-related contractors

get hired and controlled. Last but not least, a global and reputable EPCM is a solid tool enabling the executives to save face should anything go wrong. The EPCM provides someone to blame and may be easily shielded by its global reputation and structure. However, operations strategy rarely gets the attention it deserves.

- In an increasing number of projects with incredible logistical challenges and social barriers, the tendency is to appoint ex-military personnel as COOs. This is apparently in the belief that having led men and equipment under fire or at least in a comparable geographically isolated context early completion will be guaranteed. Actually, chief compliance officers are the ones who in part should monitor and support the COO in achieving the project's operations strategy. It is the author's experience that military personnel do not differ from any other professionals, but what actually counts is the ascertainable logistic operations track record in harsh environments, in addition to leadership skills. Counting on leadership skills in emerging economies is necessary, along with negotiation skills, cultural abilities, language proficiency, and nationality.

- It can be affirmed that just a few mining organizations have developed solid and integral in-house management expertise, not just finance and engineering capability. These are the organizations that often appoint the most capable EPCM organizations with whom they jointly design and carry out a consensual operations strategy. Mining organizations should give a second thought to what variables provide their projects with less exposure to risk as perceived by the global financial markets. Large EPCM firms that are well reputed and globally recognized may become a solid partner of a project developer by increasing the probability of success and easing the access to capital venture. This is provided that there is a corporate match with respect to both vision and relative size. However, this does not hinder an EPCM from having to face the same dilemmas that much smaller engineering companies confront. Such a gap can only be narrowed if executives and BOD members visualize and internalize the importance of operations for a project's sustainability. Moreover, signing on knowledgeable operations people is as critical as any other function, no matter how large or small a project turns out to be. Change, innovation, and leadership can only be developed and polished after many years of field experience. Capital sourcing indeed demands an understanding of its mechanisms, which do not differ much across the Northern Hemisphere. On the contrary, operations engulf a wide array of possibilities across the emerging world, where challenges and physical restrictions may be comparable, though never identical.

- Often, sustainability and corporate social responsibility rely on building a couple of schools for the community, donating medical equipment to the nearest hospital, paving a couple of roads here and there, providing training on certain mining-oriented tasks for the locals to get qualified to get a job, providing an antenna for the village to improve their communications, sponsoring a sports program for the community, building fast boats for the communities to operate and profit from, bringing books for the children to learn while explaining what the real environmental impact will be, and other such examples, some of which were also present in Guyana. There is of course always an impact of such things, but the challenge lies in determining what to adopt, as well as the uncharted outcomes it may produce. These are typical for any type of project when trying to get the community's approval to operate and are good things. Collaborating with the government's facilities is another way to gain state and federal support, such as providing an entire customs clearance facility both in Georgetown and Buckhall. Even if a facility already exists – which was in fact not available – then updating it by bringing newer and faster technology, air conditioners, new furniture, plenty of stationary, working cloths, and providing training for the officers to feel well treated and respected is a valuable endeavor. It is also a complement to what regular CSR practices recommend.

- An EPCM's core business is not logistics but engineering. As such, EPCM organizations consider logistics as an added profit center, at the expense of the mining organization. It is extremely rare to see an EPCM that is knowledgeable about logistics as they keep a strictly engineering view of logistics. Projects such as this one require an operational view and a logistics view that gets aligned with the manufacturing process. It also requires solid negotiation skills that may quickly generate the needed outcomes and provide certainty in a particular setting. These are aspects that EPCM organizations cannot deal with effectively. It is a new area of knowledge they do not actually take too seriously. EPCMs count on logistic cost estimators, like they do with any other function prior to commencing construction works. Frequently, these are far from reality as they lack the touch one needs to have concerning the many players and variables in the logistic world. EPCMs may provide great engineering, but their deliveries on logistics often lack innovation at the expense of the project's OPEX. One would not hire a football star to do surgery, so why hire an EPCM to do logistics.

- Guyana's project site, as well as other comparable spots around the planet, should only be operated by those mining organizations with operations talent, experience, leadership, negotiation skills, and ethics, along with an open-minded attitude towards change and innovation. The latter two are of paramount importance in challenging environments.

B. Case study: paying the bills of someone else's mistakes on a gold mine in southwest Bolivia

1. Background to the case

This case study involves a Singapore-based organization and Australian management. The project refers to a tragic mine site that experienced a series of dramatic events leading to the death of a number of workers during one of Bolivia's numerous dictatorships, long before these two companies had taken over.

Local community management was regarded as a top priority by the mentioned companies. This was why logistic operations, contingency planning, social inclusion programs, and safe operations across the Andes between Chile and Bolivia were planned considering their approval. This case study encompasses a piece of land that was historically occupied and exploited by a number of natives until a joint-venture between an American and a Canadian mining corporation acquired the rights from the federal government to undertake exploration and consequently carry out some drilling in the area. Natives were mostly dedicated to artisanal mining along with some typical primary activities such as farming and grazing. Unfortunately, the presence and initial activities of the mining companies brought about an increasing level of resistance among the communities, which led to a serious level of social unrest and violence. A typical reaction is that anyone may expect to show up every time that a proper PSM program is not in place.

The interesting point here is to identify the social variables that have, incomprehensibly, been overlooked first by the initial foreign-based firms and second by the latest investors. The latter organizations operated other projects, both in the developed and emerging world, this being the reason why one might well assume they should have acquired enough knowledge to start the Bolivian project based on cooperation, collaboration, and mutual benefit. The following presents a brief chronology of facts that led to the complete halt of this project some years ago and set a negative landmark for many projects to come in this country. It is also a good example of how global organizations sometimes improvise not only concerning the SLO, but also with respect to engineering and supply-chain decisions.

2. Program in detail

To better comprehend the magnitude of this case study, it is necessary to examine a series of events that took place near the job-site, which impacted both the former and present project developers. The tragic nature of the way the events unfolded set a negative landmark all across this country, which made it practically impossible for any newcomer to overcome the existing social barriers in the area. The whole process became a local myth, an aspect that no PSM can successfully deal with, as one needs to enter into territory often dominated by beliefs, religion, and prejudices. The term "myth" may fall beyond human comprehension and therefore may become highly difficult and time consuming to understand and work for the benefit of the projects. The following is a series of events that the original project developers had to face when trying to establish the exploration rights they had obtained in good faith from the Bolivian authorities.

First, the communities refused to leave an area they considered to be their own, given their long-standing farming and artisanal mining activities. One may assume that there was no consultation program in place, or the mining corporation's complete indifference towards the communities' concerns. In today's PM practice, this is unviable. The communities felt they had strong roots in this territory and developed a strong sense of belongingness based on history, culture, codes, and norms. This is precisely one of the significant topics a professional PSM should identify and work on from day one. The local people were not willing to give up their status to foreign interests that would take over what has been theirs for decades or longer. Once the miners realized they would be facing serious social resistance, they proceeded to try and talk the communities into reaching some sort of understanding. Unfortunately, the damage was already done.

Remediation tactics are much harder and take longer because of the indifference shown by the mining organization. Negotiations, after the damage is done, have only around a 50/50 chance of success once a project fails to consider local societal issues. Joint-venture miners and community leaders signed a private agreement by which the natives were guaranteed working stability, social benefits, construction of sanitary facilities, labor seniority for artisanal miners, revamping of the entry road to the site, and general betterment of the area. The Bolivian government had never addressed these aspects, given the artisanal nature of the mining and the predominant agricultural profile of the area. So, there was a significant gap between the governmental interests and the communities' concerns, prior to the mining company.

Even though the agreement had worked acceptably well for some time, the mining company stopped paying royalties and taxes to the state government in view of the communities' growing lack of cooperation. This also suggests that there were internal differences between the tribal chiefs making the decisions and the aboriginal workers. This suggests that the federal government did little or nothing to enforce the signed agreement. Unfortunately, this is also very typical across Latin America and is definitely an issue for natural resources companies to watch out for from the very outset.

Social unrest became a serious matter, leading both the federal and state governments to send police and army troops to the site to contain the protests. Despite this action, some 150 policemen were disarmed and their weapons distributed amongst the natives. This could probably be regarded as the worst possible scenario right before generalized gunfire, an aspect that no shareholder or investor would tolerate in today's intertwined world. As a consequence, the mining corporation hardened its position and demanded that the natives give up their crops and animals, and leave the area at once. This suggests a kind of federal support to the mining organization.

As one can begin to understand, the heart of this endeavor was not technically challenging; it was a social and political quagmire. When governments avoid straying into such areas, it is contingent upon companies that enter to recognize that they may be alone, with no legal or government support. In fact, in some instances it is a benefit to be seen as separate from the government, especially if there is some history to the dispute between the locals and the government. Here a foreign company wades into a centuries-long dispute, with a year's long horizon for profitability.

Existing cocaine plantations were also an alleged reason for the mining organization taking over the entire area in order to undertake a complete cleaning operation and set up a modernization plan. This again suggests that the organization was acting on behalf of the federal authorities in order to clean out the area. Even if this was not the case, it is easy to see the collusion perceived by the locals. The government was unwilling to step in, but they have a foreigner do their work. It seriously compromises the ability of the mining organization to build any sort of trust.

The community decided to reject any foreign investment in the region by defending their natural resources and existing opportunities. Around 3,000 regular police, rural police corps, antinarcotic police members along with elite army forces were sent off to the area to confront the communities. The results were nine dead and 20 wounded. Since then, the name of the project has represented a landmark in the minds and spirits of Bolivians, given the public exposure this unfortunate event had in the media. The federal and state governments forced the mining organization and the community leaders to sign a peace agreement to halt the hostilities. Consequently, the communities promised to free the site and to dispose of their weapons in pursuit of future mutual cooperation.

The above events took place a couple of decades ago. Yet still today the current owner of the property, who did not have any involvement in the events, is struggling to obtain its SLO, despite having invested a significant amount of money and time. It is interesting to go back and have a look at Figure 2.4 to see what type of risks were not duly considered by the initial joint venture. It is apparent that from an SLO standpoint three critical components have been coarsely bypassed: the market, political and social, and environmental. It is no secret that the Bolivian government had never taken good care of their own workers for decades, given the various military rulers this country had to face. This probably was one reason why the joint venture had decided to move forward without deepening the working conditions, instability risks, riots, strikes, or civil commotion risks. On the other hand, the very same government that encouraged the joint venture to move forward transferred to them all sorts of labor contracting and social obligations with respect to those who were engaged in activity either on or near the project site.

As a consequence of the above events, even today it is a time-consuming effort to obtain an SLO in Bolivia, where an entire team of professionals needs to be deployed in the field, including psychologists, anthropologists, archeologists, journalists, and social scientists. This sometimes requires years of effort prior to even thinking of commencing drilling operations. Furthermore, it is common practice in Bolivia, as well as across Latin America, for communities to obtain as many social benefits as possible from mining projects – regardless of their actual present or future involvement in the various stages of the project life cycle. This is an aspect that sooner or later is likely to affect a project's sustainability. Far from becoming a diminishing phenomenon, it always tends to increase and lead to a conflict of uncertain resolution.

Normally, both nearby residents and far away communities will almost always try to get a stake from any newcomer. This is a detrimental outcome that in this case study was generated by the mismanagement of both the governmental authorities and corporate executives with little operations or field experience.

Leaving ethical considerations aside for the moment, the adopted strategy in this particular case is obviously not a cost-competitive option. Neighboring countries like Chile and Peru, to name those with an indisputable world-class mining culture and tradition, have found ways to clear the permitting obstacles in a more reasonable, safer, and shorter timeframe. Yet, that does not mean they are free of conflicts. However, mismanagement on the part of the investors is not limited to granting the SLO, but also extends to the supply chain when it comes to identifying the available logistic infrastructure to be utilized during the construction stage of a project. Improvisation arising out of insufficient knowledge of operations, or just indifference to the challenges to be overcome, will be detrimental to a project's value. And, a lack of corporate concern about operations may also have a negative impact, as shown in Figure 4.4.

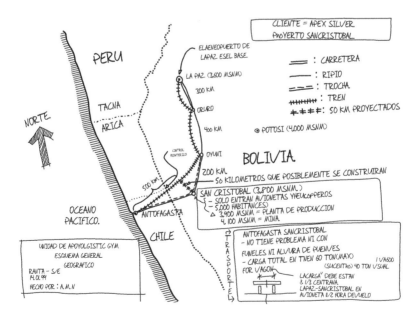

Figure 4.4 Projects infrastructure, preliminary layout 1.

Figure 4.4 exhibits the degree of informality displayed in a preliminary drawing of a given project's available logistic links made by a couple of geologists who first drew up a sort of sketch or initial impression. This drawing does not refer to this particular case study but rather to another that later became one of Bolivia's most important silver mines. Logistics was one of the great challenges for this project, especially given the early involvement of communities, suppliers, and their interaction with EPCM contractors and other stakeholders. It clearly shows the way natural resource corporations tend to regard the potential physical obstacles by just sketching critical variables such as existing railways, altitude, gauge type, existing roads and planned roads, dirt or paved, distances, tunnels, bridges, and so forth. That these facilities may actually exist does not mean they are ready or adequate for anyone to come and make use of them. Latin American countries are full of infrastructure, though much of it is outdated and too often useless. As we have indicated before, it very much depends on the type of project being undertaken. Figure 4.5 shows a better image of the available railway facilities where all the other variables have been put away for further analysis. This suggests that the operations team must have found the previous sketch quite inaccurate or purposeless as far as the construction stage was involved.

Figure 2.4 lists the sources of risks that are normally evaluated for any type of project at the initial stage, in addition to the technical and operational issues that were not professionally evaluated in this case. The more risks an organization overlooks, the longer and more expensive a project becomes. The Social License to Operate, as well as the operations, are deeply intertwined. And mismanagement of a risk may lead to a complete halt or potential conflict. This will have a damaging impact on its OPEX, CAPEX, shareholders, BOD, corporate executives, and, ultimately, the organization's brand value around the globe.

Figure 4.5 Projects infrastructure, preliminary layout 2.

Many well-known global natural resources organizations have suffered from serious operational mistakes. As a result, they have gotten rid of a number of projects in order to preserve brand value and gain sustainability in other parts of the world, where outcomes can be better predicted – or, in other words, where operations were better anticipated and planned. It should be clear that the challenges in the developing world are significantly different from those in the developed world in terms of challenges to overcome when planning or executing a project.

To achieve economies of scale, however, to become more and more cost efficient, and to outperform other global players organizations one cannot avoid doing business in developing countries. Operations may be global, and therefore global teams need to be trained and specialized by region and by specific country, if at all possible. This acquired knowledge then needs to be duly transferred across the organizations and duly internalized, so it becomes a competitive advantage. Operations' knowledge sharing and transfer management are also of paramount importance for both global executives and companies holding an international commitment to project development. In this way, they can take advantage of their global talent and experiences. Regional or country-focused organizations should first try to thoroughly assess the operational pros and cons and learn from the global organizations.

Divesting is what invariably happens next if these recommendations are ignored, at significant cost. A wrong operational decision taken by a global organization can always be worked out by selling, spinning off, or partnering on the premise that the project's scale did not match the organization's portfolio. Sometimes an organization will decide to focus on its core business and divest secondary assets. In other cases, an organization may need to protect its working capital, and in others it may alter its strategic goals by deciding to move into or out of the operations business. Some may be genuine business decisions, but sometimes it is simply executive management's intent to save face. A smaller organization may pay for its mismanagement with the ultimate failure of the entire project, as infrastructure improvements cannot be made without heavy investment – a typical case of operational underestimation.

3. Suggestions and conclusions

Cultural understanding and respect are fundamental parts of any PSM process and was clearly absent on this particular project. Today a wise cross-cultural management strategy is regarded as an essential part of any project, not only across the emerging world but also in developed nations. The difference lies in ways that different cultures ascribe value, ethics, norms, and behaviors. The British are considered to be a global society, as they dominated a great part of the world until World War II and still led a Commonwealth of Nations. They managed to learn and capitalized from their presence around the world in terms of culture, language, customs, norms, idiosyncrasy, codes, norms, and so forth.

During World War II, the British recruited an anthropologist from Oxford who was an expert on a tribe located on one of the many islands in the Philippines. He was given a two-day parachuting course and was literally pushed out of a plane over that very island and left alone to find his way. The gentleman spotted the tribe, befriended them, and managed to eliminate more than 1,000 Japanese soldiers in three years' time by using human-made weapons – blowguns. Obviously, empathy and, most important, a certain culture matching ability on the part of the Oxford professor worked for the

British army. But this example shows how powerful it is to master cultural dimensions of empathy, leadership, trust, and the like.

Global projects, regardless of the hemisphere and regardless of the level of development, require a CPE lead, business analysts, CEOs, and BODs, which require curiosity about the planet we live in. A strong leader will know him- or herself and be able to adapt to local conditions. Having women on a team in Saudi Arabia or Japan, having untouchables on a team in India, and having any two cultures that are still in conflict are common. An astute and strong leader will be comfortable working with and through such issues and with myriad others when languages, customs, values, habits, and norms differ. As we suggest, a CPE lead must be comfortable in his or her own skin, fearless, and ready to embrace other ideas and ways. A global business leader needs to be like water, liquid, gas, and solid depending upon local circumstances. Whether in Stuttgart or Uyuni, one must seek to understand and adapt.

The project does not need to hire an expert in Bolivian southwestern cultural habits, but a reasonable PSM should have been designed and put in place prior to undertaking any physical movement across the area or initiating contacts with suppliers and federal authorities. Other cultural dimensions on the part of the project developers could also have been examined here, such as arrogance, indifference, greed, ignorance, or corruption, as well as the way communications flow across a project team. As economies develop, the considerations become more complicated. Korean EPCM companies are becoming far more prevalent, so it is not just a concern for the local society but also for the members of the CPE. The cultures of all of the participants need to be understood, communicated, and celebrated.

One related point should be made here. In our experience, organizations from developed countries tend to look down upon the capabilities of those from developing countries. Our experience shows that there are intelligent and creative people everywhere, even in parts of the world that have never seen technology or Western people. Our advice is to simply listen with an open mind and with the intention of learning with respect. We have learned some important lessons from those who never lived through the industrial revolution or the IT revolution.

Stories are a handy way to engage people from other cultures and to communicate your values as a leader. Rather than telling people "trust me," you can tell them a story about you in a previous situation. If you need to engage in a conflict, or to correct inappropriate behavior with a person who is very aggressive, tell a story about a third person and how the results of such behavior ended badly. Or if you have a complex idea to convey, such as my culture looks upon all life as sacred, a story about what the feelings are may help the idea be understood much faster. It is also an effective method for difficult and contentious negotiations by again using third-party actors to convey emotions in a nonthreatening manner. And one should listen to theirs with interest and curiosity.

As we noted earlier, another important attribute for a CPE lead is adaptability. When we were teaching at the university in Asia, students would not ask questions because of the culture and their upbringing. We could see the questions leaking out through their eyes, but none were forthcoming. So, we gave everyone post-it-notes and asked them to write their questions and stick them on the wall, and then we left the classroom. Returning, we found dozens of questions, the answers to which were crucial to understanding the concepts of the course. Cultural tendencies make a difference. Think about the body language of an Italian and the stoicism of a Finn when explaining a passion for football. A CPEL must be able to look past the immediately observable to be effective in global communications.

The authors experienced a discussion about a potential project in West Africa where a practical solution was badly needed. It was interesting to see that cultural dimensions might become either a self-imposed barrier or a bridge towards innovation. The discussion was about our participation in an upcoming infrastructure feasibility study. Cameroon, Gabon, and the Democratic Republic of Congo host huge iron ore deposits that demand large capital endowments for infrastructure in order to make them viable. In Africa, roads, railways, energy, and ports need to be constructed and supplied for most projects.

A London-based mining companies run by British engineers, along with their local partners and Chinese investors, were considering a project. One of these companies wished to engage a South America-based team to develop a logistic feasibility; yet another company felt reluctant to do so because of a recent bad experience with a regional contractor. They had hired an Australian team to work in Cameroon and Gabon where they had to face serious communication difficulties with their French speaking colleagues at the job-site. One problem led to another, and they could not get along with the locals because of growing differences regarding language, habits, gestures, food, and customs. Problems grew larger as a result of poor communication. The London-based COO looked upon this situation as an impossible barrier to overcome for a South America-based team, given a previous failure with the Australians. Moreover, he considered that our presence in South Africa would be a valuable asset if we wanted to be considered in the bidding process.

We explained to him that there was no need for our offices and personnel in South Africa to commission a logistics feasibility study, as no physical operations were going to be carried out. Moreover, South Africans are regarded as a double-edged knife across Africa, given their history and influence, especially across the southern part of the continent. There is no doubt that South Africa is the more advanced nation on the continent. Yet that seems to be changing, but it may not be well regarded across the region. The British COO never gave serious consideration to this matter.

We had to convince the British executive that as long as the consulting company representatives mastered French, there were numerous things that South Americans and West Africans had in common: Such things as being developing countries, having infrastructure limitations, world-known soccer players spread all over the developed world (an incredibly powerful tool to bring people closer and ease communications), corruption of their respective politicians (which turns out to be as competitive as a sport), and a history of colonialism followed by independence, to name a few.

The South America-based team went to Cameroon and Gabon and successfully completed their job by collecting data in the field in record time. This, along with many vital pieces of data that were gathered by the locals was sent off to their offices for detailed evaluation at a later stage. This process often takes longer than expected, given the lack of commitment on the part of the officials at the job-site once the consultants leave the project area. Here, empathy, communication, trust, and common interests did play a fundamental and intertwined role. This was difficult for a developed country manager to internalize, comprehend, and put into practice, given their too often structured or limited vision of the world in terms of human interaction.

Many global projects today look and feel like the United Nations. In a global economy, having dozens of cultures on a project team is quite normal. Some are co-located, some virtual, some both. English is the common denominator, but that does not mean that it should be the only language spoken or used. Diversity is a great asset, not an easy one, and the differences in language can offer opportunities to improve effectiveness and understanding. Figure 4.6 provides one example of a typical global endeavor, what we have called a CPE. As with this case study, having a team from South America studying a project in Africa benefited from a fresh unadulterated view of conditions. The key to success is celebrating and utilizing this diversity. It is not easy; it requires leadership and the ability to gracefully deal with conflict.

Where there is diversity, there will be conflict. The CPE will need a leader who is comfortable with conflict and who deals with it promptly, sensitively, and fairly. Ignoring conflict often leads to the end of a project and wasteful expenses. From practice we recommend that the CPE agreements enacted contain a structured time-constrained protocol for dealing with contract disputes. An outline of the suggested protocol follows:

- Disputes will be settled between the project managers in good faith discussions for a period not to exceed 30 days.
- If not resolved, the dispute is then booted up to the sponsors (managing director, vice president, and so forth), who negotiate for a period not to exceed 30 days.
- If the dispute is still not settled, the parties retain the services of an independent mediator. Mediation must occur within 30 days, and is non-binding.
- If the dispute is still not resolved, the parties go to binding arbitration within a period of 3 months.

As the old saying goes, justice delayed is justice denied. Time is important, for unresolved conflict will most assuredly contaminate the CPE, and it will cast a long shadow over the leadership. The main point here is that the relationships get damaged

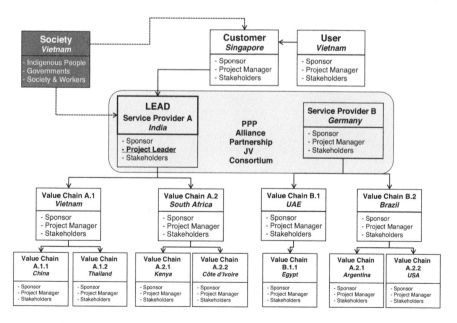

Figure 4.6 Typical global CPE.

if conflict is not addressed in an open and just way, which is what unfolded in Bolivia. We have seen many projects where an initial conflict went unresolved and spread like a cancer to other conflicts, miring the project in an endless series of disputes that cannot be managed. The message to the noncombatant members of the CPE is "get yours and get out."

We have learned from our years of stakeholder management and contract negotiations, as well as from our experience in arbitration, that the focus on conflict resolution should be on preparation. Understanding the difference between your needs and wants, and those of the other participants, is critical, as is being fair and balanced, and respectful of the other participants. It is not wise to abuse your power in the case of a global EPCM or customer. And, as you can easily see in Figure 4.6, a conflict between two parties, say Service Provider B and the user, can easily contaminate a multitude of other parties. The way a leader deals with conflict is as important as how it is resolved. We have been involved in projects where the disputes equal the value of the project, and most often the money is not what the dispute is about.

5 Mining and regional infrastructure operations in volatile contexts

What operations executives should first consider when deploying resources

In this chapter, we will focus on two different case studies that have different types of participants. First, we will analyze the operations from a unique functional perspective, within the operations for a lithium-potash mine located in northwest Argentina. Its nearness to Chile's infrastructure and its remoteness in the Andes make it a leading case for all those projects facing comparable conditions.

Second, we will describe a multiregional land-bridge logistic project that turned out to be very successful during its planning and implementation phases, despite having faced serious cultural challenges. Cross-cultural issues had to be identified first and worked out later, and had a clear impact on the operations. This case study proposes an innovative way to handle cultural conflictive projects, in an attempt to demonstrate its early importance in the project development of a project with a multicultural profile.

A. Case study: a promising way to address complex operational constraints in a lithium-potash project in northwestern Argentina

1. Background to the case

This case study involves a Canadian organization and a logistic feasibility study that comprise practically all modes of transport and modalities across the Andes between Argentina and Chile. The scope includes trucks, railways, full-container shipping, dry bulk shipping, barging, truck-rail-barge intermodal operations, border passages, bilateral customs clearance, environment, communities, and health and safety-related topics. Unlike other case studies, this mining corporation had actually undertaken a logistic feasibility study (LFS) in an attempt to ascertain the channels through which construction and operations-related logistics could be effectively carried out, and to identify the main infrastructure constraints that could ultimately prohibit achieving a cost-efficient operation.

Efficiency was considered to be intimately related to achieving economies of scale, along with consideration of the human factor. An innovative way to address the existing difficulties in a poor-infrastructure emerging economy is to have both a complex socioeconomic present and huge future growth potential. The latter almost always represents more a desired trend or path that an economy should follow rather than a concrete reality.

Many mining project operations on the Argentine Andes are dependent on Chile's existing infrastructure, as Argentina's infrastructure near the Andes is actually far from the Atlantic Ocean and consequently far away from ports, highways, paved roads, energy, and even utilities of any kind. The northern strip of the country has tremendous potential in terms of natural resources, which have been restricted and limited owing to decades of political instability and continuous divestment. Projects of this kind are rarely seen around the world from an infrastructure standpoint. However, they can be found across Bolivia or Paraguay given their landlocked geography, with no direct access to ocean ports. Other places like Central America, Africa, Asia, or Central Asia nations often make use of the infrastructure of neighboring nations when theirs is poor, unreliable, or simply nonexistent. This aspect increases a project's risk, its financing cost, and its sustainability.

For this case study, as well as for comparable projects around the region, intermodal transport operations become critical to making efficient a given logistic operation both during construction and operation. Chilean infrastructure and suitable transport means are all available, and organizations are eager to cooperate and profit from upcoming projects from the other side of the Andes whereas the Argentine side encompasses outdated means that need both to be revamped and effectively combined with that of the West in order to make a project sustainable.

It is often argued on both sides of the Andes that Argentina could easily add various percentage points to Chile's GDP, should Argentina decide once and for all to become physically integrated with Chile and make good use of the available infrastructure. Integration is a concept that is becoming more important and applicable to other regions around the world, especially Africa. Sustainability can be accomplished from a socioeconomic perspective, as no major obstacles or conflicts exist. However, the main threat at the regional level arises from not being capable of creating efficient inbound and outbound logistic operations. This is the reason to commission a logistic feasibility study (LFS) in the first place.

A good example is the world's largest bilateral gold project located in Chile-Argentina developed by Toronto-based Barrick Gold, known as Pascua Lama. Personnel, drilling equipment, crushers, conveyor belts, ball mills, tax agreements, cranes, truckloads, railways, aircrafts, customs clearance facilities, border passages, border police facilities, and further equipment and services were jointly hired, designed, formulated, acquired, and supported by the federal and state governments of both countries. Like the Pascua Lama project, the lithium and potash project not only needed an efficient approach towards the logistic process, but also an agile customs clearance process to make both the inbound and outbound logistic operations competitive and sustainable. This is a key consideration for this case study.

2. *Program in detail*

Customs clearance and border passage facilities are too often the very last aspect corporate managers or EPCM organizations actually think about. They tend to believe it is just a process that will be supported somehow, by whatever piece of infrastructure is available. In other words, corporate executives regard customs clearance as a matter of taxes, duties, and paperwork, not wrong in principle though definitely insufficient for the real world. Even though it may be considered as an interaction between a process and the available infrastructure, it varies substantially, depending upon the country and the type of commodity or capital good to be exported or imported.

Unlike developed economic regions, South American countries tend to distrust one another for long-standing historical and cultural reasons that are beyond the scope of this book. On one hand, customs officers in Argentina are very jealous when a given capital good comes from overseas through Chilean territory. On the other hand, exports from Argentina may be subject to stricter than usual controls by the Chilean authorities. The authors understand that project planners may not understand local practices, but they should know that failure to learn them will impact the construction and operation stages of a project. We rarely see such issues taken into account, even by the largest, truly global, and most professional EPCM firms or mining companies.

This is the case with a long list of products where the two countries compete in international markets for such products as wine, dry fruit, canned fruit, berries, apples and pears, asparagus, and garlic, as well as export commodities with strategic value. In this case, lithium is a rare earth element (REE) and has a number of industrial uses, including the automobile industry, electronics, and guided missile manufacturing, to name a few. It is scarce and valuable and produced in both Chile and Argentina, whereas Bolivia turns out to be a world-class potential producer. Although potash has no comparable strategic value, Argentina's neighbor Brazil is the world's largest importer of potash, a raw material for manufacturing fertilizers for its ever expanding agricultural sector. Yet, far away Canada is its main supplier. Both lithium and potash have to find their way out through Chilean roads and ports, bound to Asia for lithium and to northern Brazil for potash. Southern Brazil's supply however, has to find its way through an intermodal option straight from Argentina's northeast border passages.

Customs clearance operations may act as a facilitator or a burden, from both a process and cost standpoint, depending on where and how the clearance is carried out. It is of critical importance for those planning a supply-chain operation because even though a given country may have a mining regime or law where all the applicable taxes, duties, and levies are set forth, its applicability and cost impact may vary substantially. Brazil has a federal customs clearance law, but every State has its own regime of exceptions and particulars that make it literally a different system or a country within a country.

Argentina has a federal law that governs the entire country, though the severity or strictness of its application may offer a number of surprises. These surprises, if well anticipated, may grant a substantial advantage to the project's COO not only in terms of clearing customs timing, but also with respect to its cost impact upon construction planning and commissioning. For example, there are ports of entry, border passages, and airport stations whose customs clearance personnel are more familiar with the gas and oil industries than mining, and others more flexible with import temporary admission paperwork and verification. Then there are others that rarely deal with such temporary schemes and are more comfortable dealing with final import processes. Yet others are very knowledgeable about exportable commodities and are therefore unlikely to produce any sort of delays that may affect the export cycle of a project in a predetermined window.

Local application of laws, processes, and customs may mean the difference between success and failure. When one adds the probability of having to face potential corruption among customs officers because of discretionary practices, following a federal interpretation of rules and regulations may cause a PM to face unpleasant surprises along the way. Every PM should keep an open-minded approach and have a back-up plan.

These are just a few examples to underscore the importance of doing a special assessment prior to initiating any operation or acquisition. Getting to know the procedures in advance may also become a sales tool for those financers who struggle to capitalize a project. Here the knowledge can be a competitive advantage rather than just drilling, planning, getting a partner to jointly undertake the development phase, commit to an alliance in order to become globally exposed, or just add value to it to sell it out at a later stage. Operational certainty and project sustainability are two solid concepts one should always keep an eye on when developing a project.

Most natural resources projects lie far away from industrial centers and even smaller cities. Examples can be found all over the developing world in Latin America, Africa, and Asia, often in huge territories with a concentrated population along a bordering strip, coastal area, or flat region owing to climatic, topographic, historical, or socioeconomic reasons. Consequently, customs clearance operations often fall under the control of a faraway customs house branch that may regard a project of this kind as an impeccable opportunity to generate profits, at the expense of the project's OPEX of course. It is precisely at this point that corporate executives should deploy only the best of the best of their resources to negotiate with the customs house authorities. And this should be done without jeopardizing the project sustainability and at the same time considering ways their project could officially cooperate with the customs institutions. Creativity is a competitive advantage.

Deploying strategies at the state level in the field is always advisable rather than attempting to exert pressure and make demands at the federal level. But this is often the way global organizations either directly or through their embassies in the host country actually proceed. In fact, asking the investors' country's embassy in the host country to work out a given problem like bribery, corruption in its many varieties, operations, security, infrastructure, and taxes is probably the worse strategy. It only guarantees that the official channels will first deny that any problem exists. Then the government will often set up a commission to investigate further, which is almost a guarantee that nothing useful will come out of it. Then, the government can freeze any response long enough to be of no practical use. What is even worse is to make any possible solution nonviable due to the official channels already being made aware of the problem. Embassies may be useful channels at the early stage of a project, but it is always advisable for organizations to keep their distance while the project unfolds. Once you are in the ballroom, you must dance.

It is the authors' experience that it becomes easier, and better accepted whatever strategy is chosen, to keep a low political profile as well as an advisable distance from the media, while at the same time attempting to improve the intervening customs officers' standard of living. Organizations need a strategy that excludes bribery or any comparable tactic, but rather focuses on a more sustainable and transparent approach. Customs clearance processes, and their associated costs, should always be broken down and carefully assessed, as the efficiency of the entire inbound and outbound logistics operations may depend on them, especially on the regulations' fine print. Typically, customs clearance may be carried out in a number of ways:

a. At the job-site

In this particular case, the job-site was located some 500 KM away from the nearest city. Customs officers needed to be provided with regular transport and adequate facilities at the job-site. This cost should be regarded as an investment, as it is a way to keep the customs officers happy and make them feel useful and proud of the job they do. Good offices, air conditioning, adequate furniture, updated IT systems and computers, good food, friendly atmosphere, satellite TV, and good communications are just a few low-cost tools available for a PM to consider.

Experienced local executives often make use of such tools when dealing with customs officers in remote settings. Depending on the mine's location, this option is often the most convenient, as inbound truckloads may access the job-site straight from the border passage without first having to deviate to clear customs at the nearest city's customs house facility. In this case, it was far away and could have a significant impact on the turnaround time of the units and associated costs. No matter how high the customs officers fees and logistic costs turn out to be as a consequence of having them at the job-site, it is often far less expensive and more effective – provided of course that by clearing at the job-site the turnaround rate is efficient.

If a massive ground export operation is to run efficiently, a smooth customs clearance must match the planned turnaround speed and the availability of truckloads at a given moment in time. One of the most negative cost impacts ground transport operations often have is delay arising out of complex paperwork and time-consuming clearing customs procedures. All this may lead to a cumulative impact both on truck availability at the job-site and congestion at the port of loading given its sequential nature. Lack of motivation, poor transactional leadership, and isolation often are the causes of low productivity.

Figure 5.1 provides a general impression of how precarious and isolated a border passage facility may be. This is a solid and strategic reason for any organization to improve living conditions for the customs agents and the overall infrastructure to facilitate long-term sustainability. In such locations, customs officers have plenty of time on their hands. So, it is far better that they play with a play station or watch satellite TV instead of getting bored and become a hindrance when trucks do show up.

b. At the nearest city's custom house

As long as the customs house is located on the way to and from the border passage, this option might be workable. Alternatively, clearing customs at the nearest city might also be an option when customs officers are reluctant to be transferred to and remain at the

Figure 5.1 Jama border passage facilities on the Argentine side.

job-site for a given period of time when an import lot is to be delivered or an export cycle begins. Either way the customs officers should feel comfortable with their upgraded job-associated facilities, either at the mine site or at the nearest city's customs house. This has always proved to be a very sensitive strategy to bring peace and certainty to a remote project setting. Investing in the community in terms of roads, schools, hospital equipment, community centers, communications, or public lighting is by a typical, and always advisable, way to gain community support and the government's empathy and approval – especially if elections are closing in. Spending monies on facilities that the project will benefit from at a later stage and on a continuous basis also makes sense if the project's sustainability may be at stake for not designing a preventive strategy.

As we have said before, empathy and servant leadership are critical attributes for a CPE leader. The most successful CPE leads avoid problems rather than try to remedy them. Building trust in local communities, organizations, customs officers, and politicians is essential in doing this. Empathy shows that you and the CPE care about the well-being of the local people and want to help make their lives a little better. Servant leadership provides help and does not expect something in return. Of course, avoidance of problems and willingness to help will hopefully come from the investment. But, we suggest that for the long term that is not the reason to do it; the reason is that it is the right thing to do. Having consideration for the customs officers and their families is the right thing to do. Naturally, if one plans to invest in a project-related facility it is better, safer, and wiser to widen the spectrum to the CPE and share the investment effort with those stakeholders who can also benefit from the short- and long-term use of such facilities.

c. At the border passage

In this case, the mining organization had to either hire or set up a bonded warehouse for the customs officers to perform their duties, such as documentary and physical verification, cargo visual inspection, payment check on import duties and fees, sanitary documents, health and safety, truckload certificates and permits, mechanical safety, and further paperwork. Two border passages were necessary as one was suitable for oversize and heavy-lift inbound cargoes, whereas the other linked roads on both sides of the Andes capable of operating regular unitized and containerized cargoes. Under this scheme of diversified traffic, customs officers were usually less willing to cooperate as they saw no tangible advantage for them to expedite the process.

Lack of regular movements, a limited number of operations, geographical isolation, and strategic commodities behind a given project are all perfect ingredients that encourage bribery in its various forms. Customs officers are usually well aware of the importance of timely delivery of a piece of equipment, as well as how critical it is to keep exports going smoothly to catch a sailing vessel in Chile. Again, customs officers located at border passages often live and work under precarious and hard conditions, which if integrally improved should be considered as an investment and not an expense.

Improving living conditions in high-altitude settings often proves to be worthwhile, as it is always a welcome strategy and valued by both the intervening personnel and the state customs house authorities. Making these actions public in the media is also of paramount importance to strengthen sustainability and avoid facing hidden agendas on the part of competing mines or affected industries. Figure 5.2 provides a rough impression of topography on the Chilean side right after the export customs clearance process has been completed.

Figure 5.2 View of the existing topography around Paso de Jama border passage.

d. At a nearby third-party organization holding a bonded warehouse

This is where the inbound and outbound cargoes could clear customs for a fee not so far away from the mine site. This was the last option that was looked into for this case study, though it was not taken for two reasons. First, there were no possible credible improvements to do for the customs officers to work and live better, as the existing facilities already were in a pretty good condition. Therefore, no room was left for an upgrading strategy. Second, the strategic nature of the exportable commodities made it unadvisable to depend on a third-party facility regardless of how inexpensive the fees might be.

Even at remote and tiny spots, confidentiality plays a role as one cannot trust third-party employees who could also be considered as being at the same level of need or interest as a customs officer. Lithium carbonate is a valuable and scarce commodity that is only produced in a small number of locations across the world, and demand is looming large. Consequently, one should be prudent enough to avoid information from spreading all over the area. Access to information is not the topic this case study focuses on, but it is definitely linked to the facilities a project makes use of, especially in a remote and isolated setting, and especially if the commodity is precious. A systemic approach is always recommended given the nature of the resource.

3. Suggestions and conclusions

Further to any other operational analysis, imports were cleared at the border passage facilities, whereas exports were cleared at the mine site. Both strategies demanded a certain level of investment and expert negotiation tactics undertaken by local executives who were born in the same province and even the very same locality where the project was being developed. Culture, norms, codes, values, language, food, and other patterns were common for both parties, with the outcomes being probably ideal for both sides without having to sail in murky waters.

On the issue of local practices, it is strongly recommended that the CPE lead hire local expertise to educate themselves and the CPE on how the processes work or do not work. National jealousies, practices, attitudes, and corruption all play a part in clearance practices. And memories are long. If a local subcontractor who has a grudge against the customs officials on the other side of a border decides to inflame the officials, many other organizations may have to pay the price. Also, things done during the pressure of construction deadlines will survive into operations. Frequently, again, we see short-term thinking and pressure to get the work completed, which can have long-lasting consequences for operations. Retribution is a human trait.

Once the upgrading is done, it would be a mistake to believe that happiness and joy will automatically spread over all the workstations. This also needs some convincing on the part of the mining executives in order to make the system work for everyone. The speed at which this may work will depend entirely on the ability of the executives to bridge the cultural gaps. Consequently, it is better not to send a Canadian, American, Australian, or European executive to the workstation, as it would simply neutralize the intended outcome unless they have cross-cultural leadership intelligence. And sending a local employee to deal with the "locals" may also entail running a different kind of risk; they become too close.

Our preferred strategy is to utilize a CPE lead who has global experience and has learned how to learn about locals. This takes some time, but the dividends are quite large. We would then add in a local person. If the CPE has not yet been engaged or if he or she is not duly authorized, then an executive with the same skills will need to be present. In our experience, it is best to have a person who has a vision of the entire project engaged in negotiations for such critical components. That person must understand the culture, circumstances, practices, and politics, and be able to determine if the local consultant is too well connected and trustworthy. We prefer to have the locals see who they can trust and negotiate with, the person who has the authority to make decisions. This will set the stage for future issues, conflicts, and negotiations throughout the construction and operations.

Naturally, corporate auditing of customs fees and processes, through an appointed CCO, was carried out regularly at both customs clearing spots. This was to ensure that the cultural nearness, and the friendly atmosphere of the executive team did not become too near or merge into a single entity. If the CCO turns out to be a rather outcome-oriented square-minded individual, it would be better to leave the task to someone else with more flexibility, not only in terms of language skills but also personality and contextual adaptation.

In remote locations where large projects are infrequent, the bonanza alters how normal people see themselves and their opportunities. Border crossings into Russia or the Caspian area are not for the faint of heart. Guns and corruption make for difficult conditions. Imagine that one hires a local official in Georgia to be the representative for negotiating clearance and living issues. Customs officials can work like waiters in the USA, collecting tips with little or no salary. Helping people earn a living for their work is certainly the humane thing, but in many countries this is considered a bribe and is not acceptable. Imagine then, keeping track of it on the books, which are open to scrutiny and can show up on a Facebook feed globally, showing proof that a global company paid bribes. It is a bit complicated globally and really needs serious consideration and a strategy as to how the entire team will deal with such issues.

Critical here is the effort to foster a friendly atmosphere between the two parties and to defrost tensions from time to time. Perhaps all executives are good. but they are better if well audited. Even though this case study is about picking out the best location for clearing customs in a remote project setting, it becomes apparent once more that culture holds a dominant role to play. One may have in place the right strategy for customs house facilities, but not being able to read the signals may cause the project to fail.

B. Case study: a challenging multicultural land-bridge project linking the old and new worlds

1. Background to the case

This case study includes construction of new infrastructure as well as utilization of existing infrastructure that involved Brazilians, Argentines, Israelis, Spaniards, French, Germans, Italians, and eastern Europeans. The land-bridge project between Mediterranean ports in Europe with Chilean ports on the Pacific, through Buenos Aires, encompasses a ship-truck-rail modality along with a truly international team of professionals. This project was intended to compete with those direct shipping services sailing from Europe to South America's west coast via the Panama Canal – before the canal had been enlarged.

Figure 5.3 shows three different alternatives that were considered. Alternative A shows the existing regular full-container liner services linking Mediterranean ports with South America West Coast (SAWC) ports. Alternative B encompasses the essence of the land-bridge model by linking Mediterranean ports on a ship-truck-rail mode with Chile's industrial areas in Santiago and Valparaiso, and with continuation service to Callao in Peru through the port of Buenos Aires. Such a routing intended to outperform alternative A by shortening the transit time, avoiding the Panama Canal, reducing freight rates, and providing importers with a better ship frequency out of Europe. This alternative provided greater economies of scale on South America East Coast (SAEC) as compared to SAWC. Alternative C represents the continuation services to SAWC by operating coastal feeder vessels. This service turned out to take too long, became risky owing to the strong prevailing Patagonian winds, and was too costly when compared to alternatives A and B.

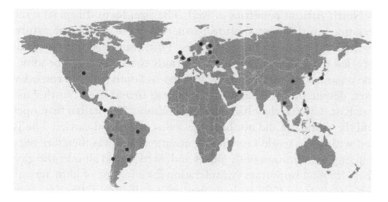

Figure 5.3 Land-bridge layout.

2. Program in detail

This project organized different modes of transport across continents by combining operations management teams of various nationalities under a common umbrella. Even though the organization and its lead were of Israeli origin, its vessel allocation scheme, vessel traffic system, operational center, and marketing and pricing policies were shared with other shipping organizations. These were of Italian and Argentine origin and became partners in a joint venture.

Driven by the need to face the typical global trade fluctuations, shipping companies tend to get rid of their excess tonnage and try to adjust to a more modest world trade scenario by getting rid of vessels and joining forces with other shipping companies. This is a cycle that repeats itself as its origins are trade imbalances and world economic fluctuations. When shipping companies are in a downward trend, they are compelled to face the new business environment by flagging a great number of vessels (tonnage reduction), while entering into joint ventures, alliances, or partnerships to optimize their fleets' space utilization, or load factor, while reducing their commitment to assets such as vessels, containers, marine terminals, trucks, chassis, yards, warehouses, and cranes.

Consequently, shipping companies have to share operations, marketing, administrative facilities, and management around the world in order to optimize their return on assets. Fleet rationalization becomes, on one hand, a must for both global and regional operators in order to survive the decreasing cargo demand cycle. On the other hand, the land-bridge project promised to become an innovative strategy to compete by reducing costs rather than by cutting rates. This is common practice amongst shipping lines to generate short-term cash flow during economic downturns.

This case study does not pretend to explore the various operational sides a joint venture of this kind may encompass, but it focuses more attention on the cross-cultural leadership topics that a truly international project may entail. Shipping can be regarded as the derived demand of international trade and is therefore one of the most international industries full of tradition, uses, and customs that find common patterns worldwide. However, these common patterns refer basically to accepted international operations and business practices, and therefore are far from guaranteeing a smooth operation when the mix of nationalities and cultures is so diverse, especially when the available infrastructure and logistic means are not precisely world-class.

The leading shipping organizations along with its joint venture were from Israel, with a good part of South American and European nationalities in the joint venture. That later expanded towards North African countries as well. The size, focus, financial standing, and business expectations of the joint-venture partners were of a different nature and therefore exerted a different strain on the operations. This, combined with societal culture and personality, led the various teams to face serious conflicts across the joint venture. The Argentine organization was regionally focused, as South America turned out to be its natural market, despite the fact that it operated lines to and from North America, Europe, and the Far East. Clearly, they had broad aspirations. The Italian firm operated various lines around the world but did not have the status of a global carrier. The Israeli organization ranked within the world's top 10 organizations and was therefore regarded as a truly global shipping organization with offices and assets spread all over the globe.

This sort of imbalance is an important consideration for any type of joint agreement. Agreements run on a scale from CPE to joint venture to alliance. CPEs are normally multiparty agreements that are bound together through a lead of some sort. Usually, there is no formal charter that encompasses all of the organizations. Joint venture are formalized agreements between two or more organizations that bind themselves together for some tactical or strategic reason, most often for a medium-term endeavor. Alliances are usually long-term agreements. The dimension we use for considering the type of leadership required for each is intimacy the closeness of the parties when it comes to sharing information and knowledge. CPEs often have no interlinking legal connection between the parties, so the desire to share is often driven by the CPE lead. For alliances, the parties are likely be far more successful if they share information. For joint ventures, it is somewhere in the middle and highly dependent upon the leadership. Also, more conflicts are possible when there is a great disparity between organizational strength and reach.

A large project in India had a joint-venture structure similar to that of this case study. In that case, it was actually a public private partnership (PPP) with four partners, one being the government. Of the other three, the margins for their respective work were 30% (largest company), 15% (medium company), and 3% (smallest company). All of the companies were global corporations, just different in financial strength. Imbalances such as this lead to awkward negotiations when changes happen. Those with 3% margins expect those with 30% margins to step forward. Also, the 3% margin people may have a disproportionate share of the power to make the project a success or failure. Which was the case.

Leaving the operations aside, a project of this kind demands a careful approach when it comes to define the joint venture and functional leaders, given the nationalities, languages, codes, norms, and idiosyncrasies. However, what usually happens in critical business environments where the cargo-carrying volume tends to drastically shift from one year to the next is that decisions are taken fast, tonnage oversupply and financial needs being the indisputable reasons for an urgent reengineering. Culture then has to somehow adapt to the circumstances. When the initial attempts to bridge the cultural gaps fail, problems surface, leading the joint venture to face inefficiencies along the entire supply chain. If cultural gaps are not taken care of, it can hamper operations to the point of no return.

Often the assumption is that Latin Americans are all alike, but Latin America encompasses a variety of cultures. Spanish- and Portuguese-speaking nationals can communicate reasonably well with one another, even though they speak different languages. Brazilians like to say Argentines speak "Portuñol," whereas Argentines counterattack by alleging that Brazilians do what they can by speaking "Espagues," which is a mix of Español and Portugués. Other than this, jokes and cooperation end here between them. Brazilians are more responsive to authority, whereas Argentines are less responsive and rebel against orders. Similarly, there are commonalities in Europe and Africa, but many differences as well. As we like to say, there are 7.4 billion cultures on the planet. We are the same, genetically speaking, yet we have developed bodies suited to our environments and cultures that enable us to live in societies.

Figure 5.4 shows data from Hofstede in the 1980s for what he called power distance, or the tendency people have to defer to authority (Hofstede 1980). Countries with large populations tend to be more receptive to being instructed on what to do. In this same figure, we have provided two other data points from the GLOBE survey published in 2004 (House and Javidan 2004). Power distance was again the topic, but in this study people were asked how things are currently (practice) and how they think things should be in the future (values). Notice first for Argentina that Hofstede showed Argentines to be balanced, but look at the GLOBE. How things are is very much greater acceptance of

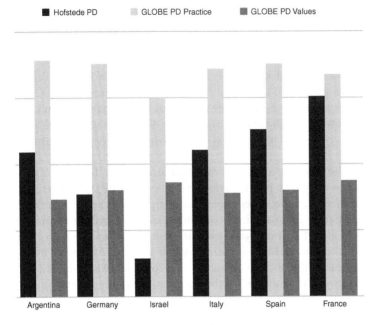

■ Hofstede PD   □ GLOBE PD Practice   ■ GLOBE PD Values

Argentina   Germany   Israel   Italy   Spain   France

Figure 5.4 Hofstede and GLOBE comparison.

power, yet people thought it should be quite a bit less than what Hofstede found. Then look at Israel where GLOBE is in the opposite direction from all of the other countries.

In part, we believe this is a function of societal and political movements within these countries and in part to the result of the globalization of ideas and beliefs and of the ability to look at what others are doing and whether or not that seems to offer more happiness and stability. There is a normalization of attitudes as a result of globalization and the Internet. Look at the GLOBE PD Values bars, and you will see very little difference. The point here is that personality, where people were raised and educated, what gender and age they are, what company they work for, and the team (in our case joint venture) they work within will shape their individual cultures. In our experience, the tendencies and trends between Hofstede's initial work and the GLOBE survey are real. GLOBE indicates that people in Israel are three times more strongly in favor of having their own say in things.

However, when it comes to operations and emergency problem solving, the Israelis have proved to be the best in this particular joint venture. But they also proved to engage in endless discussions on how to do a given task. Opposite to these characteristics, Germans tend to show a rather high rate of uncertainty avoidance as systematic planning is part of their lives both at home and abroad and at both professional and personal levels. The Israeli lead and a good number of his collaborators have a rather low uncertainty avoidance rank, according to Hofstede, compared to the Germans, who are surprisingly similar to the Argentines. This could be explained by the permanent state of alert under which the Israelis live, as well as the continuing economic change and uncertainty Argentines have experienced for the last 70 years. Both Israelis and Argentines are good at taking quick decisions, on the spot and right before an event takes place, but owing to very different reasons and motivations.

It is interesting to compare the way Americans and Japanese dealt with their suppliers on the automobile industry, Ford and Toyota. Ford used to prefer to select its suppliers by price, whereas Toyota preferred to engage in a sort of collaboration. It turns out that the Japanese outperformed the Americans and became the champions for quality. This had to do with continuous improvement, *kaizen*, as well as power distance. But it also has to do with individualism and collectivism, and for the Japanese this means cooperation and collaboration. From our experience, recently we have been engaged in helping global Japanese businesses become global in their business culture. The speed of American business is supported by short-term decision making that is quite fast but not conducive to building long-term consensus. The Japanese go in the opposite direction, which is too slow. Everyone is looking for a Goldilocks, just right, balance between what are two extreme choices.

In a ship-truck-rail land-bridge global joint-venture project, such as this one, not only project-related issues are effected by culture, but to some extent so are ongoing operations. Such differences are a bit easier to deal with if a project requires a completely new team to be recruited and assembled, like one of our mining case studies. This is not easy, but easier than attempting to merge business cultures. A joint-venture team is more like a merger than a project. On an international joint-venture undertaking, cultural differences are of critical importance as they may impact the way nonproject business operations are conducted.

In a merger, the blending of business cultures is a well-known and well-studied challenge. We had an experience a few year ago when two global European companies merged through a sort of joint-venture arrangement. Doing training for them, we found that the differences were stark. One group represented a long-term conservative manufacturing company, with most in our session over the age of 50. The other side was a tech company of people in their 30s. At the end of the training, there were the beginnings of a dialogue and recognition of the differences. Fast forward 10 years, and we are back with the same company for different training. Nothing had changed, and the cultures had caused a multitude of operational problems, just as we have suggested above. Both companies were Northern European, so the societal cultures were not that dissimilar, but the corporate and age cultures were.

Interestingly, the perception of cultural differences is quite amazing. A Nordic bank had asked for cultural training. To begin a session, we always do a needs assessment to determine the viewpoints of the participants, so that we can adjust the material accordingly. We were shocked to learn that a Nordic bank with branches in Nordic countries and a similar business culture saw the differences between the societal cultures, as described by one participant, as "radical." For most, the difference between Japanese and American culture is radical; seldom do those who travel consider the difference between Finlanders and the Swedish to be large. These two examples illustrate why culture is important and difficult: it depends on the people and circumstances.

We will describe the impact of each GLOBE dimension for this project as follows:

a. Gender egalitarianism

Gender egalitarianism refers to the degree to which an organization or society tends to deal with gender inequalities. Typically, a land-bridge project involves railways, truck-loads, oceangoing vessels, marine terminals, warehouses, crane management, transfer stations, surveys, customs brokers, customs house officers and other tasks and players across urban centers, mountains, deserts, and oceans. All these activities require a good deal of exposure to weather constraints and demand a certain level of resilience for which people in good physical condition are preferred.

Here is where the first difference becomes apparent between South America, Europe, or North Africa, which is one extreme of this dimension. Europeans tend to be the most open about hiring women for open-air jobs, though Latin Europeans tend to show certain similarity to the South American nationalities. Germans, Austrians, or Swiss tended to rank rather high, whereas Spaniards, French, and Italians had a relative lower rate, though higher than that of their South American colleagues.

There also were differences in South America where Brazilians, Chileans, and Peruvians tended to be unwilling to give women an opportunity for a job in the operations, whereas Argentines showed a bit less reluctance. This pattern repeats itself on any other project with an operations profile, regardless of its nature, suggesting a clear cultural preference that varies from country to country even within the same region. Malaysia has three distinct and very different cultures: the Malays, Indians, and Chinese. In China, there are well over 50 different subcultures, and in India, hundreds.

b. Institutional collectivism

Institutional collectivism is the degree to which an organization or society encourages and rewards the collective distribution of resources. Huge differences can be found here not so much because of the many nationalities, but owing to the very nature of a joint venture. A group is organized based not on an organic corporate growth strategy, but rather on the imperative need to survive in a difficult global economy. Israelis, Italians, and Argentines may have their differences on this dimension, but they were within a comparable bandwidth.

Looking only at the values from the GLOBE survey, we find that Israel rates 4.27, Italy 5.13, and Argentina 5.32. It is interesting that Israel ranks lower than Argentina because of the Israeli idea of Kibbutzim and Moshavim. The Kibbutzim was an idea from the 1950s that supported the idea of collective ownership of land, food, water, and the like. Later, the Moshavim idea took hold where there is a collectivistic coming together to share resources, but each person owns land, food, water, and so on. Think about 21st-century politics in Argentina, where the distribution of wealth has been disproportionate. It is easy to see why people may want more sharing. As we continue to say, a lead needs to understand the global context within which they work – not just culture, but also how it became what it is.

As we noted above for the project in India, however, the difficult global environment and differences between Europe and South America caused the teams to have very different attitudes on the pursuit of individual corporate goals. The degree of independence, or dependence, on the joint venture and its members, and the reward system, if collective or individual, had a significant impact. The project and the targets may be clear, but both the corporate and individual cultures cause team members to have very different expectations and commitment to the corporate JV goals. This aspect is of crucial importance when operating multinational teams spread across the globe.

c. Humane orientation

Humane orientation refers to the degree to which an organization or society encourages and rewards individuals for being fair, altruistic, friendly, generous, caring, and kind to others. Possibly there is no other dimension that presents so many differences than this one. Each nationality had to confront the very nature of a harsh global business environment, while three organizations of different size and strategic reach had to cooperate, aiming just to survive until the next positive business cycle.

The Israelis, in general, did not fit into the friendly, generous, and caring definition. They tended to lead the operation as if they were running a military operation in Gaza. Brazilians, Chileans, and Argentines tried to impress one another and gain leadership, both within their own structures and across the board. The Italians, Spaniards, and French did their best to contribute to the general confusion. The Germans, and their neighbors probably ranked the highest by just waiting for the disputes to come to an end and then come up with a sensible solution. Sensible is often a difficult commodity when under pressure and with diverse cultures. The GLOBE shows values between 5.44 and 5.68 for all these cultures. So, other factors were clearly at play.

People find themselves strained on this dimension when survival of the organization or society is at stake. When markets are stable and less stressed, people can perhaps feel that they can afford to be more humane. Humane orientation is a dimension that benefits projects; the question that arises is if stress, complexity, and conflict will override humaneness. Put in other words, human nature is not designed to be humane when the boat is sinking. A Chinese proverb says that you do not know another person until you have had a argument with him. Here is when leadership can make a huge difference.

People's real personalities, not the cultural masks we all wear, tend to be exposed when stress, anxiety, fear, lack of belonging, and uncertainty are present. We are all, as a species, designed to secrete such things as cortisol into our bloodstreams. And this trumps culture, which is more a domain of the cerebral cortex, logic and cognitive functions, rather than the amygdala, emotion. One of the key attributes of a project leader is fearlessness, which builds trust. Think of any war movie where the hero is the one who fearlessly confronts danger, and the other soldiers tend to follow. Trust causes us all to secrete oxytocin, serotonin, and more, which make us feel safe and happy. Leadership starts on day one and builds trust so that when the problems strike, the joint venture, CPE, or team can rely upon the leader to show the way.

d. Assertiveness

In a corporate world, assertiveness refers to the degree to which a person expresses confrontational or aggressive behavior with his or her subordinates, peers, or superiors. Assertiveness was high when operations had to struggle to overcome the lack of existing infrastructure and ongoing bureaucracy in order to complete a logistic cycle, typical in South America. This dimension had a close connection with power distance, as strain tended to be present regardless of nationalities, culture, or corporate position. Assertiveness tended to substantially decrease across Europe where the existing infrastructure, overall organization, and communications largely outperformed South America's. Even though little cultural differences may be found between Latin Americans and Latin Europeans, and even Israelis, it was the business context that set the pattern towards holding a rather high rate of assertiveness.

Here the differences in the GLOBE values ranges from 4.08 to 4.48. This is not a large bandwidth relating to culture alone, but is related as we said above to fear. When people fear, they tend to want someone to tell them what to do, which is the idea of power distance. But, as we noted above, this is likely more related to biochemistry than to culture. The problem is that we are very complicated organisms, so with each individual the calculus is different, and again different with each situation. It is complicated.

What we found in our own research was that assertiveness is seldom conducive to leadership. Assertiveness works well in command structure organizations, like the military, where people cannot afford the time to discuss and come to a consensus, or in high-power-distance cultures like Korea. The GLOBE survey values, for everyone including Korea, show that people want a lot more volition. But when things are scary, biology can take over.

e. Performance orientation

This reflects the extent to which an organization encourages and rewards innovation, high standards, excellence, and performance improvement. This dimension was the one with the least differentiation amongst the many nationalities. All tended to regard training, development, competitiveness, and performance improvement as important. This suggests, again, that it was the global business environment that governed the feelings and attitudes of the many JV partners and participants. It is also a function of the globalization of culture through the businesses. To be a global enterprise, companies must embrace what the Japanese call *Kaizen* or continuous improvement.

GLOBE has some interesting findings about this dimension. Argentina practice ranked at 3.39 and values at 5.54. These values reflect a trend showing that performance should be given more emphasis. For Israel, 4.08 was the rank for practice and 5.75 for values. For Germany 4.09 and 6.01 were the practice and values ranking, respectively. The global economy demands that countries and businesses within those countries become more productive. GDP per hours worked is a measure of productivity. In 2013, that number was 13.84 for Argentina, 59.24 for France, 57.36 for Germany, 38.99 for Israel, 49.59 for Spain, and 67.32 for the USA. If a company is a global enterprise, there will be more board members from more countries, the strategy will be more global, market fluctuations less severe, and productivity more normalized across countries. If a company is Argentinian, with global connections, it will likely be more like the statistics we just noted. If they are global, it is likely they will not be.

f. Uncertainty avoidance

This is where outcomes and conditions are unknown or unpredictable, and where some people may feel more comfortable than others. Uncertain and ever-mutating business conditions are common events for Latin Americans. The Argentines are experts at getting things done, whereas the Israelis feel comfortable to lead the Argentines across the business battlefield. There is little doubt that the business context track-record of every nationality plays a role in establishing its rank on uncertainty avoidance.

Typically, a huge gap existed between the Europeans on the one side and the Latin Americans on the other. It became apparent that Latin Americans tended to adapt faster and to return to a stable condition every time they had the opportunity to do so, whereas the Europeans tended to either take too long to adjust or reject even trying to adapt to an unpredictable environment. These need to be lessons of value for global organizations to consider when allocating their human resources around the globe.

GLOBE found that the Germans won the race for the least willing to accept uncertainty, with a practice score of 5.22 and a values score of 3.32. Germans don't like disorder and want less. For Argentina the numbers were 3.65 for practice and 4.66 for values, and for the Italians 3.79 and 4.47. Imagine you have a team with these three cultures and attitudes toward uncertainty. A leader might well use the Germans to show the way if more order is the long-term strategy, since Argentines and Italians want more. If the conditions are wildly fluctuating, on a short-term basis it might be better, as we noted above, to put the Argentines in the lead. This is not a game of some sort, but simply an effort to use a team's strengths.

g. Power distance

Power distance measures the extent to which the less powerful members of an organization accept and expect that power is distributed unequally, leading their members to react differently to the authority of a superior. This dimension was of paramount importance, as it had a direct impact on the operations performance. Immediate decisions were necessary concerning the frequency of the various modes of transport, reception, and transfer speed at the port of loading and discharge, empty container availability, customs clearance process, turnaround time of equipment, and so forth.

Buenos Aires was the inbound node through which a critical ship-shore interface had to be coordinated and where regular bottlenecks tended to take place, owing to port and road congestion, in-transit customs paperwork delays, shipping documents errors, railway strikes, weather constraints, and so forth. In an environment of regular conflict, it was common to witness difficult discussions amongst the Latin American teams and the joint-venture lead regarding the way operations should be conducted and bottlenecks overcome. Brazilians and Chileans tended to show a greater relative power distance attitude towards their leader, whereas Argentines did not easily accept the authority of the leader, or even their regional peers with respect to what they regarded as being their own jurisdiction (Buenos Aires ship-shore interface).

The GLOBE survey found the following rankings for this dimension. The largest measured was 5.80 for practice, and that was from Morocco:

- Italy, practice 5.43, values 2.47
- Israel, practice 4.73, values 2.72
- Argentina, practice 5.64, values 2.33
- Germany, practice 5.25, values 2.69

As you can see, the place most cultures want to be is where they have more personal decision-making authority so that they can determine their own way. Argentina shows the greatest gap between practice and values. And Israel has the lowest of the practice ranks. This is interesting because of the conscription requirements in Israel. Men must serve two years and eight months in the military, and women two years. Not everyone serves, however, and there are different rules for Hasidic Jews. Regardless, the relationship between a commander in the Israeli army and the troops is quite different than that in the USA. In Israel, the commander is more like a team member, and the relationship is more like peers rather than subordinates. Also of note here is that the GLOBE survey provides T-E-N-D-E-N-C-I-E-S of different cultures. Each person brings his or her own as we have noted.

However, the Argentine member of the joint venture who was expected to take a more active role in operational coordination at the reception and transfer operation opted to remain cautious by leaving the lead to the joint venture. This aspect may be attributed to organizations' lesser relative power and influence within the joint venture.

The Israeli joint venture lead and its Haifa-based team tended to remain more willing to defer to power than their Latin American colleagues. This was perhaps because of their military background, or lack of it, and opinions about authority in their own cultural system.

3. Suggestions and conclusions

Power distance along with assertiveness can be regarded as critical dimensions on an extreme project, whereas uncertainty avoidance and performance orientation can provide a uniting role, given the economic downturn the land-bridge was experiencing. Keeping a tailor-made cross-cultural management strategy is always important for international projects. It is even more critical when a global project unfolds in an unstable business environment, while it is striving to stay afloat to see the cycle upturn.

The same way a project deploys a Chief Cultural Officer (CCO) over the job-site to ensure that corporate policies and protocols are kept in place and are duly observed by both foreign and regional-based executives, perhaps there should be another CCO. Multicultural projects involving multi-regions across the world are highly advisable to hire a CCO whose main mission is to identify cultural gaps and design the strategies to bridge them efficiently. This is an issue that the authors have seen too often and that project developers seem to ignore, presumably because they believe that with time things will eventually work themselves out and heal any wounds. Time may help, but it is not the best possible solution. Projects by definition do not have time to waste, whereas wounds become too clear along the operations. A Chief Cultural Officer may be of great help in avoiding getting hurt in the first place.

A certain analogy might be made with Colombia's Cerrejón coal project. This is one the world's largest open-pit coal mine operations, involving a land-bridge in the northern La Guajira province close to Venezuela. This is where a 150-KM-long railway runs from the job-site up to the loading port on the Caribbean. The operation itself is quite efficient, despite its rather low transit time of around 13.5 hours. It has a loading rate of 7,000 tons/hour at the pier, to fill out an 180,000DWT CAPESIZE vessel in some 25 running hours, weather permitting. This loading rate is not bad at all by international standards. The railway runs through a number of indigenous communities, with a right of way duly endorsed by a timely permitting process. However, every time a community member passes away, the community throws the corpse on to the tracks so that they may claim some compensation from the mining company as if it had been an accident.

Even though the army is hired to watch, the entire logistic operation is run without major threats or contingencies. Compensation is often claimed by the communities, ranging from just a number of goats up to a complete fleet of motorcycles depending on the communities' mood at a given point in time. Both parties know well that all this is part of the game intended to keep a costly operation moving on, especially when the price of coal is so low and environmental pressures are looming large. Consequently, bargaining may be regarded as part of their culture or part of the show. Whichever it is, it must be taken into account and dealt with, both during the project planning and development phase.

This process now happens because the mine operator failed to take preventive measures at the beginning of the project. It begins with a consultation process in order to identify who is who at first sight, and a meeting face to face with the tribal chiefs.

Perhaps appointing a CCO to assist with the indigenous communities, army, executives, operations people, railway operators, and further participants would help avoid such issues. Cultural gaps not only need to be understood and classified by PMs and operations teams, but also must be bridged by professionals prior to the deployment of any assets and before starting construction. Hiring a good CCO is as difficult as finding a competent COO. But their fees will always turn out lower than whatever update on the OPEX becomes necessary.

As we have mentioned, there is societal culture, corporate culture, global culture, microculture, and individual culture. All are blended into the unique people who populate our planet. Culture, according to Margaret Mead, is "a body of learned behavior, a collection of beliefs, habits and traditions, shared by a group of people and successively learned by people who enter the society" (Mead 1955). This is the definition that we used in constructing Figure 5.5, with a few liberties in the use of the word "society." Mead was thinking of societal cultures, but our concept extends this idea to include CPEs, individuals, organizations, joint ventures, and what we call the emerging global culture. Those with teenagers may be surprised to know that it is becoming more difficult, relating to cultures, to tell the difference between a person raised in Bangkok and Zurich.

This means that there is no quick easy way to determine what tendencies a particular person may have; it requires conversation, listening, and time – no shortcuts. With this caveat, the work of many, including ourselves, starts with generalizations and tendencies to help people begin to engage in conversations with the intention of empathizing and listening to learn. The world has become far more complex in the last two decades, with increasing access to the Internet and social media. Old habits like greetings have fallen prey to new ways of doing such things. So the key is for leaders to have a high level of emotional intelligence (EQ), know themselves, and be willing to don new clothes in different cultures – like a chameleon.

Figure 5.5 Cultures.

Now let us look briefly at how to learn and the level of cultural intelligence (CQ) that leadership requires. Staying with societal cultures for a moment for CPE leaders and JV leaders, we see that there are different levels of CQ, and in our work XLQ (cross-cultural leadership intelligence) that means green belt, black belt, and master black belt:

- Green belt is basic knowledge of such things as geography, history, government, languages, religions, demographics, time zones, appointments, business entertaining, greetings and titles, gestures, dress, and gifts – the sort of information one may glean from basic books (Morrison, Conaway and Borden 1994).
- Black belt is a more nuanced view of such things as religious beliefs, family structure, small-group behavior, public behavior, body language, traditions, food and eating behavior, social class structure, rate of change, organization and work ethic, aural spaces, roles and status, humor, and arts – the sort of information that Hofstede and others worked with. There is also the work of Gannon who dealt with cultures through the use of metaphor (Gannon 2004). To fully appreciate his work requires knowledge of the basics described above. As one example, the metaphor for India is the Dance of Shiva. It provides a more nuanced view of the society and the trends that shape and change it.
- Master black belt is easy; one must live in a country. In our expat assignments, we are always amazed at how much we learn from breathing the same air, marketing, navigating the rituals, trying to speak the language and such. There is no better way to learn a culture. The trick is to engage with a sense of curiosity, and respect.

Most of the case studies we describe involve projects with people from multiple cultures who have worked and been trained in cultures outside of their origins. Many global citizens are very difficult to read and understand quickly. Our advice is to select the key stakeholders and learn them as completely as possible. For the others, do your best to learn those if time permits. In general, we think 80% of a CPE leader's time should go to people and 20% to all the rest. On large projects with thousands of stakeholders, it is essential to determine who the key stakeholders are, as we have repeated on many of the case studies. We strongly recommend you devote your immediate attention to this step, day one.

References

Gannon, M., *Understanding Global Cultures: Metaphorical Journeys Through 28 Nations, Clusters of Nations, and Continents*. 2004, Thousand Oaks, CA: Sage.

Hofstede, G., *Culture's Consequences: International Differences in Work Related Values*. 1980, Beverly Hills, CA: Sage.

House, R.J., and M. Javidan, *Overview of GLOBE, in Culture, Leadership, and Organizations: The GLOBE Study of 62 Societies*, R.J. House, et al., Editors. 2004, Thousand Oaks, CA: Sage.

Mead, M., ed., *Cultural Patterns and Technical Change*. 1955, New York: UNESCO.

Morrison, T., W.A. Conaway, and G.A. Borden, *Kiss, Bow, or Shake Hands: How to Do Business in Sixty Countries*. 1994, Holbrook: Bob Adams.

6 Ocean and river logistics in emerging contexts

Variables PMs should pay special attention to in order to accomplish a sustainable operation

In this chapter, we will focus on two case studies that are similar, though of a different dimension and different type of participants. First, we will analyze the operations from a leadership standpoint on two joint ventures that were formed more by necessity than by diversification strategy on South America's east coast. Both studies refer to a number of both regional and global shipping companies that had to face a slump in their respective markets, leading to a significant tonnage surplus. Indeed, they were forced to reengineer their structures to match the new market conditions, and to find a new leadership formula and business scenario. A complex supply-chain operation designed for a large transnational corporation demands attending to a number of variables that are of utmost relevance in project management as well. The uniqueness and complexity of the Parana-Paraguay waterways in the heart of South America makes this case study a sort of compendium of qualities PMs should have prior to accepting an assignment in complex emerging environments. Both case studies are useful for the reader to observe what the major variables are with respect to both ocean and river logistics.

A. Case study: a threatening scenario leading to a compulsory shipping operation reengineering on South America's east coast

1. Background to the case

This case study is about two joint-venture projects between various regional and global shipping organizations intending to rationalize their fleets and bring costs down. Their effort was aimed at the typical regional economic crisis which caused significant trade imbalances between South America's east and west coasts and Europe, as well as the USA and Canada's east and west coasts. Israelis, Argentines, Brazilians, Greeks, Germans, and Koreans were the main actors, along with the Americans and Europeans working from their respective overseas stations in a matrix-type organization. Here, both personalities and culture did indeed play a role.

This could also be a case study that focuses on cross-cultural leadership topics, given the array of different nationalities that participated in the two joint ventures. Thus, it is more like the common global project. However, this case study is more related to CPEL and how to decipher the way common strategies are formulated and put into practice for a group's benefit – this, despite the resistance of those relatively smaller organizations that had to strive to adjust their existing systems, structures, and management to match those of the larger and more global organizations. Unlike the previous land-bridge case study, the shipping organizations' decision to enter into two different joint ventures was based on increasing tonnage surplus vis-à-vis a decreasing cargo tonnage demand, which led ocean freight rates to slump, within an overall economic downturn scenario. Global shipping is always subject to global market forces given its international and intertwined nature. This aspect would probably place the industry on top of a volatility index.

As it usually happens in South America, imports for dry van containers tend to surpass exports three to one, leading to a huge excess of empty containers spread all over its coasts. Thus sooner rather than later they have to be evacuated from the area and repositioned where a given demand level can be guaranteed. Opposite to that is the situation for reefer containers (utilized to carry refrigerated and frozen cargoes), where exports from South America surpass four to one imports from any overseas markets, thus, leading to a continuous repositioning of empty units into South America. These variables are the very essence of a serious operational inefficiency that has its roots in the structural imbalance trend in the region.

Naturally, evacuating an empty container, no matter whether it is a dry van or reefer unit, has an operational cost that is made up of storage, handling, loading, and transport – all this until the containers reach their final destination, where other charges will have to be borne by the ship owner in order to make them ready for the client to pick up. Special equipment to carry out-of-gauge equipment also deserves a certain level of planning and repositioning (e.g., open top, flat rack, open side, high cube), as inbound traffic always tends to be five to one or even more, given that machinery and equipment is a typical import segment with little countertrade, e.g., South America. Consequently, the greater the number of empty containers, the greater the immobilized capital will be – pretty much comparable to the principles of inventory management where keeping a high turnover ratio is required to minimize both immobilized and working capital. Losing track of the container fleet around the world has led many respectable shipping companies to face bankruptcy when combined with a global trade slump. All shipping companies need to safeguard against this issue.

2. *Program in detail*

As we just mentioned, probably one of the main causes many shipping organizations went bankrupt in the recent past is the existing lack of optimization in their worldwide container allocation tracking system. Thousands of containers spread over a long list of ports and almost endless inland spots worldwide are too often regarded as the trigger for a liquidity crisis, especially if it is a global carrier. This is exactly the point at which operations management plays a crucial role.

To avoid being exposed to its financial and operational impact, clearing curves have to be established and monitored in order to reduce the turnaround time of the container. This management begins the moment a laden container gets discharged, up to the moment that it is sent back empty to the port terminals storage yard in order to be reutilized in a new cycle somewhere else in the world. Figure 6.1 shows the time a given number of inbound units take to get cleared and ready to be utilized in a new export cycle. The longer it takes for a unit to be cleared, the more costly it becomes for the shipping organization as that container remains unavailable, which leads to a negative opportunity cost. Keeping a high container turnover rate is the golden rule.

This process obliges the shipping organization to reposition a new unit from somewhere else, increasing its variable cost; otherwise it just loses market share and misses an

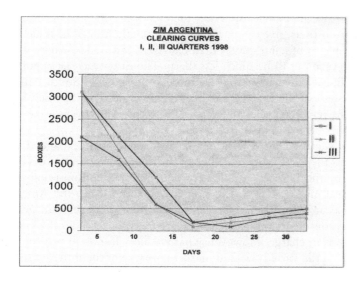

Figure 6.1 Ship owners clearing curves, quarters 1–3, 2000.

opportunity to offset its variable cost and make a gross operations profit. Naturally, reefer containers are worth around five to eight times a dry van unit because they carry higher freight rate cargoes (e.g., beef, seafood, fruit, chocolate, and wine). This is why efforts should be directed to optimize their turnover rate, without losing track of the dry van containers since they provide critical mass. Special equipment such as flat-racks or open top containers is also designed to carry higher value cargoes yielding much higher revenue. For this reason, worldwide availability should also be managed by the operators, if they want to avoid the negative impact an imbalanced traffic produces on the operating capital.

A joint venture that is driven more by necessity and transactional short-term rather than long-term strategy often brings together organizations of a very different structure, culture, management, and market share. In volatile market conditions, the pressure on organizations to optimize their scheduling of containers for example, can alter the way that joint-venture partners react to one another. Since they are in different markets, with different economic trends, shortages in one area may seriously jeopardize the short-term profitability of one JV partner, while it has no effect on another. And if one partner is embarking on a long-term global strategy, outside of the joint-venture agreement, that can also change the short-term goals of the various partners. It may be a rather volatile relationship in a joint venture, as it is relatively short term, and it is not possible to run a business with just short-term thinking.

Organizations in this particular case got downsized and flagged out a number of ships in order to try to adjust their structures and pursue a new balance between tonnage demand and supply. They also managed to reduce the variable port costs by holding joint negotiations as a bloc, instead of individually facing a long list of marine terminals on the various lines they were servicing. The leading joint-venture partners, such as the Israeli and the Korean global container lines, exerted pressure on the port operators, as they operated other lines around the world with some of the same port operators in South America. All of this brought about a greater volume to negotiate with for the groups' benefit.

Service rationalization turned out to be greater in those organizations servicing regional markets compared to the global carriers, which enjoyed different or more benign market realities given their global scope. Typically, South American trade is by definition more susceptible to ups and downs than east-west-east trades, where supply and demand imbalances turn out to be much less sharp. The east-west-east exportable supply was and still is hugely diversified and far more complex than South America west and east coasts. To successfully face these market realities, global companies should first try to understand the regional cycles and demand patterns. And this requires close cooperation between marketing and operations.

The global operators were led by American management, which expanded their view and influence across the joint ventures. Most of the inbound and outbound cargo volume was generated by the USA, as a pole of production and consumption. Such a cargo volume or critical mass gave a sort of nonwritten authority to the American executives, who, being aware of it, tried to spread their vision, strength, management systems, and skills across continents and participating organizations. Under this system, it was easy to see who was in charge. However, what was not clear at all was the type of management used given the varied size and market coverage of the different organizations. The various nationalities and cultures created confrontational attitudes, with the American dominance based on market influence and technology and, most importantly, the grounds upon which these joint ventures were formed. The joint ventures were transactional short-termed operational necessities, and not longer-term corporate strategy.

It has been the authors' experience, around the world, that power in a joint-ventures framework is mostly driven by two factors, technology and organization and regional knowledge. Both tend to temper personalities or cultural differences that may exist. Technology and organization may be accounted for (IT, marketing, cost monitoring, compliance, reporting, quality, economies of scale, etc.) simply because they are essential for any global organization, and certainly for a JV. Regional knowledge held by the minor partners' executives, and the recognition of it by the more global firms' executives, changes the power within the joint venture. Earlier we described the imbalance on the project in India; here the issue is the value of knowledge.

Think of the potential of insider trading. The USA permits senators and congressmen to buy and sell shares of stocks, using the knowledge gained from closed hearing testimony and from lobbyists. They know what is going to happen before it becomes common knowledge in the press. Savvy global leaders understand the importance of local knowledge for exactly this reason. Reacting to new stories is a poor tactic, especially in a joint venture where short-term profits and thinking are more prevalent. This changes the balance of power within a joint venture. There is reward and punishment power, position power, knowledge power, and referent power (respect). IT and organizations would fit into the knowledge category. So you can see that local knowledge is only one part of knowledge power in the joint venture. This then leads to conflict and more negotiations.

Transactional leadership is based on the short term. Transformational leadership requires people to be inspired. Both types of leadership were present when negotiations were held with port authorities, large accounts, shippers' associations, container suppliers, fuel oil suppliers, intermodal transportation suppliers, time charter ship owners, warehouses, logistic operators, major accounts, and bankers. However, it was the market knowledge and situational certainty, provided by a few senior managers, on the way the traffic imbalance was going to unfold during the uncertain years to come that contributed most to keep the two joint ventures united. Their capability to clearly read and anticipate the current market trends, based on past experiences around the world, along with their true understanding of the changes in the business environment and the competition made them unique in our experience.

It is always interesting to see how teams, especially joint ventures, respond to different head businesspeople. We use the word "head" to describe a person who is at the apex of an organization, like a CEO. That person may also be a leader, but in English that term can easily be misinterpreted. Here, the head people showed strong management skills, understanding the numbers and statistical trends. They also displayed judgment and understanding of markets, governments, and competition. That knowledge, in our opinion, is a combination of management and leadership. The ability of the head people to be fearless in making decisions, to inspire others to be like them in their curiosity to know, and their ability to inculcate trust in the members of the CV are transformational leadership.

3. Suggestions and conclusions

Leadership is no doubt an asset for a joint venture, CPE, or alliance. At the same time, the head organization or person (meaning the person or corporation in charge of the joint venture) may conceal misleading facts about the business environment or about their personality and cultures. This may be an advantage or a disadvantage, depending on the way the integration process had been completed. Integration of the joint venture is fundamental, as it brings together all the functional areas of each joint venture organization in order to identify who will be in charge. It will also determine what departments will have to be discarded, which ones will need to reengineer for the new structure, and which systems and processes may have to be imposed on the JV organizations. All this entails a phenomenal adjustment process on the part of the organizations with respect to the way they do business and perceive the market, and may need to adjust their organizational culture. How different the situation would have been if this joint venture had been based on corporate strategy, and not on an urgent need to get by.

PMs on any international venture should have a global vision and must be credible when making their arguments with suppliers, creditors, partners, and other stakeholders. Whatever the situation may be, necessity seems to be a powerful motivator to align nationality, culture, code, norms, ethics, operations, finance, and environment into a single entity, like a joint venture, most often governed by the ones with greater economies of scale or critical mass.

Cooperation, leadership, mutual respect, understanding, and cultural flexibility or tolerance are not minor variables. They turned out to be the pillars upon which this, and any other multicultural and multiregional joint ventures should be based. Necessity may be the triggering factor towards accomplishing a multiplayer and multicultural joint venture. But to become a successful undertaking, the joint venture needs experienced PMs from all the participating firms, as well as a great dose of tolerance and humility – obviously, easier said than done. Leadership and culture become intertwined concepts here and do need time to evolve. In other words, projects should prepare their executive and field teams to cope with uncertain, unexpected, and truly changing contexts by holding an integrationist view of knowledge.

In considering a structure, and a lead organization for global agreements, it is our experience that they must be an organization with global reach and a strong economic foundation. No matter how well informed or insightful a person or organization is, it is not possible to forecast with complete accuracy what will happen in this fast-moving global economy. Changes will happen, losses will be incurred, conflicts will arise, and people will leave for other opportunities (turnover). The lead organization needs to have a long-term strategy in our view that they can and will share with the joint venture, alliance, or CPE. Ideally, the lead organization can field people who are transformational leaders. These people can not only lead a successful venture, but can also help the participating organizations improve their own efficiency after the venture is completed.

This idea of servant leadership and empathy, giving without expecting something in return, takes time but has a low cost/benefit ratio. Being transparent with information, including members of the joint venture in decisions, soliciting opinions from the stakeholders, builds trust. Demonstrating the skill to deal fairly and openly with conflict, showing consideration and respect for the cultures and people on the joint venture, and being fearless in making decisions all lead to trust. And, in our experience trust is essential for success and for transformational leadership.

B. Case study: a demanding and uncertain river logistic operation design: the abilities every PM should have prior to committing to complex project scenarios

1. Background to the case

Iron ore and magnesium reserves all over Bolivia's Mutún region are estimated to total 40 billion tons, according to recent prospects carried out in the region.[1] Those located in Brazil's Mato Grosso do Sul are, are another large source of supply of these key raw material utilized in the steel industry. Mutún's iron ore deposits are considered to be the world's largest.[2] While Brazil is a significant producer and exporter of this strategic mineral, Argentina lacks it and is therefore increasingly dependent on Brazil as a supply source to manufacture steel tubes, rolls, and slabs to be exported all over the world.

Traditionally, this manufacturing role has been mostly dominated by a single industrial Argentine multinational group, whose supply sources were spread all over the globe. They have done this as a way to avoid too much concentration of supply, which might negatively impact the manufacturing cycle should anything go wrong in the supply chain. Thus, disregarding any quality assessment of the material itself, their supply sources were utilized as needed by making good use of the opportunity cost concept. About one quarter of the supply needs were consequently allocated to each of the following historical supply origins:

- Mato Grosso do Sul, Brazil. This source of supply was rated as supplying a good product quality but with a poor or unpredictable logistical performance. Its main advantage, quality, often was offset by a complex river logistic operation involving barge convoys sailing 2,400 KM along the Parana-Paraguay waterways across four countries. Getting the raw materials on time, on budget, and at the plant often proved to be impossible. Therefore, the steel plants' critical stocks often had to increase, to offset occasional shortages of iron ore that would ultimately lead to overseas sources gaining a relatively higher share of the required supply.

- Newcastle and Fremantle, Australia. This lower relative quality iron ore was regularly supplied on oceangoing vessels in shipments of up to 40,000 tons on PANAMAX-type ships of 60,000 tons deadweight. Even though these vessels had more capacity and were therefore underutilized, owing to the ongoing River Plate draught limitations (which are explained later in this chapter), this resulted in higher ocean freight rates per ton, or in other words, a waste. However, this was still useful in offsetting any supply shortfalls arising out of the waterways recurrent logistic bottlenecks and service interruptions. A full shipment from Australia generally supplies of 40,000 to 45,000 tons with a 30-day sailing time. In contrast, a full convoy on the waterways often supplied tonnage ranging from 18,000 to 30,000 tons (depending on seasonal draft) and a sailing time ranging from 15 to 60 days, depending on a number of operational variables. It was clear that the waterways' variability, in reliability of supply, was high, leading to low loading volumes and poor sailing times. This was without even considering port congestion at the Brazilian river terminals as well as a modest loading speed. River draft variability was subject to a dynamic seasonality that made planning risky and tricky, precisely the project phase at which corrections can, and should, be made with relatively little impact. Constraints related to the existing regulatory framework regarding convoy fractioning,[3] night navigation ban, and safety controls also played its role in tightening the operational window even further.
- Mobile, USG, United States. Although the product was of high quality and the sailing time and/or certainty of physical delivery much better than the two options previously mentioned, the existing draft limitations on the River Plate limited the size of the vessels to the underutilized PANAMAX type; therefore, logistics economies of scale were only partly accomplished – another case of forced waste if looked from an operations standpoint. Consequently, this supply source was very similar to the Australian option in terms of operations and productivity. However, Mobile turned out to be an efficient supply source capable of quickly offsetting a shortfall of any other sources, owing to both its relative geographical proximity and ample ship tonnage availability (unlike far away Australian ports and problematic river services). These variables were reinforced by an existing easy access to the commercial or negotiating channels to reach both shipping companies and qualified shipbrokers capable of giving the right response on short notice. However, this supply source also started allocating an increasing degree of preference to those orders coming from China and India. These two markets represented markets of much larger volumes and higher prices than the River Plate. Australian suppliers also showed the same tendency with respect to the Chinese market.
- Sepetiba, Tubarao, Carajas, northeastern Brazil. Product quality here was not the best, but both product delivery response by the producing mines and sailing times offered a result being close to optimal. However, continuous labor strikes, unannounced port lock-outs, and the ever-existing draft limit on the River Plate, affecting all ocean sources alike, restricted this source of supply to no more than one-fourth and often even less of the total required.

2. Program in detail

On the river logistic side, the waterways were dominated by a number of traditional barge operators displaying great variability as regards barge and tugboat technology, management, operational versatility, financial standing, and reputation, all of which led the Argentine steel company to exploit those asymmetries by playing one river operator off against another as a way of negotiating lower freight rates and short-term contracts in their favor. Service commitment was not a variable present at this time. Therefore, the Argentine steel manufacturing group historically supplied their needs of iron ore from four regular sources across the world by combining a number of variables that they always tried to optimize according to the ongoing business environment and operational considerations like:

- Level of critical stock to avoid production shutdown.
- Total transit times from supply source to destination.
- Mix of freight rate levels and type of services.
- Mix of product quality to allow a competitive end product.
- Draft limitations and its ratio to the critical stock level.
- Operational constraints of any nature, such as strikes and lock-outs.
- Stranding, collision, sinking, and so on.

Ocean shipping operators supplied their vessels in a normal fashion with relative stability and predictability. Time-charter rates varied within a range that was considered reasonable, whereas ship owners did not hesitate to engage in one-year contracts for carrying iron ore from Australia, the US gulf, or northeastern Brazil. They did this in view of the return trip, often backed up by grain shipments from the River Plate up to the origins nearby locations. Both ships' hiring rates and bunker prices, two critical interrelated cost factors for any shipping company, remained under control throughout most of the 1990s.

All the above can be considered as the normal ongoing circumstances that historically had governed the supply chain of this organization with respect to a commodity or raw material. These were not seen or regarded as strategic variables in a supply chain but rather as a fact of life one has to accept and deal with in the best possible way. Consequently, one may anticipate that the supply-chain management of this group could be regarded as sensible and reasonable within an international environment of relative stability. In stable circumstances where suppliers did not fail to honor their delivery commitments, no supply source was a major or dominant player, and the ever-existing operational constraints were always, to a lesser or greater extent, under control. And demand for steel products and its price levels were relatively stable, logistic suppliers were abundant, and logistic bottlenecks of any kind were mostly manageable.

A business environment that is relatively stable and certain, with no drastic or major changes during the 1990s, suddenly experienced a structural shift for the following reasons:

- China's economy increased demand for various commodities, two of which were critical for the steel-making firms' supply chain, iron ore, and soy. An increasing demand of iron ore caused this firm's historical suppliers in Australia to shift to supplying Chinese buyers because of higher prices and long-term commitments based on price adjustments. China's proximity and its shorter financial cycle also played a part. China had growing demand for soy products, of which Argentina, Brazil, Paraguay, and Bolivia were and still are large exporters. This changed the commercial priorities of the barge operators on the waterways. The barge operators gave up carrying iron ore to load a much better profit-yielding product, soy and its by-products, which, despite being seasonal, offered them the typical commercial advantages of a product mix that was heavily demanded on the other side of the world. Even though the barge operators did not disappear and kept carrying iron ore along the waterways over 2,400 KM, their commitment, compliance, and reliability left much to be desired. Service informality then loomed large and became a common practice.

• Even though the Gulf War triggered soaring oil prices in the early 1990s and introduced a certain element of uncertainty on the river and shipping markets worldwide, this crisis alone impacted neither the market structure of the shipping companies nor that of the river barge operators. Bunker costs were duly adjusted according to their respective bunker adjustment clauses, and suppliers kept carrying iron ore in a regular fashion. However, the situation in 2004 with respect to soaring oil prices and increasing global uncertainty found its causes on different roots. The difference can be explained by the pressure that China's economic expansion exerted on a critical and drastic business scenario change through:

  • China becoming the first priority as a long-term customer.
  • Ship tonnage supply being mostly committed to China.
  • River tonnage supply giving preference to supply China.
  • Ocean time-charter rates and river freight rates tended to increase sharply owing to a supply shortage, and excessively high bunker rates, which made operators retreat and cancel new-buildings orders.
  • Short-distance sailing being preferred to long-distance sailing by the shipping companies as a way to reduce their financial exposure due to the fluctuating price oil had on the time-charter rates across the world.

Steel prices had increased by more than 70%, leading the steel manufacturing firm to increase its physical assets by investing in an entirely new plant to cope with the growing global demand. At the same time, the fluctuations in the oil price made barge operators become cautious, and they avoided engaging in new buildings. A perfect storm was by then closing in.

The waterways market linking Brazil, Argentina, Bolivia, Paraguay, and Uruguay were, until the 1990s, dominated mostly by Argentine and Paraguayan barge companies with significant capital investment in barges, tugboats, river terminals, handling equipment, and specialized management. This was historically so that when the currency parity of the Argentine peso to the US dollar became one to one, the Argentinian economy started to open to the world. Thus, Argentina received a significant flow of foreign direct investment in practically every infrastructure segment or economic activity of interest, including railways, ports, electricity, hydrocarbons, water, grains, foodstuff, mining, and power generation, to name a few sectors.

Both private and public national firms saw a bright opportunity for capital investment, thanks to the high valuation that their assets enjoyed, based on the existing one-to-one currency parity. Barging companies were not the exception, and a deep and rapid process of capital concentration took place, first from the USA and later from Chile – two aggressive investors in the country at that time. It is interesting to highlight that project teams and EPCM firms tend to get confused and somehow disoriented when rapid and aggressive economic change leads to strong investment flows. Actually, it is difficult to anticipate the dimension of rapid economic change, especially when the business climate seems to lean so clearly towards the positive side; yet it is Latin America, and therefore a cautious approach is always recommended.

Traditional barge operators with interests along the waterways started to retreat, they sold their assets, and either reengineered their businesses or disappeared from the market. Most of the few existing Paraguayan operators sold off their companies and gave up the river business too. By the end of the 1990s, the market was mainly operated by a strong and financially solid, though unskilled, foreign barge company whose only competitors turned out to be a bunch of small independent persistent operators from both Argentina and Paraguay. During these periods of adjustment, good and bad things can happen. In any case, a precautionary approach becomes advisable as the local operators, the ones with the knowledge, decide to sell off their assets and cash out. One may wonder why not stay, or enter a joint venture if the market was so promising. As it often happens when a project terminates, it is highly advisable to avoid team members leaving, as training and induction take too long and have a negative impact on the operations.

Even though the main barge operator engaged in one-year contracts, it was normal practice to break down a convoy and split it to carry soy products and iron ore or other goods. This left the steel company without badly needed supplies. On the one hand, the penalties for breach of contract were often substantially lower than the additional income soy freight rates generated. On the other hand, the soy exports' seasonality did not hinder the barge company from operating informally, as the competition was not important, given the large available iron ore volume in the marketplace. Therefore, the steel firms' critical stock was fed from Australia, USG, and northern Brazil, as a way to cope with the ongoing river market informality that dominated the waterways in those days, the economies of scale remaining modest.

It is useful to visualize some navigation distances, convoy formation structures, and draft limitations to allow the reader to better understand the formidable operational constraints the waterways presented. These, along with the constraints faced during the planning stage of a supply operation, included the following:

- Total river navigation distance was 2,450 KM.
- Convoy formation structure was 12 barges on a 3 x 4 mode basis. They were 200 meters in length, 45 meters in width, and had a carrying capacity of up to 2,500 tons each, for a total of 30,000 tons.
- Tugboat pushing power of 4,000 HP equipped with bow-thruster and having an optimal operational draft of 10 feet 6 inches.
- Draft limitations from March through September were 12 feet, from September through December 9 to 8.5 feet, and from January to February 8 to 6 feet.
- Critical passages[4] marking trends in the river are often identified at various spots all along the waterways. However, there are 500 kilometers on the Alto Paraguay river (KM 0 to 500) that show certain particulars that are worth highlighting: KM 485 rocky bottom where barge convoys could not dredge the river bottom by just pushing forward and making use of the tugboat power, or becoming fractioned to facilitate individual barge (rather than barge convoy) passage; KM 415 rocky and sandy bottom where barge convoys could not dredge the river bottom, but could be fractioned and facilitate passing carefully right on top of the sandy bottom by leaving rocks on either side; KM 184 rocky and sandy bottom similar to KM 415, but also including strong currents that posed serious constraints to a safe maneuvering of both tugboat and barges.

The above clearly shows that every voyage had to be carefully planned in advance and the convoys loaded with as much cargo as possible. But bearing in mind that the type of data nature provides to the experienced eye on navigational hazards that lie some 800 KM away may suddenly shift for better or worse. Therefore, data readings in advance of the journey often resulted in a disastrous round trip for all those who participated in the sailing adventure because of inherent uncertainty of weather and river and other relevant factors that need to be expertly read. This uncertainty may be avoided or diminished by making use of technology or by improving the infrastructure. However, the expert eye must always be there to overcome whatever constraints the technology or civil works fail to foresee and to adjust to the conditions in real time.

A geologist working on an offshore rig in the North Atlantic may be consulted to give his opinion on data produced somewhere off the South American coast. Actually, this is what BP often does when it has to compare data and reach a conclusion. However, not even the expert eye of a skilled geologist can be regarded as bulletproof, given the data variability and its uniqueness and the changing conditions. Something comparable occurs on a 2,400-KM-long river navigation. Whatever the data available, one must face it during the planning phase and avoid carrying the problem over the execution stage. This is what happens too often on the waterways, no matter how skilled the expert eye turns out to be. The environment and limited infrastructure makes it too hard, even for the expert eye.

Even if data readings were correctly interpreted and expertly put into practice by the barge operator, much was left to the operator's tacit knowledge of how to successfully navigate these turbulent waters. This kind of operation suggests the importance of traditional knowledge, as it provides a company to project a certain level of certainty to its supply operations. In other words, it plays a critical role to achieve sustainability. Navigation in the Indian ocean is highly dependent upon the latitude and the season. Sailing in the "roaring 40s" is challenging, even for an old salt. Sailing into India and Sri Lanka with heavy loads must be scheduled before or after the monsoon season. The trouble with both is that with the planet warming, changes are often quicker and more severe than they were even 10 years ago.

In an attempt to bring both certainty and efficiency to the global supply operation, a highly customized project was designed by vertically integrating the river barge operation within the company's supply chain. River barge transport remains the most financially viable mode of transporting for such materials. An important facet is that case study participants shared a past history of business interaction and collaboration, which, despite being limited, tended to cement trust. As we have said, this is essential for any project, as well as the necessary relationship commitment to discuss a vertical integration option in this case. This project comprised the construction and operation of fully dedicated barge convoys to carry iron ore supplies from Brazil to Argentina, commencing in 2003 and phased over six years. The first phase comprised development and acceptance of an innovative logistics design solution, and its realization through the construction of new barges and leasing of existing barges. The project had in-built replication possibilities to roll out a series of similar projects. Figure 6.2 was the proposal agreed upon to describe the broad scope of the six-year project, with the prospect of a larger follow-on project.

The first barge unit required 90 days to be built, with a maximum of 30 days for every subsequent built barge. A group of 12 leased barges was sourced, surveyed, approved, and chartered from one of the smaller barge operators. A reliable river operator

One fully-dedicated barge convoy twelve months a year	Building 12 barges of 2500 tons each = 30.000 tons capacity
One suitable tugboat of "pusher" type basis 4500 horse power	Port Loading at: Ladario, Corumba, Sobramil /
Speed 5 to 6 knots up-river and 8 to 9 knots down-river	Port Discharge at: San Nicolás /
12 days sailing up-river; 11 days sailing down-river; 2 days loading/unloading; 1 to 2 days open	Gross operational time: 25 to 27 days; 1 trip every month.
Total annual volume 250,000 tons + or - 10% basis 6 years contract	24 hours loading / 24 hours unloading
Barge dimensions basis 65 metres length by 15 metres width	Building of new barges basis USD490,000 each

Figure 6.2 Proposal.

was introduced into the project team, and persuaded to operate the convoys under strict efficiency standards throughout the six-year contract duration. Three potential shipyards were approached in Argentina, Brazil, and Paraguay and invited to bid for the barge-building contract, using steel sheets for the barges to be supplied by the steel manufacturing company from one of its plants in Brazil.

Figure 6.3 shows the structure of the joint venture. It involved three principal players who formed the joint venture with several other instrumental secondary players that influenced the final joint venture design. Although this project and therefore this case study addresses a number of players which made possible the implementation of the project itself, only those who played a key or critical role will be analyzed from a PM

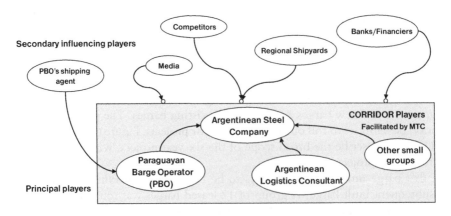

Figure 6.3 Joint venture showing critical primary players and instrumental secondary players.

perspective. Those having fulfilled a secondary role will only be mentioned to let the reader identify both the number of participants embodied in the project, as well as the different dimensions that made up the project, leading to a rather complex decision-making scenario. Critical and instrumental players are described as critical players or primary stakeholders and instrumental players or indirect stakeholders.

First, let us look at the three critical players or primary stakeholders. The steel manufacturing company is based in Buenos Aires, with 4,000 employees and an annual turnover well in excess of USD1 billion. This firm belongs to a much larger industrial conglomerate with annual sales of USD3.2 billion, with 16,000 employees worldwide. The company's corporate booklet cites Stanford University's Business School Professor John Roberts, who introduces this company as a global leader by highlighting some of the attributes of this company:

> Historically, large transnational corporations pursued two great targets to achieve good outcomes. First, achieving larger economies of scale as a way to reducing unit costs and remaining competitive. Thus, companies tended to sell the very same products world-wide and keep costs going downwards. Second, customization capabilities for each country resulted in expanding their markets and keeping achieving economies of scale. These two goals were traditionally difficult to accomplish simultaneously, and just a few firms made it reality. The Argentine steel manufacturing company is an excellent example, as at present it operates with global efficiency, counts on global cooperation, and works on a global basis without overlooking what the many market needs are and by integrating their supply of products and associated services worldwide.

We can confirm that this company has a high level of explicit knowledge that transcends their domestic offices and that they play an indisputable global leadership role.

The logistic consulting company is a Buenos Aires-based firm specializing in the formulation and implementation of relatively high complexity logistic designs. It has offices throughout Latin America to provide industrial conglomerates with assistance in their logistic campaigns, in landscapes characterized by difficult physical access. It specialized in oil, gas, power, and mining, infrastructure for customers represented by large transnational corporations with projects undertaken throughout the region. This company can be said to possess a great volume of tacit knowledge, which provides them with a competitive advantage position as described by Porter of low inimitability, along with an ever-increasing market-focused positioning (Porter 1998).

The barge operating company is based in Asunción, Paraguay. This is one of the various river transportation firms that went through a reengineering process during the 1990s by getting rid of most of their floating assets and shore facilities. However, this operator kept running a very efficient and rather small operation, based on deep knowledge, solid planning, and sound strategy. It can be said that this operator was probably the only one left on the waterways skillful enough to undertake a project of this nature, as well as being daring enough to challenge larger and more resourceful global operators.

Second is the instrumental players or indirect stakeholders. These are organizations that were not part of the joint venture but had an influence on it. The primary and secondary shown in Figure 6.2 are what we would call a CPE. The barge operators' ship agent is based in Buenos Aires and could be considered the barge owners' right hand in Argentina. A barge owner himself during the 1990s and ex-partner of the Paraguayan barging company, this ship agent has become a shrewd and intimate translator of the various meanings and codes that are often hidden behind people's facades, attitudes, phrases, and cultural behaviors. The ship agent acted mainly as a cultural bridge and managerial interpreter between the Argentine steel transnational and the Paraguayan barge operator. Both the current operational and regulatory frameworks on the waterways were well-known fields for the Paraguayan operator. This actor played more of a role as a cultural enhancer than as a technical advisor on operational topics that were of tactical relevance.

Regional shipyards in Argentina, Paraguay, and Brazil played their respective cards by actively lobbying critical and instrumental players alike. Technical skills, social contacts, governmental lobbing, and community impact were some of the variables cleverly utilized by the shipbuilders and the client, suggesting a fluid interaction at the Corridor roundtable forums.

Main competitors were wary of capital concentration, enabling too much dominance over the waterways market. Competitors' retaliation to impede the accomplishment of the project was no less significant than their seemingly short-sighted strategy of relying on their prevailing market dominance. The Corridor also provided a dynamic scenario for interactions to occur between all competitors who were members.

Banks were purely instrumental in approving or rejecting the project from a financial standpoint, although their understanding of the waterways business may be regarded as important.

The media also became instrumental in supporting the location where barge-building was going to take place, as well the facilities the steel was going to be supplied from for the shipyard to build the barges.

The project's logistic design was formulated by the Buenos Aires-based consulting company on the basis of carefully assessing the existing contextual conditions and the steel manufacturing firms' strategic position at that given moment. Such an assessment entailed a deep review and study of the following aspects:

- Australia's increasing commitment to supply China's growing demand for iron ore.
- USG suppliers' growing preference to meet China's increasing demand for iron ore.
- Northeastern Brazilian suppliers' preference to supply both China's and India's expanding markets for iron ore.
- Inauguration of a new plant on the River Plate to cope with a steady increase of demand for steel-made end products from all over the world, including the Asia-Pacific region.
- Existing relative indifference on the part of the steel-producing firm with respect to becoming more actively involved in controlling their own waterways-based supply chain.
- High levels of capital concentration of river transportation companies operating on the waterways, linking the Brazilian suppliers with the Argentine buyer, leading to both price increases and service informality.
- High levels of ongoing variability and a future uncertainty scenario for oil prices, impacting negatively on oceangoing vessels time charter market.
- Steady increases in demand volumes for soy products arising out of China's formidable growth, leading to a river transportation imbalance and a general rate increase in barging services.
- Slow reaction and limited innovation capacity on the part of the Argentine steel-producing company, despite its global structure and well-reputed international management.

In view that the waterways market was to a great extent dominated by a major player and that no independent barge operator was at that time in condition to successfully compete on a sustainable basis, the logistic design shown in Figure 6.2, was formulated and submitted to the steel company for their evaluation. It was intended both to bring an achievable solution to the multinational and to make their executives visualize the opportunities lying in the long run in terms of market dominance, ship-building, and supply, as per the scheme outlined in the Figure 6.2.

The building project schedule was expected to be 90 days for the first unit, and a maximum of 30 days thereafter for every barge, bringing the total construction time up to a maximum of 12 months. In the interim period a group of 12 barges was located, surveyed, approved, and chartered from one of the smaller river companies that were still doing business on the waterways. The steel-manufacturing firm signed a contract for six years, this being a requisite for the financial institution to even start talks, and carry on with the process. A reliable river operator was brought into the deal, and convinced to operate the convoys under strict efficiency standards throughout the duration of the contract – despite the well-known operational constraints of the fluvial system. Three potential shipyards were approached in the three countries, Argentina, Brazil, and Paraguay, and were invited to bid for the building contract. It was agreed that the steel sheets for building the barges would be supplied by the steel-manufacturing company from one of its plants in Brazil, in view of it having the most adequate sheet cuttings and lowest cost.

The moment this information appeared in the media, things started to change, and the project ran into serious danger of running aground and obstructing the realization that a second larger contract was already being negotiated. A Memorandum of Understanding (MOU) on a six-year contract was made public to the media by March 2004.

It is interesting, and it helps to look at the context within which this project emerged and to analyze from a leadership standpoint how the sequence of events influenced the players' decision making and shaped their final agreement. It reflects a typical project multiheaded stakeholder quandary, which needs to be managed and in some cases resolved. It also illuminates the reality of those involved in PM, and the reality of its uncertainty, planned responses, as well as coping mechanisms to achieve results. As we described earlier, one only really knows another company or individual when there has been a conflict. And, a conflict between any two of the players, 11 secondary ones, may contaminate all of the joint venture. Look at what followed:

- The dominant and largest river company lodged a formal claim on old pending issues against the smaller river operator and proceeded to seize some of the barges that had been chartered to the steel-making firm for the transition period of 12 months – this until the new buildings were launched and ready to operate. Thus, the first shipment of 25,000 to 30,000 tons of iron ore resulted in a failure.
- The steel-making company's shipping manager threatened the large river operator with no longer chartering their oceangoing vessels from northeast Brazil; the company also provided shipping services from overseas, unless an amicable solution to this issue was found.
- No threat was made, however, with respect to the ongoing barging operations of this dominant player. Despite being informal and therefore inefficient, the steel-producing firm needed to maintain raw material supplies in any way it could

to avoid having to make use of critical stocks at the San Nicolas port terminal for its plant in Argentina.

- The Paraguayan operators reinforced their distrust of the smaller river operator by maintaining that one never knows what legal or financial problem lies behind this firm's floating equipment assets: maritime liens, embargoes, outstanding moneys, material deficiencies, unsettled casualties, and the like. In the meantime, the Asunción-based company had positioned a tugboat in San Nicolas while waiting to proceed with the voyage, thus incurring heavy running costs.
- The Paraguayan operator offered to personally talk to the smaller river operator and convince him to pay the pending moneys, lift the embargo, and carry on with the river adventure while getting capitalized with the still pending 12 months' charter. Instead, the smaller operator proposed that the Paraguay-based company advance the said pending monies in order to immediately free the barges and to jointly exploit other extracontractual barges that were also trapped by the embargo to carry the other party's cargo with their tugboat. After some robust negotiations, the deal was accepted and the first convoy departed from San Nicolas towards Asunción. All the same, the Paraguayan operator continues to harbor a high degree of distrust.
- While performing the third day of navigation, a new embargo emerged and resulted in the seizure and retention of 6 out of 12 barges at an intermediate river port. This time the plaintiff was the Argentine Government, which claimed reimbursement of some loans that were destined to construction but were in fact utilized in running their daily operation. Lawyers had to be appointed, and guarantees were submitted to let the convoy proceed. However, the efficiency with which the whole transition process of the river operation had been planned was already void and deserved an urgent reengineering if economies of scale were to work on their side instead of becoming burdensome.
- The dominant river operator let the market know that a huge building order had been initiated for 40 barges in each of the potential shipyards with which the steel-making firm was negotiating. The most likely shipyard, located in Paraguay, acknowledged having read the news and being in advanced negotiations to build 40 barges as informed by the media. At that time, the players did not know whether this was a distractive operation or a strategic move to keep control of the waterways market.
- The financial party started to delay the final signature for releasing the funds in view of the recent events. This brought about uncertainty, and they made public their concern as to whether or not the appointed shipyard would have enough building facilities to carry out the job on time and within budget. These were two variables of paramount importance in a project characterized by efficient operations based on low margins.
- The steel-producing company instructed its lawyers to speed up the proceedings of some old claims for barge sinking and total loss that it went through on several occasions against the dominant river player, which it found to be responsible for. Clearly, this acted as retaliation.
- The media gave nationalistic coverage to the fact that an Argentine company was placing a construction order, not in Argentina but in Paraguay, and that it would supply steel sheets from its Brazilian subsidiary and not from any of its various domestic facilities.

- The Paraguayan operator finally lost the support of its financial partner and had to call for the services of another bank, which imposed less attractive conditions, causing margins to lower even further, though it was still feasible.
- The Paraguayan shipyard, though the best qualified, was eliminated by political motives, and thus two Argentine shipyards became shortlisted. One turned out to be very knowledgeable and counted on respectable facilities and availability to start work immediately and guarantee strict construction schedule compliance. The other shipyard was once a large yard specialized in building railway wagons, and its CEO happened to be an old schoolmate of the steel-making company's owner and chairman. In spite of not having the right facilities and giving no certainties with respect to construction timing or delivery dates, this shipyard was invited to participate in the bidding process.
- The new bank, despite having little knowledge of naval construction engineering, was the first party to oppose the appointment of this new shipyard by alleging its lack of expertise and commitment. Banks tend to be quite pragmatic.
- The Paraguayan operator let the others know, confidentially, that should the bank pay a visit to this shipyard's job-site, the deal would be over. It was clear that their facilities did not match the basic needs for a safe construction process.
- The steel-making firm's managers had no other option than to consider this shipyard's proposal, since the top tier of the organization favored it.
- Such a proposal was delayed over and over and caused the Paraguayan operator to give final notice to the steel-making firm, alleging the company could no longer wait for a final decision, if an operational scheme based on efficiency and productivity was to be accomplished.
- Finally, the inexperienced shipyard delayed so much in matching the necessary technical requirements that its offer was dismissed, despite giving assurance that it was the most competitive. Despite the fact that it was previously disqualified, the bid was won by the Paraguay-based shipyard while it was agreed that the steel sheets supplies were to be sent off from an Argentina-based facility. This was a way to cope with the media and pacify potential critics, referring to the fact that the whole project remained as a MERCOSUR deal, with no extraregional participants, was a way of coping with the media and potential critics. However, at the very last minute, the board of the steel-producing company decided to proceed and place an additional construction order with the most qualified Argentine shipyard, and therefore commit to the fully dedicated operations philosophy to be applied on a second convoy.
- As by-products of these first two contracts, a potential third identical contract was awarded to the same Paraguayan barge operator through the consulting company, with shipyard works completing monitoring and the carriage of steel sheets being awarded to the consulting firm.
- Related business possibilities emerged for the consulting firm with respect to developing a dedicated convoy for a large soy exporter and new river traffic for the same steel-manufacturing firm.

These simplified vignettes of the complex and energetic interactions between stakeholders provide a glimpse of the complexity of the situation. Delivering this kind of business transformation is fraught with uncertainties, but often ignored obvious risks, and the politics of stakeholder management that can only be summarized. The point of highlighting the above is to illustrate the complexity, richness, and tentative nature of the variables involved. Such studies are necessarily filtered by the personal observations and experiences of those contributing evidence. However, despite these limitations, the lived experience advances our knowledge of repertoires of behavior and responses to such situations, and so this is what constitutes the value of these business transformation project management studies.

Two driving forces for this joint venture become clear from this case study. One is the global dimension of the primary stakeholder, the steel manufacturing company, and the other is the complexity of the logistic operation itself which gave relevance to traditional knowledge of strategic relevance. One might assume that the steel company, having a business presence in so many countries, with access to countless databases and logistic experiences, would not source domestically but rather globally. However, even though a number of functional aspects such as financial engineering, insurance, port operations, and barging services were often contracted by the steel company in diverse geographical settings, the knowledge specificity and viscosity of the logistic design caused this firm to source these features entirely at home. The unique geographic and operational particulars embodied by the waterways seems to have found fertile ground for these various actors to get together and become interested in one another's needs, potential, and proposals.

The steel company's Procurement Managing Director and head of the waterways project within his organization eventually submitted the project for the board's approval, once the consultancy firm had rounded off the logistic design. The Director headed a division of more than 20 engineers in charge of the many logistic segments needed to keep various plants running across Argentina. He admitted that his team was more focused on setting new key performance indicators and improving or securing their supplies from various origins rather than on innovating new supply channels or creating the conditions for new logistic suppliers to emerge. When asked about this particular logistic design, he was categorical in his response: "The parties to talk to were so many, their interests and points of view so diverse, and the traditional knowledge so deep and attached to every single player, that I find an alternative setting to develop a project this complex simply unrealistic."

When a major river operator representative's opinion was requested on the above comments, he stated that had this individual and his team taken a more modest attitude, or exhibited better receptivity with respect to those with the specific operational knowledge, the project would not have been so time consuming.

> With this I confirm my own suspicions in that representing a large multinational may give oneself negotiating power and a high self-esteem I suppose. This person, along with his team, took a long time to evolve and understand that here the key to the project was accepting others' views and experience coming from so many years of working on the waterways, and not that much engineering performance ratios and indicators that proved successful somewhere else. The authors are convinced that this was always about who held knowledge and not so much about relative power or global dimension.

The operator's opinions and views, based on their experiences on a number of different functional aspects (e.g., loading speed at Brazilian river terminals, controlling procedures by the national coastguards, port congestion impact on freight rates, casualty probability, and seasonality impact on round-trip performance), helped to dissipate the doubts or fears of the steel company's management in a scenario in which it could not dominate, anticipate, or even entirely assimilate. Induction would have taken too long for the steel company, and the risks would have been too high.

Even though this whole exercise was not an easy journey, such a process provided the various players with the possibility of double checking with those who were not parties to the project on certain operational issues. Otherwise it would have meant that the project was not feasible because of the doubts with respect to operational or financial aspects, hidden agendas, or lack of trust. A complete breakdown and full exposure of the critical variables, along with the input from both the stakeholders and collaborators, helped the project to avoid becoming a nonstarter.

We tend to agree with the direct participants and observers who commented on the uniqueness of this project, as well as the great number of variables that had to be considered on a 12-month basis for operation. In this regard, we would like to add that a river operation has a tight connection with its geographical environment, which cannot be extrapolated in view of both the existing topography and the traditional knowledge that often comes attached to it. Otherwise, why not to bring Mississippi River operators down to the Parana-Paraguay waterways and assign them a fully dedicated convoy five-year contract? Naturally, traditional knowledge acts as a natural barrier.

It becomes apparent that operating convoys in both the Amazon basin in Brazil and the Orinoco basin in Venezuela has little to do with operation of the Parana-Paraguay waterways. One can always find certain analogies, though they often turn out to be the exception and not the rule. In those locations, traditional knowledge turns out to be absolutely critical, while both the operational variables (tugboats, barges, terminals, cranes, berths, buoys, people, culture, etc.) and the geographical particulars (depths, tides, currents, sedimentation, seasonality, rains, fog, temperature, etc.) tend also to be unique.

3. Suggestions and conclusions

Certain aspects clearly stand out in this case study that did not play such a dominant role in the previous examples. One is represented by the fact that once this project was designed, formulated, and put into practice, the worst of the globalization impact on the region had already been experienced or absorbed. Therefore, the driving motive of this project does not find its sources in the first globalization wave over the region but was a sort of globalization impact by-product that brought about a specific supply-chain problem for a major regional player.

The traumatic moments that hit each and every national and regional logistic player and compelled them to reengineer their business or give up were over by the time the steel company had engaged in construction. It can be argued that the high level of traditional knowledge a project like this one needed to develop and become a reality played a determinant role here. However, had not the marketplace required those few critical regional players, with a deep knowledge of their business context, it is extremely unlikely that this project would have progressed the way it did, regardless of the contextual or global circumstances. Bringing together independent actors with a common interest or rationale to collaborate, exchanging views and impressions, and transferring knowledge to produce a remarkable business transformation would have been unthinkable without identifying the existence of a solid traditional knowledge platform upon which to build. PMs often ignore such considerations.

This project knowledge specificity and viscosity, and its apparent dependence on traditional knowledge, also suggest that a certain degree of maturation amongst both the primary and secondary stakeholders was needed to overcome the many managerial and operational barriers. One may assume that this project would have failed had it been undertaken in the early 1990s, when the system was just beginning and little experience was available in terms of interactions, networking, knowledge sharing and transfer, cooperation, and collaborations.

The way stakeholders (direct and indirect), and others collaborated and shared data and information on their own functional experiences shows that further to traditional knowledge, face-to-face interaction, along with a degree of maturity in the system itself, also had a leveraging effect on the project completion. It seems clear that trust, commitment, leadership, motivation, collaboration, and innovation have all played their part within a common setting.

In our privileged role as direct observers, we can affirm that when the impact of the Asia-Pacific economies had been felt, the regional players had already, to a great extent, reengineered their businesses to cope with the new business context that gradually impacted the region during the 1990s. This entailed a great deal of business transformation, along with vision, knowledge sharing and transfer, and leadership on the part of the members with respect to both their own internal or regional reengineering, and their alliances and partnerships with foreign-based companies. Such a degree of evolution has apparently helped the steel company to quickly realize it had to open up and push its executives to interact in a more proactive manner in search of knowledge to transform their business limitations into strategic opportunities.

To this end and given the project's complexity, the maturity accomplished mainly by the direct stakeholders by the early 2000s seems to have helped the steel company transform a threatening supply-chain context into a more predictable operational context, leading possibly to a dominant market position in the waterways.

Leadership, knowledge transfer capacity, cooperation, collaboration, transformational attitude, and innovation are all features of utmost relevance for PMs to develop, in ever-evolving emerging contexts where the only linear variable is uncertainty. Projects should train PMs by bearing these variables in mind if achieving economies of scale and sustainable operations is the goal.

As we have said before, the lead for a CPE, joint venture, alliance, or any other structure must act as if he or she is a CEO. As in this case study, many organizations had no written or verbal commitment to all of the other players. The joint venture certainly did communicate to one another and the secondary players to those members of the joint venture with whom they were contracted. The PM for the lead joint venture organization only has his or her leadership skills to rely upon. The lead needs to have a wide range of interests and reasonably good knowledge of local and global conditions. The lead cannot know it all and must know how to find those with adequate local knowledge to anticipate, avoid, or mitigate the risks. Politics, especially, must be on the agenda whenever a project has the potential to garner attention. Empathy and understanding for the other members of the joint venture, not just what is required by the agreement, will facilitate open dialogue. Building trust will enable the project to overcome obstacles more smoothly, with less animosity. We believe a global PM needs to be a renaissance person, with wide-ranging interests.

Notes

1 "Will Evo stick?" Mines and Communities Website. www.minesandcommunities.org. Retrieved on 2008–03–29.
2 "Serrania Mutun, Chiquitos Province, Santa Cruz Department, Bolivia." www.mindat.org. Retrieved on 2006–10–20.

3   This means splitting or separating cargoes into smaller loads to lower the barge draft (depth from the waterline to the underside of the barge) or to cope with narrow unobstructed channels. Fractioning is critical where the barge is travelling over rocky and shallow waters or through narrow navigable channels within the river. Fractioning cargoes produce inefficiencies in carrying capacities but are necessary to avoid grounding risks.
4   A critical passage is one that shows a lower draft than average or where a convoy needs to make special maneuvers to avoid a physical obstacle during its navigation.

Reference

Porter, M., *Competitive Advantage: Creating and Sustaining Superior Performance.* 1998, New York: Free Press.

7 Mining operations in emerging Asia and Oceania

Variables beyond the ordinary PMs should render a special look before committing technology and financial resources

Here we will focus on two distinctly different case studies with different locations. The first case study relates to gold mining on a remote island in southern Indonesia, where a number of variables have to be assessed and solutions developed. These variables, being of a different caliber, must therefore be aligned in order to accomplish operations in a timely manner. Communications, gestures, filters, manners, and cultural features must all be refined in order for operations to move forward as planned.

The second case study encompasses an entirely opposite vision of how projects should be run from an operations perspective, as it encompasses a sort of institutional assessment approach in an emerging economy such as Papua New Guinea (PNG). It explores to what extent a weak institutional profile may endanger the success of a given project in a remote setting, and it sets forth a number of measures for PMs to take to avoid project development constraints that remain hidden in the decision-making process.

A. Case study: a truly extreme project setting that requires a tailor-made approach to survive on the Indonesian archipelago

1. Background to the case

This case study is a gold mining project located in a delicate ecosystem within Gorontalo province in Sulawesi. Logistics turned out to be both complex and atypical in that the project involved coastal shipping operations, minimum infrastructure, coastal zone management, and a rather intensive PSM. Australian and Indonesian executives were the main project participants, but the participants also included Europeans and Latin Americans and a long list of suppliers for both capital goods and services. The main operational topics were procurement-related oceangoing and barge operations, rotor-craft management, health and safety, and port development. But the project also included the development of a forestry-dedicated area under the strong presence and influence of indigenous communities, as an attempt to provide the project with both operational certainty and overall sustainability.

This case study encompasses a typical gold-rich area located in an almost inaccessible spot on an isolated Indonesian island whose inhabitants formed part of ancient tribes dedicated to forestry and farming. These are two typical activities that often are deeply rooted, and in principle, contrary to what brings foreigners, technology, and change to their living patterns. The entry access is represented by a s7-meter-deep concrete-made wharf with no gear and connecting to dirt roads that go right into the jungle as soon as leaving the wharf area. Calling this facility a port of entry would be optimistic.

Some oversized rope conveyors were purchased in Austria and had to be transported all the way up to the job-site in Gorontalo. The project's operational feasibility depended on whether suitable barges could be hired from Jakarta, the primary point of entry and a transshipment hub, or if a charter party had to be signed to complete a full ship from Singapore, or another major transshipment port, to sail straight up to the site's wharf. Like previous case studies, the place to clear customs became of critical importance to optimize the lead time and avoid incurring unwanted delays at both the port of transshipment and final discharge location. Even though not the topic of this case study, customs clearance was an issue with respect to where and when to clear customs, given the existing coordination difficulties on the logistics and its associated delays along with elementary infrastructure at the job-site.

Even though the project's artisanal port lay on one of hundreds of islands across Indonesia, a huge territory with islands of different shapes and sizes, it may be compared to an inland port terminal in South America, where neither the available infrastructure nor the existing topography provided the developers with the minimum to carry out a predictable and safe operation. However, the analogy starts and ends right there, as operations are always deeply influenced by uses and customs, culture, and factors that are inherent to the specific project site. And Indonesia can be considered a very special place to work.

2. *Program in detail*

Several operational obstacles soon emerged, for despite regular barges being available, none had the necessary configuration and seaworthiness to undertake a coastal navigation with overdimensional rope conveyors and some heavy-lift and out-of-gauge (OOG) capital goods. A berth crane, along with a job-site crane, had to be acquired and positioned at the port and the mine site, respectively, to make the necessary movements to put the equipment in place. Roads had to be surveyed and upgraded where necessary to make them passable for heavy-lift pieces and overdimensional equipment. Furthermore, the design and approval of a contingency plan also became necessary, along with its logistic-related environmental impact assessment. We often see risk assessment and development of contingency plans bypassed, despite of their tremendous importance in terms of the potential damage risks may have on a project's timeline and budget. We often hear project planners or engineers, give the following statement as a reason to ignore or dismiss risk analysis: "no worries, there is no barrier our engineers cannot lift." This reply reflects arrogance or ignorance – and in our experience, probably both.

The operations were conducted under the close watch of the indigenous communities, which far from being simple spectators were getting ready to actively participate in an upcoming stakeholder consultation process. Helicopter operations to carry both personnel and cargo from the port area up to the job-site turned out to be one of the communities' main concerns given their dedication to primary activities such as farming and hunting. These aspects could be negatively affected by noise and the typical intensity logistic operations often reach once construction begins.

Figure 7.1 describes what the five PSM strategies should be to successfully deal with the various types of opposition a project may face prior to its construction stage. The model in itself does not vary from place to place, but its application and outcomes may bring about huge differences. It is here that we recommend that a project deploy a CQO (cultural intelligence officer), ideally the lead, in order to bridge the cultural gaps and to find ways to get closer to the vision and concern of the people at or near the job-site.

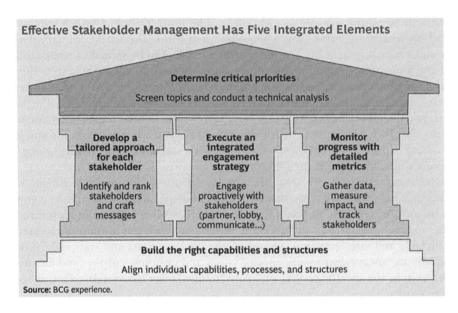

Figure 7.1 Stakeholder management model.

Naturally, the need of either hiring or developing a CQO will greatly depend on the number of regions a company deals with, as well as the type of projects it develops.

A Canadian gold mining company faced a comparable situation in northern Indonesia. It hired a former Canadian diplomat who was raised in Indonesia and spoke not only spoke Indonesian, but was also familiar with the country's complex culture. Even though he held an engineering degree, mining was not on his radar. What do you imagine was more important: his technical expertise in mining or the cultural background he brought to the table? The former could be replaced from home without major constraints, whereas the latter turned out to be the right tool to enable the former fit into the planning stage. One may wonder where one is going to find an executive holding such an interdisciplinary and dual cultural background? This is precisely one of the main concerns PMs should bear in mind before deploying resources on the field. (Some suggestions are provided at the end of this section.)

Early identification of both negative and positive leaders is crucial to formulating a persuasive approach. These tactics are not aimed at gaining one little advantage here and thereby playing tricks. To the contrary, this allows the PM lead and staff to start on solid ground and to keep an eye on the long term without neglecting short-term issues. Both long-term goals, such as caring for the forest and the communities, as well as short-term issues such as noise levels that spike on a particular occasion, are both required consistently.

The Boston Consulting Group (BCG) model proposes a few steps that appear sensible if applied across the Western world, where the setting of critical priorities, identification of stakeholders interests, engagement with stakeholders, or alignment of individual capabilities fit into a social framework where one can anticipate reactions, gestures, or leadership trends. However, an ancient Asian society, ruled by tribal values and led by caciques, requires more understanding and effort to enable the team to at least try to understand reactions, gestures, and what the local people consider leadership. As we have said, a leader is defined by those inspired to follow. This is again a reason we prefer to have the CPE or joint venture lead become as much of a cultural expert as is possible.

Australians have a good understanding of their neighborhood when it comes to project development and investment opportunities, as Asia is their backyard and main client for mining and energy projects. However, undertaking and completing a successful PSM program in a setting like this one may take too long and therefore expose the project to face unexpected and unwanted delays. The time span of a project cannot be regarded as everlasting because its CAPEX will withstand it. Discouraged management, angry shareholders, revisionist BOD, negative media, inquisitive suppliers, along with a weak global corporate image, may all lead the host government to exert pressure on the mining organization. It may do this to ease its guidelines in favor of secondary stakeholders, or what is even worse, force a governmental associated investment agency to become a potential partner. This is a derived effect of ineffective planning.

Having the government become a partner is a maneuver that sometimes is deliberately sought and generated, though it may also happen accidentally. Either way, it should be anticipated by undertaking a professional risk strategy throughout the planning stage and always prior to initiating construction. We suggest that this not be left to the engineers. Not being able to show concrete progress on a PSM process may provide an open invitation for a tricky state or federal government to take advantage and step in, which is dependent on the project's nature and geographical location. This is exactly what happened in this case, as the PSM process did not show any progress despite the organization's efforts and allocation of resources. The problems that surfaced were negative leadership, hidden agendas, environmental concerns, social issues, economic fears, apparently unbridgeable cultural gaps, communication problems, and lack of cooperation. The local investor had to become part of the project and lead the communities to relax, trust, and cooperate.

Trust is a major component in any project undertaking, and this project was indeed not the exception. It was like considering the payment of a royalty in exchange for letting the project move forward. This practice is often seen across Latin America anytime a strategic mineral or rare earth element (REE) is to be exploited by a foreign organization. This suggests that both cultural gaps and geographical isolation, along with rareness, may easily become project inhibitors. Every project should have a contingency plan to address such issues as the project going off course or causes of it going aground. A corporation must be realistic about the risks it is running when operating in such extreme settings. Looking at these places with Western eyes and values is a huge mistake. The CPE or joint venture lead needs to exercise empathy, patience, and compassion for the local people and environment.

Communication also plays a key role in any project, though especially in those where Western culture is rare at the project site. Harkins says that communication is "an interaction between two or more people that progresses from shared feelings, beliefs, and ideas to an exchange of wants and needs to clear action steps and mutual commitments (Harkins 1999). A powerful conversation produces three outputs: shared participation, shared knowledge, and a strengthened relationship." When communicating with another person, the person sending the message is responsible for assuring that the person receiving the message not only heard it but understood its intent.

This is not a quick process, and it requires that the receiver and sender share a common context. If I am excited about the *Century* I witnessed in yesterday's cricket match and want to share my joy, the receiver must understand what the term signifies, or what I say will have little meaning, and will be stripped of emotion. So I must first explain that a *Century* is an individual score of at least 100 runs and a significant achievement for a batsman. Once there is context, the information must be internalized by the receiver and converted from information to knowledge. Nonaka described this process, with explicit information being the words spoken and tacit knowledge being the understanding (Nonaka, Toyama and Konno 2001).

This process requires that both the sender and receiver actively listen for ideas, thus producing shared participation. There also must be an interest in the other person. My colleague may not give a twit for cricket, but since I do, if he actively engages in the emotion and empathizes, it also builds our social bond. While there are numerous tools and techniques to enhance communication skills, the most important one is to listen actively.

Imagine a typical dialogue in the field between an Australian PM and an Indonesian who makes his living in the bush. They are waiting on a delivery, and the PM asks what the fruit is hanging on a tree. The Indonesian answers durian and begins to explain, in broken English. If the PM has curiosity, he or she will ask more questions such as is it tasty, how do I prepare it, and is there a season for example? For the Indonesian, if the curiosity is genuine, he or she will get a shot of oxytocin and feel good that the PM has taken the time and shown the interest. The Indonesian then tells his colleagues about this interest and desire of the PM to share personal time. This builds trust in the CPE, as the reputation of the PM will spread. Also, the PM learns more about the culture of the people on the team and can then better engage the next time. In doing so, it prepares for the inevitable disputes and lays the foundation for leadership.

Communication filters exist, and it is necessary to find ways to either drop them, or work around them. Filter biases include a Brahmin's view of a Dalit in a caste system, or blacks and whites, or rich and poor, or educated and uneducated – unfortunately, the list is a long one. Overcoming such biases begins with EQ and the recognition that we all have filters. Few people can mask their internal emotions, and Paul Ekman found that the facial expressions for emotions were common around the globe (Ekman 2003). A genuine smile in the jungles of Indonesia or Papua New Guinea looked like those in Europe. Eckman's work provided the foundation of facial recognition technology. Emotions leak out through the eyes and body language, and it is far better to be genuine and honest than to feign interest. But first we all must learn ourselves and learn how to empathize and listen actively. It takes practice, but it can be learned. And most importantly, it definitely pays off. Between the authors, we have experience in well over 100 countries and can tell you that effective communications are critically important everywhere.

As we mentioned above, listening for ideas is a critical skill. In our experience with well over 600 companies in a variety of countries and industries, we often see cross-disciplinary problems in communications – for example, an IT person explaining the technology to a business person, or a finance person explaining a balance sheet to a biotech physician, or a project logistic operator explaining a given operation to a banker, or a construction person trying to understand an operations person. Professionals have their own language and revert to disciplinary vocabulary that is efficient as a default. The trick is for both parties to attempt to communicate in a common language and to help the other party articulate ideas that they may not have the language to say.

Moreover, PMs and staff should also strive to deploy a kind of urban language, as well as a bush language, by identifying ways to communicate differently with office and field workers across Indonesia, which may turn out to be critical. We have seen too often the arrogance of Western PMs when interacting with locals in nondeveloped or developing countries. Apparently, they think Westerners know everything, since they have the technology. We have seen the creativity of local people, who know how to find workarounds for their entire life, and who can often pick up technological ideas quickly. In fact, we have on occasion asked the locals to use their ideas globally. Imagine the impact that has on the team.

Creativity also includes the ability to tell engaging stories. Steven Denning has authored a number of books that we find very helpful in learning how to tell more engaging stories (Denning 2005). Denning suggests that stories should provide the listener with the following:

- Trust – tell where and when the story happened and make it a true story.
- Relevance – reflect the type of person you are.
- Clarity – make your values clear.
- Distinctiveness – reflect your uniqueness.
- Consistency – reflect your conduct. "Walk-the-walk," meaning it must match with your actions.
- Happy ending.

All cultures use stories, so it is a very strong method of communications; it goes straight to the limbic brain, which has no capacity for language, only emotions. It is the part of our brain that keeps us from being eaten by tigers. The beauty is that storytelling is something all people enjoy and do, everywhere. Here is a great opportunity to engage with the members of the team. As with the durian, you better ask to be told how that person learned about a particular story. It is also a way to correct behavior, by telling a story about a third person who was acting improperly.

This is not easy, but think about the potential advantage a project could achieve should it use these concepts in an integral way starting with the planning stage. At the end of the day, project management is about doing business, and those capable of outperforming competitors in challenging environments will gain the respect of peers, shareholders, directors, and most important, bankers!! These are a few tools that, if well observed and internalized, may lead a project to substantially shorten the PSM and SLO processes as well as gain sustainability.

Gestures, attitudes, looks, words, tones, the way we dress, what we eat and drink, the way we walk, what we think, our tastes, and preferences on sports and entertainment all come together to make up who we are. Genetics plays an important role, as does where a person was born, raised, and educated. We believe from our experience that 80% of the time in leading a global project should be devoted to people and 20% to process. A solid understanding of the people and cultures will often overcome a poor schedule, estimate, or disregard for operations. A great operations plan will not overcome a poor understanding of the people on the project.

No two projects are the same, and while standardized processes are useful, they should not overshadow the necessity of leading and making plans specifically for the project at hand. We see this as a typical mistake that even global and highly reputable corporations repeat again and again. As an old operations executive with global experience once told us: "It takes about five minutes of my time to realize the type of individual I am chatting with." It is essential that a leader understand him- or herself and be able to relate to, or read, others. Communication is an essential skill, especially when the cultural gap is big.

It is of course easier for a project to overcome PSM stage issues if both the developers and stakeholders are from a similar or compatible geographical and cultural region. It is consequently more likely to avoid delays when conflicts occur, no matter what their nature. Naturally, these gaps can always be narrowed by hiring a team of knowledgeable professionals with respect to both PSM and operations management. But it is often not easy to combine these two fields, as they entail dominating various knowledge dimensions within the PM profession, especially if the job-site lies in such an atypical region as this one. We suggest having a person with strong leadership skills and then supplementing him or her with the necessary technical expertise. Technical expertise is relatively easy to find; leadership and the ability to read people is not.

Project delays may also be attributed to other factors like those that are engineering-oriented or have a strong operational component as shown in Figure 7.2. There is no doubt that this project was in need of rope conveyors to fit into one of the many production processes for efficient gold manufacturing. However, what was not well defined was the logistic method by which overdimensional pieces should be carried from Austria up to the job-site, after overcoming a risky transshipment operation in a major hub port, a complex lifting, and on-carriage operation alongside the wharf in Gorontalo.

EPCMs are too often awarded to projects that tend to hire a logistic operator that is a company they trust, rather than a specialist in the target region. This leads the project to face a number of risks and operational inefficiencies that translate into increased OPEX and CAPEX. Risks and insurance premiums, as well as the professional responsibility of those in charge, play a role in deciding on how operations should be carried out. It is the authors' experience that hesitance to make decisions is what usually occurs when no technical skills are available, or when too many ambiguous views are given about what should be done without providing any commitments. Lack of knowledge, or the unwillingness to develop a knowledge base prior to starting a project in a challenging location, is a bad idea indeed – like firms that disbelieve environmental investment pays off. Corporate strategists tend to erroneously believe that by outsourcing these areas of knowledge they can keep costs low and sustainability high. When they do, costs tend

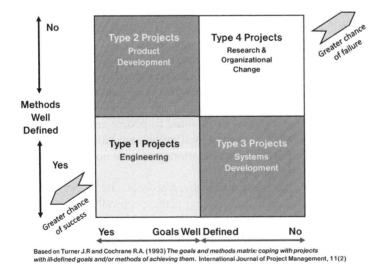

Based on Turner J.R and Cochrane R.A. (1993) *The goals and methods matrix: coping with projects with ill-defined goals and/or methods of achieving them.* International Journal of Project Management, 11(2)

Figure 7.2 Project types – procurement.

to rise and sustainability suffers, both scenarios that shareholders and BOD hate facing throughout the life cycle of a project.

The engineering may have been well defined, but the method of shipping encountered a physical impossibility to engage suitable barges, tugboats, cranes, transshipment facilities, and specialized out-of-gauge haulers. All of this ultimately made the entire operation face great failure. Again, there was a clear disconnect between engineering and operations, or at least an underestimation of the role operations would play in the initial phase of a project execution. Planning is a process that does not limit itself to engineering aspects of construction but relates to the PSM stage as well as the logistic operations right before construction. And it must be ongoing as changes will occur. Overlooking integrated planning within a CPE or joint venture may lead to time-consuming challenges, while leaving the door open to attract unwished or unplanned potential partners, these being variables neither shareholder nor director would like to hear about.

3. Suggestions and conclusions

As with all the case studies, global projects include numerous stakeholders and participants who have areas of expertise. The primary role of a CPEL is to create and nurture a communications network where knowledge is shared openly, quickly, and accurately. It serves no one's best interest if engineering does not talk to procurement or if operations does not talk to the local people, as is illustrated in the next case study. Many projects have faded away at an early stage owing to a poor communication strategy, inability to speak the local language, no translator, or the indifferent attitude of the CPE leader and his/her team toward learning the local conditions and culture. Both executives at the headquarters and local team members should keep in mind a number of essentials, notably:

- Communication. One should always consider who is going to be the receiver of your message. Such things as their language, culture, background, technical training, and personality should be discovered. Filters exist in all of us, and to be effective, one must learn to recognize them and either eliminate them or reduce their interference. Communicate humbly and with respect, and be as clear and precise as possible. Also, use basic simple words whenever possible. Dress simply, share time during lunch or dinner, and learn who the other people are, especially those you will need to communicate with regularly.
- PSM. Do not get delayed beyond what was planned for this stage of the project. There are early indicators of potential delays during the PSM consultation process. Hire a CCO and ensure that the process fits into the allocated time during the planning phase. Most of the time project developers include people from developed nations who have CCOs spread all over the world. Learn to spot them and bring them onto the project team if possible. Do not blindly rely on those with technical backgrounds, as they often see the world as a mechanism that should be how a project should be designed and put to work.
- Engineers. Who doubts that without the contribution of engineers most projects would run aground. Actually, one may find a long list of projects that fade away because of engineering mistakes that had never even started the PSM or SLO phase. Though engineers would probably never admit it in public, they would tend to think of themselves as a superior entity, given their professional education. Do not mistake our meaning here: engineers are extremely intelligent individuals, but this

is both their strength and their weakness. Our advice is to talk them into broadening their vision of the world. They need to become more flexible and receptive by incorporating the board of the utmost importance across the emerging world. Arrogance based on technical knowledge may be regarded as a good thing in the developed world but certainly not across the emerging world. And natural resources mostly lie in the emerging world. Project integration or the PMO may help ease the complex decision-making layers a global organization has to face, but it is not helped by arrogance or a feeling of superiority. Engineering, operations, environment, and social variables should all be aligned to accomplish a project on time and on budget. This is what theory says, and this is precisely what does not often happen in the field.

- Trust. It takes time to build trust; it must be built as grains of sand on a scale. But it is also fragile and is not to be taken for granted. One has to shape it, invest in it, and be consistent in order for trust to flourish and work in a project's favor. If you give priority to technical matters, without paying attention to those areas that might help you and your team build trust among the locals, you are most likely not only to face delays but also to be discredited. Such an action may open unwanted opportunities for agencies or individuals who wish to exert pressure on the project, to become part of it, on the grounds of excessive delays or unmet social needs. Further to the practical outcomes, gaining trust makes one feel good.

B. Case study: a state-of-the-art offshore mining project in Papua New Guinea requiring a political assessment approach

1. Background to the case

This case study is Papua New Guinea's only offshore mining project. This project includes variables from both an operational and environmental perspective, given its location and delicate environment. The caliber of the technical partners and shareholders for this project, along with its challenging setting, make project-applied knowledge management critical. It also sets forth a path to follow for other offshore operations in the future. Innovation and expertise in operations are the two words that define this project, without disregarding the importance of a sound risk analysis prior to engaging people and capital goods. Australian, Canadian, and American management was in charge of the planning and execution phases of the operations off the coast of Papua New Guinea, which may be considered as a kind of Australian protectorate. One cannot be sure whether or not this is an advantage, especially when gold and copper are the targeted resources. Political and economic ties may not necessarily help a project, but to the contrary it may become a heavy burden.

2. Program in detail

Given the global relevance and knowledge of the participating companies in this offshore mining undertaking, we would like to first introduce the players:

- A well-known Muscat, Oman-based oil and gas organization, with a sound knowledge of mineral processing, became a significant shareholder providing both liquidity and knowledge. Here, a new Middle East cultural profile is added on top of finance and technical knowledge, which presupposes an adjustment by the Western project developers.

- A Cyprus-based iron ore producer and steel manufacturer, with a leading position across Western Europe and Russia, also became a significant shareholder, and brought both copper processing knowledge and marketing contacts. This is valuable expertise on massive handling of ores, with different commercial profiles. The firm also made a significant contribution to the project's technical feasibility, but it also entails a cultural challenge at the managerial level.

- A global British and American mining organization with a leading position in gold, platinum, diamonds, base metals, and other products also joined the group as a minor shareholder. It signed a technical cooperation agreement by which their engineers could assist their partners in all aspects of operations optimization and mineral processing. This association does not in principle require the engineers to engage in a cultural adjustment, but it may demand that they strive to avoid guarding the knowledge that needs to be transferred, not so much for their partner engineers, but for the operational staff in PNG.

- A technical alliance was set up with a British organization, internationally recognized for having developed the world's best-in-class technology to deploy and make use of underwater remote operated vehicles (ROV) to scan and extract the minerals from the seabed. They commissioned two ROVs, along with their technical assistance during its programming, operation, and maintenance. In our opinion, even though technology may become a project enhancer, it needs to be introduced as if it were a new team of professionals about to step into a new and remote project where language, culture, and valued could not be more different. Technology by itself may be a great thing for investors, technical teams, and BOD, but it needs adjustment and local acceptance prior to being deployed. Again, the ideal place to make it public is a PSM consultation, not in the press. The latter may be targeted to ease project financing, whereas the former is normally aimed at easing the way around the job-site, either offshore or onshore.

- A 20,000-employee EPCM organization with global offshore operations expertise across five continents was awarded the engineering and construction contract, based on its knowledge of offshore construction and environmental protection. Being a world-class environmental protection leader may be a very good thing as it eases the planning phase of a project. However, it may become detrimental to the project during the execution phase, should doubts or potential operational hazards emerge amongst the technical staff or should they be made public. Having a stellar reputation limits the error margin almost to nil, especially in an extreme setting where the degree of stakeholder tolerance is often regulated by the local agencies and government officials.

- A well-known, resource-rich, a traditional Canadian mining organization with numerous polymetallic projects across Canada and the USA took a minor stake in the project. They brought with them a Vancouver-based firm highly specialized in the development, deployment, and testing of new deep-water electromagnetic technologies. In our experience, traditional organizations have a culture of risk avoidance, and stability. This is not always the best fit for a nontraditional, bleeding-edge technology project.

- Finally, a global offshore structural engineering organization with over 12,000 employees and operations in more than 70 countries also joined the project as a consultant. It was to provide the project with its expertise in deep-water operations optimization, such as pipelines, structural solutions, or underwater slurry pump operation. This was a critical asset to guarantee a 24/7 mineral processing operation. This organization stands out in its continuous search for technological innovation in other sectors such as aviation, health care, and offshore oil and gas operation.

It is true that offshore deep-water operations are less exposed to never-ending and time-consuming PSM processes, or complex SLO programs as the assets are located far away from the coast and normally out of sight of the stakeholders, unless a coastal community gets affected or a given industry sees itself endangered owing to a project undertaking (e.g., commercial or artisanal fishing, cruise industry, mariculture, wind energy, wave energy, tide energy). In other words, offshore projects may in principle be regarded as easygoing until an environmental or a terrorist event occurs. Actually, corporations should never relax when carrying out operations in seemingly low-conflict zones, as issues may show up unexpectedly. High-caliber technology and international management may provide a false sense of safety and solidness in terms of operations. However, meeting the local expectations and making both technology and management accepted and understood may prove to be more troublesome than expected or thought of in the planning phase.

Figure 7.3 shows the processing vessel to which an underwater slurry pipe line is connected to in order to extract and carry the polymetallic nodules by using its 1,600-M deep seafloor production tools or ROVs. It is important to point out that the term "polymetallic mining" encompasses the extraction and processing of gold, copper, silver, and other metals. PNG is one of the world's poorest countries, with a revenue-hungry government – an aspect that deserves careful assessment and close monitoring to avoid jeopardizing the project's sustainability with the stakeholders and general public. Project risk mitigation management can be considered part of the adjustment scheme global corporations having a special focus on the developed world, and a minor one in emerging economies, too often fail to observe.

The PNG government of had signed an agreement and exercised its option to take up a 30% stake in the offshore project, where the mother organization retained

Figure 7.3 Drilling vessel off coast of Papua New Guinea.

its 70% share in an unincorporated joint venture to be established with the PNG government to hold the mining assets of the project. The government's initial payment to secure its holding was some USD20–25 million, which represented its share of the exploration and development costs incurred up to the date of grant of the mining lease.

A few months later the Canadian organization, which had joined the project both as shareholder and consultant, formally notified its offshore project partner that it had elected not to participate in exploration activities in Fijian waters. This decision was not surprising, given this organization's low risk tolerance, or high uncertainty avoidance, especially since the locations of its assets across North America have provided them the necessary training, or tolerance, for uncertain business conditions. They were accustomed to a region where almost everything is clearly set forth in the planning stage, and even little deviations are rare.

Shortly after the initiation of exploration activities that offshore Fiji had started, the State of PNG asserted, unilaterally, that the project had not met certain obligations and that the project had therefore breached the original agreement. This led the project to apply the dispute resolution mechanism set forth in the agreement. One may at this point wonder why PNG, being an Australian protectorate and benefiting from financial endowments and technological support, could come to the point of threatening a world-class innovative project. This is precisely what we do suggest, and we urge the reader to bear it in mind when thinking of planning a project in such an extreme setting, both structurally and culturally. Australian involvement in PNG may be regarded either as a benefit given the degree of influence and commitment of local government officials or a weakness owing to hidden agendas that lie behind the commitments.

The immediate result was the suspension of the exploration activities not only offshore PNG, but also the construction of a new drilling ship planned for operating in Fijian waters. The company had become the first private-sector organization to be granted offshore exploration licenses covering a total area of approximately 60,000 KM^2. This caused bankers, financiers, and insurance companies to fear this would escalate further. Just a few months after the arbitration process began, the project organization announced the discovery of two high-grade Seafloor Massive Sulfide (SMS) systems, in its wholly owned exploration tenements in the territorial waters of the Kingdom of Tonga.

Diversification always turns out to be a good strategy to diminish corporate risk exposure and ensure financial support, unless the countries or regions one targets are of a similar caliber. Naturally, resources are not always available where one would like them to be but, rather, where nature or geology decides. Geological results may be great but should first be traded off with the existing institutional strength or the relative weight institutions in a given country. It is very rare to see even in global corporations. This no doubt must have sent a strong signal to the PNG authorities with respect to the organization's ability to raise funds, and capitalize on its own new discoveries. Grab samples from these discoveries assayed higher than the average for copper, gold, zinc, and silver.

Shortly after the discoveries were made public, the project faced an unsolicited takeover bid by an individual with no track record in the mining or offshore industry. Being some sort of ghost operator was the reason the project's BOD was unable to make any determination regarding the validity of the offer. The BOD's message to its shareholders was the following:

> "The BOD will consider the unsolicited offer, if and when it is formally made, and maintains its *advice to shareholders not to take any action in respect of such offer* until shareholders have received further communication from the Board. In the meantime, the management team remains focused on maximizing shareholder value by delivering on the Organization's primary objective, *being the development of the world's first seafloor copper-gold project.*"

A few months later, the arbitrator declared that the State was in breach of the State Equity Option Agreement signed by the parties in failing to complete the purchase of a 30% interest in the project. The amount to be made available by the State escalated from USD25 million to over 110 million. Arbitration clauses on these types of projects always appoint Canadian, British, or American courts as a way to produce legal coverage in their attempt to consolidate sustainability. Australian arbitrators played their role in this particular case. However, all this could and should have been avoided by better understanding what a government like PNG was after or what their hidden agendas turned out to be, prior to diversifying drilling and committing more monies in the South Pacific – in other words, more homework for CCOs and CQOs prior to committing resources across the South Pacific.

3. Suggestions and conclusions

This project is about the way technology, leadership, and operations can be brought together to generate state-of-the art innovation. It is also about how necessary a project risk analysis is. This should include operational, environmental, and social risk variables put together within a contextual political risk analysis. Poor countries. politicians hiding behind weak institutions, with or without community activists, may often become detrimental to the project's timing and may jeopardize the entire project. The project was compelled to sail into murky waters in order to get capitalized in the first place, and unscrupulous governments tend to learn quickly and maneuver accordingly. No matter how strong, globalized, and technically skilled a given partner, associate, or shareholder may be, without these considerations they are as vulnerable as anyone. Actually, the bigger and more global a company, the more likely it is to commit elementary mistakes like these. Technology and global presence as well as recognized success should not enable one to feel unbeatable or beyond the reach of a government that may be looking for a way to profit from a given scandal.

An even more intense struggle this organization had to face occurred when it tried to move forward towards initiating marine drilling operations offshore both Fiji and Tonga. As for these countries, the Australian government did not exert such a close monitoring and assistance when compared to those of PNG. Again, it suggests that carrying out a thorough project risk assessment becomes essential. It may not only help a given project identify potential political conflicts and hidden agendas, but it may also help to gain sustainability and therefore support from stakeholders worldwide. Anticipation is a key component during the project's life cycle. A politically adequate combination of leadership, technology, and operations, all encapsulated within the framework of the precautionary approach, seems to be the right project approach for accomplishing sustainable development.

The lack of occurrences or even minor incidents during entire decades of operations should not hinder a company from running, updating, and putting into practice a contingency plan. It is a bad idea to assume that since risks have been avoided in the past they can be in the future, particularly in different environmental circumstances. A good example of contingency planning, and where it can lead, is given by the Swedish chemical diving team, which by 1986 had been training for more than 30 years in the event a chemical incident affected their waters. They did not have any incident within their waters, so they cooperated in a number of shipping incidents across northern Europe and became leaders in this kind of operation.

Risk assessment must be done for all projects and must include such items as politics, society, the environment, weather, civil unrest, corruption, technology, governments, and market conditions. We recommend that every project address these risks as a minimum. We suggest the following outline for managing risks on global projects:

- Create a risk profile. This is a measure of the amount of risk different groups are willing to take, ranging from 0.0, none, to 1.0, all. The joint-venture financial group may have a very low risk tolerance of 0.2 and the EPCM a risk tolerance of 0.5. So there is a range of the amount of risk that different organizations are prepared to take.
- Create a list of risks. The identification of risk needs to be specific; otherwise they cannot be managed. The risk of bad weather is not adequate; the risk of a monsoon is adequate.
- Create a risk rank. For each risk, assign a subjective probability for 0.0 to 1.0 and an impact from 0.0 to 1.0–0.0 means no probability or impact, 1.0 maximum.
- Filter the risks. Here any risk rank that is below the lowest risk profile should be passively managed. As conditions change on a project, the risk profile of participants may change or the probability or impact may change. So we suggest keeping them on the potential list but not managing them actively.
- Risk management plan. For risks with a rank above the profile, a complete risk management plan needs to be developed. This includes who owns the risk (critical), the trigger event, the risk response, an estimate of the cost of managing the risk, and the assumptions made. For example, if PNG's government corruption were an active risk, which of the partners would be in the best position to manage it? Because of the relationship between Australia and PNG, and the islands, the organization with a close connection to the Australian government might be ideal. What might the cost be, in hindsight, the USD85 million coming from the dispute? For most projects, the total risk cost estimate can easily equal the project budget.
- Risk management. When the potential cost of risk management equals the project budget, management tends to proceed and ignore the risk. This is not a sustainable strategy, and we saw it grow to well over USD1.4 billion for a global company that chose to ignore formal risk management. For this to work, risk needs to be transparent, reported upon, and managed just like construction or operations. Think of risks as activities, and you have the idea.

In conclusion, operations, politics, and environmental variables seem to run parallel on this particular case. Furthermore, the necessity of defining risk, allocating risk in contracts, and building contract provisions that will provide a reasonably fast way to resolve such disputes is essential.

References

Denning, S., *The Leader's Guide to Storytelling: Mastering the Art and Discipline of Business Narrative*. 2005, San Francisco: Jossey-Bass.

Ekman, P., *Emotions Revealed: Recognizing Faces and Feelings to Improve Communication and Emotional Life*. 2003, New York: Times Books.

Harkins, P.J., *Powerful Conversations: How High Impact Leaders Communicate*. 1999, New York: McGraw-Hill Professional.

Nonaka, I., Toyama, R., and Konno, N., *SECI, Ba and Leadership: A Unified Model of Dynamic Creation*, in *Managing Industrial Knowledge*, I. Nonaka, Editor. 2001, Thousand Oaks, CA: Sage.

8 Mining operations in emerging eastern and western Africa

Where to keep a sharp eye on the operations and how to balance global context variables with those of a project in extreme settings

This chapter presents two case studies that have a common denominator, though different global contexts. The first one takes place in eastern Africa in what is probably one of the world's poorest countries. Madagascar has poor infrastructure where all multinational firms have struggled to provide their projects with a reasonable level of facilities to build their projects. Amazing infrastructure restrictions do conspire against the normal development issues of a mineral sands project to make projects challenging when no adequate ports, roads, bridges, tunnels, railways, or trucks are available. This is operations management in an extreme setting.

The second case involves a number of huge iron ore deposits, concentrated all within Cameroon in western Africa, which extend into neighboring countries, making this resource a potential source of both richness and conflict. It represents what some authors have called the resource curse. Infrastructure is limited and needs to be built if economic prosperity is to spread across a number of nations and will determine if these projects ever see the light of day. The potential resources are gigantic; this leads the project to face incredible long-term operational challenges that need to be tackled by skillful and knowledgeable global executives.

A. Case study: a unique project setting that is compelled to face challenging infrastructural and social barriers

1. Background to the case

This case study concerns an Australian corporation and includes a due-diligence study undertaken for a Dubai-based natural resource producing and trading organization with worldwide interests. The project lay on the southwestern coast of Madagascar where the available infrastructure is modest, like almost everything else is on the island. The weather constraints are both frequent and intense, two aspects that guarantee headaches in terms of project infrastructure and logistics operations. The intended export port of loading for mineral sands is not entirely a human-made facility but actually a reef-sheltered water space along with an improvised jetty. This means that the ship owner has to face risky shipping approach maneuvers and a tight operational window. This is a scary combination of factors in a place that lacks the minimum facilities to plan regular operations. The truck operations were intended to be carried out using 110-ton payload road-trains to run on dirt roads unfit to withstand such weight on a regular basis. Additionally, a bridge and warehouse were designed to avoid the three-month flood season, interrupting operations by stockpiling on the other side of the river.

Figure 8.1 shows the only port of entry, Toamasina, on the east end of the country. The mineral sands deposits lie on the southwest end of the island near Toliara, which also is a small container port that only operates feeder vessels and occasionally some chartered vessels and trawlers. Toamasina was intended to handle incoming cargo for the construction phase, whereas Toliara was erroneously identified as a potential port to operate export cargoes. In fact, it was only fit to operate small coastal feeder vessels along with a rather modest number of containers.

Ground transportation would play a key role during construction and operation, as the project lies far from the port of entry. And there is just a single route linking both ends, along with a few scattered secondary properties located further southwest by the coast. This case study describes the logistical challenges a mining organization needs to overcome to get the project sold, developed, and capitalized in order for them to move forward and export the concentrates. It is about the logistic variables the original developer should have considered initially, prior to any asset acquisition. This is a corporate strategic mistake often made by executives and investors who prioritize a project's financial and geological fundamentals, short-term thinking, over its operational drawbacks, long-term thinking. Short-term thinking is not strategic: it is tactical or operational.

This case study analyzes a list of operational challenges to be overcome in one of the world's poorest developing nations. It is a nation where its lack of infrastructure hinders getting a project sold and discourages potential partners. The data and information described in the following section, arises out of a due diligence study where we were commissioned by a potential joint-venture partner.

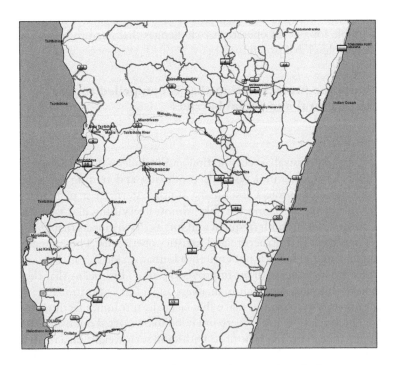

Figure 8.1 Total road extension from port of entry to the job-site.

2. Program in detail

The due diligence study focused primarily on the main logistical challenges that were represented by roads, ports, and shipping operations, both inbound and outbound. Natural resources developers often feel tempted to only assess the geological data, the opportunity cost to engage in a given takeover or joint venture, and the financial fundamentals. It is rare for these corporations to undertake a sensible analysis on what the real challenges are for operations. Surprisingly, management tends to believe there is a solution for every challenge, when in fact that solution is most often dependent on money. Actually, OPEX and CAPEX are not limitless but very tangible and finite dimensions that sooner rather than later tend to grow when operational constraints become known and perceived as insurmountable.

The study assessed the following variables:

a. Roads

The 110-ton payload road trains are specially adapted trucks to transport ilmenite and nonmagnetic products from the mine site to the Toliara storage facility. These vehicles would accommodate up to four trailers, to be supplied and operated by the haulage contractor, which was a theoretical organization at the time the study was conducted. The existing road network was a series of poorly maintained rural unsealed road tracks that served the local communities. Consequently, a purpose-built haulage road would need to be constructed by widening and resurfacing a series of such tracks, going from the ever fluctuating Fiherenana River on the islands' southwest up to the mine site. The road tracks would be sealed and consolidated by using crushed limestone sourced from a nearby dedicated quarry. The existing 350-M-long bridge across the Fiherenana River, as shown in Figure 8.2, was considered unsuitable to withstand the transit of 110-ton road trains.

Alternatively, a causeway was going to be built to safely cross the Fiherenana River. Three months' product storage was also planned at both the mine site and jetty to enable continuous operation during the wet season, when the causeway might be closed for up to 12 weeks depending on the flow of water in the river. This condition tended to vary from year to year and made operations even more uncertain and risky.

A 340-KM-long RN2 paved route linking the Toamasina port of entry and the country's capital of Antananarivo, as well as a 1,005-KM-long RN7 paved route

Figure 8.2 Bridge over Fiherenana River, 7 KM away from Toliara.

running from the capital up to Toliara seemed to be the two most important road arteries running across the country. Even though both routes were paved, its width was the minimum, and the quality of a number of stretches ranged from poor to bad. This aspect demanded a careful survey to safely carry both gauge and out-of-gauge cargoes bound for the construction. The construction phase is where any delay will most likely have a negative impact on both OPEX and capital financial costs.

Both routes run along a significant number of rivers of different sizes, which also need to be properly surveyed for 12 months a year operation. In addition to the crossings, other variables such as bridges, aerial cables, signaling, turning radius, gradients, traffic particulars, weather constraints, and so forth entailed serious challenges for logistics. The existing road distance between the port of entry and the job-site exceeded 1,000 KM across an extremely limited infrastructure having no safety standards at all. A great number of bridges, of doubtful quality and unsuitable dimensions, identified along the road, also needed to be surveyed, prior to committing to an inbound road transport operation of both standardized and oversize cargoes. This turned out to be of paramount importance to carry capital goods for the project construction phase which usually means with overdimensional (OD) and heavy-lift (HL) cargo. Topography did not seem to be a problem, at least on RN2, as it ran across flat terrain only 50 to 70 meters above sea level, whereas RN7 lay at 1,700 meters above sea level and presented a winding jungle-mountain road layout.

Horizontal or vertical road signaling, as well as guardrails or any typical safety device along the roads, was practically nonexistent. Guardrails and visuals are actually two Health and Safety (H&S) logistic variables that become critical not only for the operations team to consider, but also for bankers and insurers in view of the rolling stock obsolescence and layout of the roads running through urban and rural areas. No primary stakeholder would like to witness a project facing a lawsuit or bad publicity arising out of an undesired casualty. However, casualties are almost impossible to avoid when infrastructure and safety are on the low side. It is even worse if a series of accidents takes place that jeopardize the projects sustainability. A PM should anticipate and plan for this to happen on a regular basis. Pedestrians, a great variety of minor vehicles, loose animals, transit chaos, and a large number of settlements and villages along the roads also constitute a potential challenge to be overcome.

The RN9 route between Toliara and Morombe also crossed a great number of creeks and rivers, therefore, these bridges required a proper survey (e.g., Fiherenana, Manombo, Mangoky rivers, etc.). Rivers and rains as well as the ground transportation viability played a determinant role. Yet the number of settlements and villages tended to substantially diminish on this side of the island. This variable may be regarded as positive, given that it helped reduce the likelihood of increased social conflict in the communities near the project.

Figure 8.3 exhibits the poor quality of the existing dirt roads, which were intended to withstand intensive and regular 110-ton payload road trains. Even though Figure 8.4 shows paved roads and a better layout, there were houses lying practically on the routes' edge, which might easily lead the project to eventually face social conflicts. Building route bypasses may always be a valid option as long as it is not the rule but the exception because of cost and topography. However, undertaking a housing relocation program may also entail high cost, and what is even worse is the possibility of an uncertain scenario among the people living there. It could include the dwellers' total refusal to relocate.

Figure 8.3 View of dirt roads near the job site.

Figure 8.4 View of houses by the road.

House relocation and road bypasses can have a boomerang effect and a generally negative impact if done too frequently. No matter how well intentioned such a strategy may be, an excess of these actions may be too much for a community to bear. Once a community says no, there is no point of return. This is how drastic a logistic operation in an extreme setting may become if not duly planned, or if its environmental and social impact is not considered in a timely manner and put to work for the project's sustainability.

Logistic costs can become detrimental to the project's economic sustainability, and the living patterns around the area may turn the communities against the project for reasons such as noise, forest destruction, religion, culture, harvests, aesthetics, overuse, and change. In any case, project sustainability may be at stake unless a thorough approach is put in place well before construction; consequently, CAPEX dimensions are committed. It is at the planning stage of a project that this should be designed, executed, and monitored with the community.

Structural restrictions also became apparent, as we have mentioned above and as shown in Figure 8.5, in order to operate regular trucks for the inbound logistic operations. The type of bridges and their structural design were never meant to operate project cargoes of the required width, height, and resistance for the project. This was

Figure 8.5 Structural restrictions.

another huge obstacle to reasonably plan and carry out procurement and inbound logistic operations on time and on budget.

b. Ports

A product storage site and standalone jetty capable of loading bulk vessels was planned to be situated on the sandspit just to the north of Toliara in an area sheltered from offshore wave swells. This area would be utilized for the mineral sands storage sheds, offices, power generation, weighbridge facilities, truck unloading, and truck turning areas. The loadout facility would be composed of a raised jetty extending out into the deep-water channel to enable direct loading of concentrates via conveyors onto the waiting vessels. An earlier bathymetric study showed that the deep-water zone of the channel leading to the port area was sufficiently deep (12–16 meters) to accommodate vessels of up to a HANDYMAX or SUPRAMAX type (45,000 to 55,000 tons). However, no specific data on tides and currents were incorporated in the study.

According to the mining organization's executives, there appeared to be no navigational issues associated with the intended port operation based on the following dimensions:

- The natural channel width was three to four times wider than the recommended channel width to operate both HANDYMAX and SUPRAMAX vessels.
- The ship turning area was two to three times larger than the recommended ship turning area requirements.
- The clearance between a ship at berth and any passing ships was three to five times greater than the recommended ship clearance distance.
- The zircon-rich concentrates could also be loaded into containers and carried to the existing Toliara coastal port for export.

It was clear that the mining organization wanted to highlight the logistic variables that its management thought would be valuable for a potential JV partner or investor to seriously consider. However, the available "port facilities" and their "hinterland facilities" were largely nature dependent, which by definition is unstable, nonreliable, and therefore unsustainable. It is amazing to see how a great number of projects commit the very same mistakes of underestimating the potential impact operations may have when assessing a given project's potential. And, one should be alert and double check when reading a corporate website that emphasizes the operational and infrastructural advantages a given project may have. Far from being a corporate strength, it is actually a visible weakness for the expert eye of an experienced COO, who will undoubtedly recommend that his BOD withdraw and look somewhere else.

c. Shipping

To base the entire bulk export operation on a reef-sheltered water space, assisted only by the construction of a sort of mobile jetty, is absurd for any serious global or even regional ship-operating organization to consider. The concepts of safe port (SP) and safe berth (SB) applied on the operational audit case study developed in the Peruvian rainforest turns out to be exactly the same here. No serious shipping organization would initiate a maritime adventure where the loading spot does not comply with the elementary rules of SP and SB, no matter that a SUPRAMAX ship may fit well into the available space and safely maneuver within the reef.

Should a ship owner enter this area to load concentrates, he or she would automatically face substantial increases on hull and machinery insurance, arising out of the potential risks of ships going aground or possibly being damaged against a reef because of strong winds or current. This is the typical underestimation of operations that project developers incur while trying to make their project look attractive to investors and potential partners. The loading productivity would still be an issue, which along with the mentioned obstacles would definitely lead to longer operation time and substantially higher ocean freight rates. Due to the vessels' longer laydays and accruing daily running cost, both affect the project's economic feasibility from its outset.

Regarding construction logistics, not being able to rely on a nearby port of entry increases the complexity of the whole inbound operation. Combining all the purchase orders and concentrating most inbound cargo, say in Houston, in order to voyage-charter a break-bulk carrier is not a realistic option for two reasons. First, every manufacturer has its own delivery priorities with different lead times. Consequently, storage and handling charges might represent a much higher OPEX component. Second, if the latter case were not a problem, it would still lead to incurring huge accruing port storage and handling charges that would immobilize capital at the port of entry, as construction is done in time-consuming phases, and not simultaneously. The port of entry lay far away from the project site, and its road links left much to be desired – all of which would lead to extended turnaround times and increased OPEX.

Gathering inbound equipment in Durban as a nearby intermediate hub port in South Africa would allow the project to engage feeding vessels straight to Toliara, provided that this port was outfitted with the necessary gear to discharge OD and HL equipment, which no feeder normally counts on. Naturally, port storage, handling, and insurance expenses would also tend to accrue in Durban. Either solution was costly and risky, and conspired against the project's sustainable development.

3. Conclusions and suggestions

The great majority of mining projects around the world should rank financial assessment, market opportunity, geology, and operations at the very same level, provided that what they genuinely wish to accomplish is to transform a property into a real project. Even if they do not, to overlook operations will be a costly decision that may only be overcome by pouring in huge amounts of capital.

Examples in Madagascar have been China-based WISCO, Brazil-based VALE, London-listed Rio Tinto, and Toronto-listed Sherritt International. These organizations are global, with huge economies of scale and capable of building and outfitting their own ports of entry. They can also improve or build the access roads and even bring in and operate their own road train organizations to make their projects competitive and sustainable, provided that there is sufficient critical mass to support the concept and that the prices of commodities justify the investments. However, even global corporations and their well-reputed EPCM organizations show a tendency to underestimate the impact operations may have on a project – especially if false belief, or perhaps arrogance, causes them to believe there is nothing that cannot be solved by a solid engineering partner, either in-house or outsourced.

Enormous challenges need to be overcome if a project ever moves to the development phase, once it has assimilated all the possible constraints and become stronger during the planning stage. Financial and macroeconomic risks encompass almost all projects, as most of the countries where they are to be developed have to deal with inflation rates, fluctuating rates of exchange, absence of credible capital markets, ever-changing rules, bans on imports, forced import substitution schemes, and more such issues. It is the authors' experience that trying to assign a coefficient or probability of occurrence to each of these variables is difficult, and thus a range of possibilities is often used. What one may do is to work on different occurrence scenarios and have ready a contingency plan should any of these scenarios actually take place, especially for those risks that are considered active.

Our suggestion is to take a sensible approach to operations management not only during the construction phase but also in the execution stage. Moreover, if a corporation has already invested in an extreme project that has substantial operational challenges, there is nothing better than including a thorough operations study within the feasibility study aiming to demonstrate the various alternatives to cope with the realities and restrictions. In operations management, it is rare to see a single solution to a given problem, but often a specific problem may be worked out by making use of a set of combinations, especially in emerging economies where innovation lies around the corner. Furthermore, a realistic and complete operations study may be a powerful tool to attract a suitable partner corporation. This is particularly true for a partner who has strengths and knowledge in operations that could help a project overcome the initial phase of development and initiate construction on solid ground. All the previous case studies have shed some light on this concept.

What these models require for success is leadership, and one of the pillars upon which leadership rests is common sense. Often there is a notably scarce raw material when it comes to project design and construction, given that too many companies tend to believe that "there is no unsurpassable barrier or challenge our company and contractors cannot deal with." This has been a recurrent attitude that the authors have witnessed on a worldwide basis, suggesting that these companies' learning curves are flat and a huge mistake, as we have seen in many of the case studies. One should never step into an extreme setting without first looking into the operations.

B. Case study: a project holding huge economies of scale, limited infrastructure, and geopolitical exposure in western Africa

1. Background to the case

This case study involves a British and Australian organization focused on the development of huge iron ore deposits in West Africa. The master project entails a number of export-oriented projects in a country and region where several world-class iron ore projects are competing for both the existing and future infrastructure. The infrastructure needs to be shared amongst a number of mining organizations and also amongst neighboring nations with different interests and relative power. Railway negotiations and operational surveys play a key role in determining its feasibility. This is in addition to the government's increasing interest in making a regional social contribution, with the new railway to be constructed amongst both the scattered country's communities and neighboring central African nations. This is not an encouraging scenario if one looks at Africa's contemporary rivalries and foreign influences.

Port transfer and reception facilities in Cameroon, along with the corporate objective of achieving larger economies of scale at sea, represent major milestones for the sustainability of these projects. Iron ore is about volume, whereas the feasibility of its related operations is about infrastructure, and they are dependent upon each other. One of the projects is located within a national park and therefore demanded special considerations to ensure its sustainability. Armed park rangers, drones to watch potential poachers, along with IT devices especially designed to protect the environment, had to be engaged to successfully overcome the permitting process and get the SLO. These are two landmarks on any project, though especially important in extreme contexts like this one.

2. Program in detail

Three huge iron ore projects own properties scattered both by the coast and inland Cameroon, Gabon, and the Democratic Republic of Congo (DRC). There are potential marine terminals to be built either in Cameroon or Gabon, as well as a railway that is expected to link the three countries and extend its influence even up to the Central African Republic. These plans and related challenges go well beyond the mining business, suggesting fertile ground for regional conflicts to arise. The following projects are the ones attracting the interest of private and corporate investors, as well as some African governments, which despite the apparent insurmountable logistic obstacles wanted to keep a certain degree of influence and control on the upcoming projects. The actual magnitude of the infrastructure challenges was dictated by the huge volume that all of the existing projects were expecting to process and export, as follows:

a. Organization A

This organization owns exploration licenses in Cameroon, spanning the coastal regions near existing and developing ports. The port of Douala might be suitable for inbound cargoes throughout the construction phase, whereas the port of Kribi could operate as a deep-water facility capable of berthing dry bulk carriers. Given the far-off location of some of their properties and the lack of railways, organization A's (actual names not used) management had focused on de-risking the projects sustainability by planning a truck-based direct shipping operation (DSO) for those near-coastal properties or for deposits with good quality ores that needed no processing at all prior to being exported.

This was the chosen strategy to deliver substantial real value to shareholders in the form of low capital and operating costs, while easily developing iron ore production. Figure 8.6 shows an overall image on the relative location of the deposits shared by Cameroon and DRC, an existing, though insufficient, export dry bulk sea terminal as well as a planned railway line yet to be entirely built. Only three MTPAs were expected to be handled under a DSO scheme within Cameroon's territory.

b. *Organization B*

This organization envisaged that its project, with an integrated rail and port infrastructure across Cameroon and DRC, might become a regional mining production hub in the future. Such a hub could unlock the value of other regional assets, which would not be feasible on a standalone basis, but that could benefit due to its proximity to the richest inland deposits and related rail and port infrastructure. Once in place, the planned rail and port infrastructure could be upgraded to support regional production of up to 100 MTPAs in the long run. This is a huge volume that could entirely reshape the economic and social fabrics of this region. Organization B was confident that the region had the right geology to deliver sufficient iron ore resources to sustain production at this level.

However, its management was aware that in order to sustain a 35 MTPA DSO export operation for around 35 years, both a new deep-water iron ore export terminal south of the existing at Kribi and a 580-KM-long railway must be built from scratch. Economies of scale were close to ideal if there was capability of loading vessels of up to 300,000 DWT. Figure 8.7 shows the location of the new deep-water port and railways to be built in order to make Organization B's project sustainable.

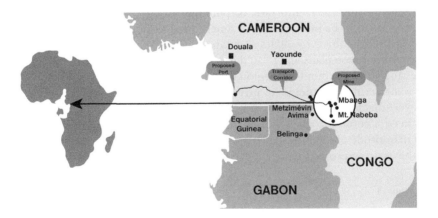

Figure 8.6 Cameroon and Gabon's inland deposits and planned railway line.

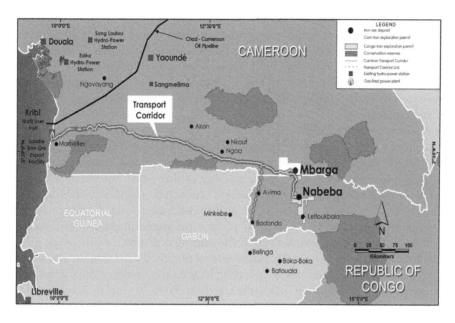

Figure 8.7 New deep-water port location and main railway line and its extension stretch into DRC.

c. Organization C

This project is situated in the Northwest of DRC close to both Gabon's border to the west and Cameroons to the north. And it would exert further pressure on the not yet existing infrastructure of the area. Access to its job-site means a purposely built 62-KM-long all-weather road, which services the site and provides easy access for drill rigs and other infrastructure and equipment. This may be workable during the prospecting stage, but by no means can be seriously considered to sustain an intensive DSO ground operation. Approximately 200–240 million tons have been identified as high-grade DSO, which might cautiously lead to an approximate DSO volume of one billion tons, which is a volume that falls outside of any present or future infrastructure plans.

The direct shipping quality ore and the enormous size of this project make it the most significant project across the region, with its development integral to the development of the region as a whole. Organization C has completed a feasibility study for the rail and port option, via Gabon, which adds a new player to the scene, as huge capital expenditures will become necessary to develop all these properties and other nearby projects. Huge potential exportable volumes, ores that originate in countries other than the port where they will be handled, as well as alternative designs and locations of the future facilities, bring about a complex geopolitical dilemma for those countries that are directly affected, as well as for those that might benefit or suffer from the course decisions.

World-class EPCM organizations and suppliers of all types might also envisage upcoming regional conflicts on the horizon and decide to withdraw their interest or increase their demands for safeguards. Organization B and C have signed a memo of understanding (MOU) that opens up further possibilities for cooperation regarding shipments of iron ore from their respective deposits. It includes the possible sharing of infrastructure capital costs on the basis of two transport corridors, along with deep-water port options via Cameroon and Gabon. This option makes perfect sense from a project design viewpoint, but it could feed regional rivalries, leading to a lack of cooperation in a region that desperately needs foreign direct investment, growth, development, and employment.

It is clear, considering the projects of the three organizations and without taking into account about half a dozen other nearby projects of lesser relative impact, the level of demand hugely surpasses the existing supply of logistic infrastructure. And the infrastructure is limited to some ports and a number of dirt roads capable of withstanding a modest DSO export operation. The host countries and interested neighbors – Cameroon, DRC, Gabon, African Central Republic, Equatorial Guinea – have their own vision and agendas. These agendas include infrastructure, economy, social, and political issues that may or may not match the mining organization's interests, given the huge volumes at stake. The resources and business potential exist, but the infrastructure is yet to be built, and its facilities are pending negotiation amongst the parties.

Iron ore projects by definition may easily take from 20 to 30 years to develop and therefore remain subject to impact by a number of variables that tend to drastically shift either abruptly or in cycles. There is a strong correlation and volatility between demand from places like China, Japan, Korea, and India, and supply from Brazil, Australia, and possibly West Africa. Under the ongoing geopolitical circumstances, China is not only actively positioning itself by acquiring assets across the emerging world and investing monies in development-hungry countries but is also jointly developing projects with the host countries across Africa. So it seems reasonable to expect a sort of logistic infrastructure expansion process across West Africa sooner rather than later. In this scenario, much depends on China and India on the one side and the USA as a counterbalance on the other.

Operations in these particular deposits become an opportunity to attract a natural resource-hungry customer like China, which is capable of pouring in capital to develop whatever project is desired, provided that it is regarded as strategic for their interest. These circumstances are unique and are mostly applicable to African countries where the buyer and developer become one entity without too many restrictions. Joint ventures, alliances, partnerships, mergers and acquisitions, and any other type of undertaking with Chinese organizations seem to be the only way to work out the many formidable logistic challenges that lay ahead. China can provide capital, build the necessary infrastructure, deploy both technical and social-focused management, make a strategic use of time like anyone else, and, most important, keep control and a tight connection with the demand – this through Chinese corporations and state-owned enterprises (SOEs).

World-class project operational challenges require an understanding of geopolitics in Africa, along with China's intentions, short and long term, given their aggressive approach to this continent. Facing regional political conflicts arising out of huge CAPEX-dependent projects may also deserve a careful contextual risk analysis beyond China's financial capability and strategic interest. Operations and project logistics do play a different role when compared to Latin America where China has not yet taken such an active role.

However, it may be a matter of time when Chinese interests start to actively focus on ports, roads, waterways, ships, and railways in Africa, and also in Latin America where

Western countries still exert a counterweight to China's influence. Running efficient operations in remote locations in Africa requires huge investments that may become viable only if the producer and consumer actually converge into one entity. China in this particular case and possibly India next? And it is precisely this need that may trigger serious political conflicts amongst the host nations with weak institutions and a lack of transparency. This must be considered along with the project stakeholders' attitudes with respect to royalties, taxes, duties, levies, investment, and industrialization. Leading extreme projects encompass solid financing, robust engineering, consistent social back-up, and realistic operations. Also needed is envisaging the way geopolitics may evolve in order to make a given project sustainable.

Another aspect remains to be described and duly analyzed here: the lack of contractual responsibility. It is often represented by those project developers who cede the management of the construction and the global logistics operations to their global EPCM contracted companies, once the commissioning takes place. The latter often impose their services by alleging that they cannot accept any claims or responsibility as a consequence of working with an appointed logistic operator. This is a common tactic used by an EPC firm, at the last minute, well after design and construction engineering has been agreed upon, and the customer wants to impose or suggest their logistic operator of confidence. Such a bond between the customer and the logistic operator(s) often has its roots in the trust gained throughout the successful completion of projects in other complex environments around the world, such as in many of the cases we have so far described.

In practice, the more complex a project is, the more influential EPCM firms become in the logistic operations. It is very common to see EPCM firms impose their logistic contractors under the argument of their expertise, financial capacity, insurance coverage, owned assets (too often outsourced), rapid response to critical timing, geographical expertise, owned worldwide offices (too often unnecessary and outsourced), and so forth.

Keeping project logistics under the EPCM umbrella can be regarded as a considerable profit center for the EPCM on the one hand, whereas on the other hand it clearly demonstrates the unfitness of the customers' executives, and the amazing unawareness of many project developers. By setting up a consistent and knowledgeable operations team, customers can hold serious discussions with the EPCM contractors, impose their own suppliers, and avoid many EPCM tactics – all while lowering costs along the supply chain and without being held accountable for potential delays throughout the construction phase. Design of construction and operation always leads the parties to hold discussions. However, the more extreme a project site is, the greater the chances a global EPCM firm has to impose its conditions at the project's expense, leading to higher OPEX and CAPEX.

3. Conclusions and suggestions

It becomes apparent that in order to successfully operate in Africa, a company needs to reengineer its priorities as well as lengthen the deadlines upon which the various milestones will be established. Africa turns out to be a different setting when compared to Latin America in that infrastructure and operations are more an aspiration than a tangible reality.

Even though these features are in general visible and understood by those corporations with interests on the continent, it does demand from the PMs abilities that are critical, have a strategic value, transactional leadership, and conflict management skills.

The first feature entails the values of patience, careful negotiations, understanding, and the ability to cede when necessary, along with a flexible approach to cross-cultural leadership realities. Aside from leadership, this is practically the opposite to what one may expect to need in a project across Latin America, where one has to make the best possible use of what is readily available in order to meet the deadlines. This is precisely where change and innovation have little to do with technical matters or productivity indexes, but are 100% connected with the way life goes on across West Africa. Here cultural flexibility and adaptability mean everything.

One example may help the reader better comprehend the concept. In Cameroon where, despite an oppressive heat, spitfire-type mosquitoes, yellow fever and dengue exposure, constant rain and humidity, the consulting tasks quickly evolved for better, mainly based on football empathy as Cameroon turned out to have a strong national soccer team. And while practically no employee had empathy and admiration for South Americans, when it came to soccer they were all great fans. Charisma was a dimension automatically assigned to the South American consultants because of this, which provided a great deal of help, collaboration, and empathy. Little was discussed about project operations, but there was much talk about soccer teams and players around South America.

The little time we authors had to discuss the project's challenges proved helpful for us to make a preliminary operations layout. The project infrastructure did not change because of our mutual sporting interests, but the consultants could survey all the available facilities in record time, while exchanging views on how to make the best out of an almost useless piece of infrastructure. Moreover, information exchange kept flowing between the job-site and the Latin American-based consultants well after they had left Cameroon, which turns out to be very rare, as we mentioned earlier in our discussion of communications. Having a common context is essential if communications are to be effective and tacit knowledge is to be exchanged. Also, research shows that when people share a conversation about a common interest, like soccer, work can creep in where it normally may not.

To be effective in managing conflict, the PM lead needs to have a long-term strategic view of operations, and goals, and of course should be supported by the BOD and executive team. The BOD and executive team should be in line with the relative speed of a project of this kind in a resource-poor region. All this may and will most likely lead the project to face a conflict sooner or later, with the federal and state governments as well as with agencies and even neighboring countries given the interests at stake. All of this requires that a PM lead have very different abilities than if working in the Northern Hemisphere, Latin America, or Asia.

Some conflict needs to be managed, and some conflict needs to be resolved. Conflict that needs to be managed is cognitive or intellectual conflict, such as two possible alternatives to a problem or two ideas about how to plan the work. Creativity needs conflict to flourish and enhances empowerment. It also can bring big possible benefits to the CPE, such as a new way to get materials on site, how to deal with corrupt local officials, or how to improve living conditions in a remote spot. It also provides the CPE lead with the ability to build trust amongst the members, demonstrate empathy, and create more effective communications. The Chinese have been very effective on this topic, as they are at present outperforming the USA, Canada, Australia, and even Europe as a bloc.

Negative conflict, whether racial, class, economic, or cultural, needs to be resolved. What we mean here by negative is the cultural conflict born of bias or stereotyping. In

India, there are laws forbidding the caste system, yet it continues to exist. Likewise in the USA, there are laws banning discrimination, yet it continues to exist. There is also, unfortunately, a world filled with cross-cultural social biases between countries. In such cases, the CPE lead must show his or her mettle. Such conflicts can easily contaminate the environment of the CPE for everyone and sow discontent. We rather think of such conflicts as an opportunity to show leadership. A long-term-based leadership view on the part of the CPE lead and staff requires a global understanding of both cross-cultural topics and Africa-related geopolitics.

Strategy, long term, and tactics, short term, are how one decides to engage with the other party in a conflict. Using the metaphor of playing poker and knowledge and diagnosis of oneself and the other party determines what cards one gets. Strategy and tactics are how one decides to play them. For small disputes, where relationships are not critical, the strategy may be to resolve a conflict in a single session. For larger disputes where relationships do matter, we suggest two or three sessions, and even multiple sessions a year, when railways and port construction have to be discussed and shared among a number of bordering countries. In the political arena, we suggest quarterly or monthly discussions to keep the relationship alive and healthy. Patience and negotiation resilience are critical traits for a CPE lead to rely upon. From our experience, conflict can actually be a blessing that enables the parties to forge stronger, more durable relationships. We strongly recommend that organizations avoid win-lose thinking on conflicts and appoint skillful individuals with a tangible track record in extreme settings.

To conclude, it is interesting to cite a global executive search organization's requisites to fill the post of a CPE lead for a USD200 million power transmission line project aimed at transmitting 1,300 MW of summer surplus hydroelectric power from Central Asia to power-short Pakistan and Afghanistan: "With dedicated assets to be constructed from the Kyrgyz Republic through Tajikistan and Afghanistan down to Pakistan, the project is being implemented under the authority of the four-nation Intergovernmental Council (IGC), composed of ministers from the four countries."

The project will be implemented via multiple interconnected construction contracts, including seven country-specific and several multicountry contracts. The CPE lead is expected to provide the overall leadership needed to ensure completion of all infrastructure works and associated activities, in accordance with the established time frame for project implementation. Leadership is of paramount importance if the appointed CPE lead is to diagnose and resolve construction and logistics problems that are not quickly solved. And she or he must do this under existing contractual arrangements as they arise and before they make any major impact on overall project cost or schedule. The key is leadership grounded in transmission construction experience.

Engineering and logistics in their different stages should be jointly considered, understood, and conceptualized as they both engulf the great majority of the critical variables CPE leads have to deal with when leading extreme projects. It becomes apparent that both the project developers and the executive search organization were very well aware of the intertwined role of the CPEL for this particular project.

9   Suggestions for practice

In this chapter, we provide a list of recommendations that pull together the lessons learned from our experience, based on decades of project management planning and execution around the world. The differences we have drawn between developed and emerging markets mainly refer to how suppliers, EPCM firms, indirect stakeholders, headquarter-based executives, local managers, contractors, or BODs respond to issues and global conditions. Here, we will focus on the interactions between people around the world that may be directly or indirectly connected with a project and somehow interested in its sustainability. We will focus on what we feel positive and yet has been negatively affecting the concepts of operational efficiency and sustainability, given a wrong understanding of the Project Management Body of Knowledge (PMBOK) guidelines. Or perhaps, from a positive perspective, projects undertaken with too simplistic a contextual assessment, or disregard for the cultures and values of the citizens.

Start with the basic questions of why this project is being done, just now, and how stakeholders, all of them, define success. Every organization involved in the endeavor should know the answer to these questions. This is in addition to the scope documents which define what is to be done and which in our view is more important. As a CPE lead, we suggest you repeat it, like a mantra, at every opportunity, for all organizations. This concept applies particularly to all those stakeholders involved in a project's supply chain who should ideally mirror the corporate values and global image of the project lead. And that assumes the project lead is a leader and has values consistent with international standards for CSR.

Those who minimize the impact a faulty, incomplete, or inadequate PSM could have on a project's probability of success are likely to regret their decisions during the execution phase – precisely the stage where any error is magnified from the planning stage. Most of the case studies deal one way or the other with stakeholder issues, during both the planning and executions phases where the differences and issues become evident. As Abraham Lincoln said, if you have 60 minutes to cut a tree, spend 40 of those minutes sharpening the ax. Mistakes during planning can often be fixed with an eraser; if delayed to execution, emotions and money will be required, as has been observed in most of the case studies.

When projects are undertaken, it is essential that the CPE lead accept the fact that the goals of the project may not be clear and that the participant organizations will have different timelines and individual goals. The CPE lead's responsibility is to recognize these differences, articulate them, and work to mitigate the resultant problems and changes through leadership. A CPE lead is often not in the position to fix such problems, as he or she may not have been part of the initial feasibility discussions and evaluations, and may not have the authority. In many cases, he or she may never know about challenges that the initial team considered during the deliberations of whether a project could be viable or about what risks could be involved. That does not excuse the CPE lead from engaging in a consistent quest to understand, even if well after the fact.

Some projects move from concept to initiation quickly to follow market changes. We have described a number of these changes and the perils that can arise if a long-term strategy is not the basis for determining viability. Often, markets will push decision makers into short-term thinking, results of which are seen in many of the case studies. Consider a development bank project, perhaps for providing privatized water for rural customers in Vietnam, and then go back and look at Figure 4.6 again. It is easy to imagine that the customer in Singapore may have started doing the long-term analysis say in 2010 as a potential project. Perhaps he does a 30-year operations program that requires a short-term construction effort. After discussions with banks, society, lenders, and other stakeholders, he decides to tender for services starting with a CPE lead. We will call this the long-term example.

Now think about a mining company that believes the price of gold will skyrocket within the next two years. To take advantage of this, it must construct a new mine, and the normal cycle time for doing this is, let's say, 16 months. So the pressure is on to get started with the design and construction as quickly as possible and to sort out the operational issues as the other work continues – a so-called fast-track approach. Again look at the stakeholders in Figure 4.6. There is no time to engage them, as this is short-term thinking; perhaps one can engage while the work is ongoing or do a so-called fast-track project. Assume there is a CPE lead who sees the increased risk in multiple areas (operations, society, environment, infrastructure, costs, etc.) and now must attempt to bring in the lower-tier organizations. What does the CPE lead tell these organizations? We will call this the short-term example.

In both of our examples, the CPE lead MUST understand and communicate the goals and risks, so that everyone knows the game. This may in fact be one of the greatest challenges for a CPE lead. Many of the case studies highlight a fundamental problem: operations are not well considered during the initial planning of a project or even early in the execution, as in the short-term example. Imagine that the customer does not want to divulge information about potential environmental issues until later, not withhold but just wait. Do you make these issues known to subcontracting organizations, knowing that there is a risk it will have a negative impact upon their work? Trust is the basis of leadership, and this is a quick way to lose it for the entire CPE as people talk.

There are no quick easy fixes or some checklist to follow; it is not that simple. Global projects encompass a great diversity of geographies, cultures, nationalities, values, and visions, which risks sustainability if all this is not adequately aligned, early in a project. Our best advice is to treat everyone the way you would like to be treated. A CPE lead cannot avoid every calamity and cannot control a customer or the impact any stakeholder may exert on a project's sustainability. But he or she can stand up and offer trust, truthfulness, and empathy as highlighted in various case studies. Here then are the suggestions and guidance we offer from our experience. They apply not only to extreme projects, but also to the hundreds of thousands of IT projects done every day in developed economies.

A. Unite the stakeholders

First, we suggest that you do a stakeholder assessment regularly, as different organizations will come online at different times and team members will change. This is particularly true for long-duration projects. It is a dynamic process, and no organization should believe that completing a PSM, with only a series of consultations, will be enough. This is a never-ending process that should be kept alive from concept through planning, execution, commissioning, and operation. Expect new demands, along with changes in stakeholder's and stakeholders' opinions throughout the project. We have provided an example template in Figure 9.1. This template provides example stakeholders, titles, organization, power (to help or hurt or control), and involvement or interest (frequent or sporadic), passive versus active management, what they want as far as frequency of updates and format (electronic or paper) are concerned, and action the CPE lead needs to take for each key stakeholder. Key stakeholders are identified by a ranking (PxI) and an arbitrary cutoff. In our example, we used 40, as you can see.

For key stakeholders, with rank above 40, the CPE lead needs to learn as much as she or he can about the stakeholder. Things such as culture, personality, religion (don't directly ask this; do it with subtleness so that you know what holidays they celebrate), names of family members (same as with religion especially in the Middle East), hobbies, sports they enjoy, and so on. This is not to be intrusive, but rather to provide opportunities to open communications and build trust, as we noted in the case studies. These people hold the key to success.

On projects in tribal areas, key stakeholders are the indigenous people, and they will likely not have a spokesperson who represents all the tribes. That should not be seen as an excuse to exclude them, but rather as an additional challenge to take the initiative to bring them together, all of them. Do not divide but unite. Dividing interests may seem an attractive option in the short run, as it appears things get done more quickly, but it is short sighted. However, by uniting interests, you may ensure that your tasks will withstand the upcoming pressures along the way, despite the fact that it may take a bit longer at the outset. Anyway, it demands close monitoring and corrections along the way. Never tend to believe or accept that a solved problem cannot lead to a new set of troubles. Monitoring is critical, and the CPE lead is like the captain of a supertanker; small short-term adjustments can make large changes long term.

The other caution we would like to issue is that the CPE lead should make it her or his responsibility to build the social communication infrastructure for indigenous communities that have none. Exactly the same idea as infrastructure is needed for construction and operations. One easy example comes from the developed world, where one would expect such things to be common. A project in close proximity to stakeholders' homes, some of which were children of US presidential candidates, had no association or spokesperson. They had a great deal of power, however. Taking our own advice, we built an interest group, helped them select a spokesperson, and kept them engaged weekly for well over two years. It was still a rough ride, but as we learned, they could have easily stopped the project in its tracks.

For small projects, performing a rigorous stakeholder analysis is not necessary. On large global projects, it is not unusual to have potentially thousands of stakeholders. Even hundreds are simply too many to manage. Figure 9.1 provides a simple way to filter down to identify the key stakeholders, and since the quantification of the dimensions is subjective, one must regularly review the matrix. As we have said above, circumstances change, as do stakeholders. Think of it as what is called span of control.

What that means is how many people should a CEO have reporting to her directly? Two might be too few, 100 is clearly too many. Most agree that somewhere between 7 and 15 is just right. The same concept applies here. A single person can only handle a limited number of so-called direct reports. It is better to do 15 stakeholders well than to do 100 poorly. Just make sure you do not miss a key one.

There will be different versions of short- and long-term success, and the job of the CPE lead is to understand all of them, communicate all of them, and strive to find a balance for all of them, all of the time. And never snub a stakeholder; treat each of them as the most important organization involved in, or effected by, the project. Make time to listen to stakeholders and do not promise what you know cannot be done. As the old saying goes: underpromise and overperform. Be honest and transparent, and when you make a mistake, own it and correct it – even if at the job-site and you may not be supported at the time. But perhaps later, depending on your abilities to persuade them, your strategies will lead to success long-term. Success lies in the small details and the way you communicate.

B. Communicate frequently, openly, and effectively

Don't just rely on scheduled formal reports or meetings; also seek opportunities to communicate, as we noted above. On the example project we described above, the local community was strongly against the project, so regular forums were scheduled to provide updates and to answer questions and concerns. These were minimum requirements for us, and we sought out opportunities to engage with individual key stakeholders in informal ways as well. The informal communications proved to be more effective in getting the message out and in building trust in the overall community than the regular meetings. The regular meetings were a way to engage those we did not know existed.

Open communications are a challenge in many cases. Imagine that an environmental impact report finds that the potential damage to the environment has a probability of $1/1,000,000$, but that if it happens it will be catastrophic. Does one tell the community this and then explain the steps being taken, or does one describe the steps being taken and then avoid providing the numeric probability if asked. We can tell you from having seen it done both ways that withholding will result in a lack of trust, and that will contaminate the remainder of the interactions. It is possible to get lucky, but better to take that bet to Las Vegas, as the odds are better.

A PM that intends to succeed while making his or her project sustainable needs to assign as much time as needed to speak to every key stakeholder and deliver a concrete message with respect to whatever issues have been brought to light. No matter how long this may take, and no matter either if other important aspects of the project, like technical issues, must wait, the CPE lead must devote the required time. Do not delegate this function to others. Every stakeholder deserves to be heard, regardless of their relative importance or potential influence. Determining the key stakeholders helps to determine where a CPE spends the time available. Even if he or she turns out to be a lone rider, there is nothing more important than the stakeholders – and they know it.

C. Become culturally flexible

Matrix-type project organizations require that their PMs be able to successfully negotiate with the many functional executives who are often located in their comfortable corporate offices, while the project offices are far away from civilization. Such a distance may cause the PM to neglect or be relaxed about the corporate vision, mission, or values, given the existing level of pressure, like fulfilling the deliverables on time and on budget. Moreover, a matrix-type decision-making process may include business, personal, societal, and microcultural issues, and PMs are often not totally prepared to assimilate, internalize, or confront these issues. Actually, most of the time PMs are not up to the task when trying to apply their knowledge and skills in emerging markets. Recurrent CAPEX updates on world-class projects prove the concept.

Global projects bring together different cultures and backgrounds not only across the regions or countries, but also within the same organization. Suppliers, EPCMs, governmental agencies, communities, consultants, bankers, insurers, and many more players do constitute a real blend of nationalities, backgrounds, cultures, and realities that provide different contextual experiences that each uses to take their decisions. And, each has his or her own personal expectations. The way a PM and team identify and channel them in the right direction may mean the difference between success and failure.

PMs must prepare and keep alert to deal with different goals and values, which oftentimes are unpleasant and even hostile, in order to cope with the challenges of a project, as we have noted above. Sometimes corporate resistance at the headquarters, internally in a matrix-type organization, turns out to be even more of a challenge than those at the job-site overseas. This means a PM must quickly learn to accept these facts and find ways to adapt, to make the best out of difficult situations.

We suggest one focus on two main aspects inside the organization. First, one should determine what kind of people you will interact with at the corporate level, when negotiating the resources you will need at the job-site. This becomes crucial for both a PM and the organization, in order to avoid resources constraints, conflicting personalities, or cultural gaps between the PM and the functional level executives. This often ends in the PM asking for more resources than are needed in order to provide a buffer against potential issues. The number of people at the job-site tends to grow bigger, as well as working capital and immobilized capital, because of this potential cat and mouse game.

Second, identify the stakeholders you will have to work with, as we have suggested previously, both within and outside of the organization. Also, getting to know a given culture prior to jumping into an overseas project is critical, as we have discussed. It helps identifying attitudes, responses, and gestures leading to an early identification of potential hidden agendas. This includes CPE leads, headquartered personnel, project site management, suppliers, and stakeholders in general. Corporations tend to prioritize the PM's technical knowledge and geographic track record. This often leads the corporation to assume PMs are acquainted with the local cultural traits, which are recognized and neglected at the same time by those at the headquarters. Often it is dismissed with an "okay, we know it is relatively important but not a top issue for our engineers to deal with." We strongly recommend that this is precisely the type of attitude that needs to be destroyed. Failing to allocate time and human resources to address cultural issues and bridge the numerous gaps is simply shooting oneself in the foot.

D. Identify, evaluate, and assign risks

Project Management is about taking risks. The case studies presented in this book describe a significant number of risk, that companies have to assume when approaching the emerging world. Risks may be less serious or easier to anticipate in places like the USA, Canada, Australia, Western Europe, or other developed regions and countries. As with stakeholder and cross-cultural management, risks may be anticipated and mitigated but rarely 100% avoided. The probability and impact differ much not only when comparing the emerging world with developed nations, but also within the emerging world even in a single region. One may assign a risk manager to every type of risk, depending on the magnitude of the project in question if the CAPEX is large enough to justify such a preventive structure. Otherwise, a risk manager position may carry out the work by gathering all the potential risks under a single department or functional area. Having a risk manager available is important, but at the end of the day it is the CPE lead that must take ultimate responsibility for identifying, evaluating, and assigning the risks.

Whatever the size and organization of a project, the emerging world is packed with risks. Many risks turn out to be of difficult classification, great volatility, and unique in terms of the potential damage they may exert on a given endeavor. However, we suggest an approach that addresses the following considerations. You may want to look back at Chapter 7 and Figure 2.4 as well for typical sources of risks. Since this material is critically important, we reiterate it here, as follows:

1. Identify, evaluate, assign

We suggest a simple approach to identifying risk. Every project should, at a minimum, decide if the risks shown in Figure 2.4 exist on every project. More can be done if desired, but these are a minimum. Then it is necessary to determine the risk ranking for the customer and key stakeholders. We prefer a scale of 0.00 (risk averse) to 1.00 (risk seeker). This part is essential.

Then each risk in Figure 4.15 is evaluated for probability of occurrence from 0.00 to 1.00 and for impact upon the project from 0.00 to 1.00. Then we multiply the two together. For example, let us say that a project in the Amazon is being conducted by an organization that has a risk profile of 0.60 on our scale. Assume we have determined that the risk of pollution has a probability of 0.70 and an impact on the local people of 0.90. We then compare 0.90 to our risk threshold of 0.60, and since it is a risk that exceeds our threshold, it must be evaluated and assigned, and managed actively.

In the evaluation, we would need to determine how we would manage the risk (avoid, mitigate, transfer, or accept), what the cost of the management would be, and who would be in the best position to manage it. Think of any of the case studies, and the answer becomes quite clear: someone who knows the local conditions and the person who has the trust of the local people. A manager in Toronto cannot manage a pollution issue in the upper Amazon – it needs to be handled by a local organization. So then, who should have this responsibility? It could be a local organization involved in this type of work; it could be the EPCM, a local contractor, or anyone else. How then does the risk get assigned to the organization selected? By negotiations and contract.

Imagine in our example that it is necessary to conduct a one-year training and education process to bring the local people into the project and make them feel they are part of the evaluation. If the risk is clearly identified, it can be negotiated and priced. Unfortunately, we often see such risk implied in a contract, so that it is not apparent to an uninformed bidder. This is why we keep harping on the issue of transparency. Let's assume the cost of this is USD1 million.

There are then consequential impacts if the risk is not managed like foregone revenues or completion penalties or delay in opening. Here it is possible to procure insurance for delayed operation, but it is pricey. Let us assume the insurance premium is USD5 million. Who is in the best position to purchase such coverage at the best possible rate – likely not the local organization, but possibly the customer, along with builders all risk. And who all are covered? What if a subcontractor to a subcontractor produces a poor quality weld that causes a minor spill?

Our point is that doing a reasonable job of risk identification, evaluation, and assignment is a time-consuming effort. There are 28 risks listed in Figure 2.4, and those are mostly categories. We have seen projects that have a listing of hundreds of risks. It is not possible to manage this number. At most, 12 would be optimistic. So to return to what we said earlier, you really need a risk profile to determine if the risk needs to be actively managed. If in our example the risk of currency transfer has a probability of 0.40 and an impact of 0.80, our combined score is 0.32. This is below our risk profile of 0.60, so we leave it on the list and manage it passively. Then watch to see that it does not change. There is no need for an exhaustive exercise; take the risk and keep an eye on it.

2. *Expertise*

Don't try to extrapolate expertise with a certain risk, or group of risks, on the basis of north-south or developed-developing nations. This is a typical mistake we have seen too often, especially across those large global organizations which believe that – owing to their own arrogance or ignorance, depending on the way you look at it – their global nature grants them the needed credentials to overcome whatever risks they encounter. Our advice here is to hire locals who can transfer their knowledge to the corporate risk executives and the CPE lead. No matter how many times corporate executives have dealt with inflation rates, hard currency transfer bans, tricky central bank regulations, royalty schemes, customs clearance legislation, or public deficits, each location is unique. All these risks are culturally influenced and precisely the component that needs to be transferred from the local expert to the CPE.

We do suggest one hire or assigning a CCO, Chief Compliance Officer, to ensure that risk managers are doing their job 24/7. A CQO, Cultural Intelligence Officer, should be hired to help guarantee there are no wrong messages and interpretations, that the team understands one another and the community, and that the communications are effective. As we said before and reemphasize, we recommend the CPE lead be the CQO, unless the project is too large and complex.

Too often, global organizations make the same mistake: they proceed with the acquisition of what they regard as a fantastic project, based on its potential deliverables and a given market demand. Its fundamentals may be brilliant, causing the BOD and executive management team to move fast towards an acquisition, merger, joint venture, alliance, or partnership of some sort. We have presented several case studies about this matter across Latin America, Africa, and Asia. However, infrastructure limits posed by the ongoing economic situation in many regions are often either overlooked or minimized by assuming the project's fundamentals justify such a move. The truth is that infrastructure restrictions should be identified as a risk and that its probability and impact be duly quantified prior to committing any money to such efforts. Overcoming the lack of suitable roads, ports, railways, waterways, energy sources, or any consumables is directly linked with the political and institutional conditions of the country where the project is located. Members of a BOD and corporate executives are either seldom knowledgeable of these restrictions, or they just see them as items to be worked out at a later stage – the fast-track idea.

Again, no matter how global your experience may be or how knowledgeable your engineering team has become over the years of global activity, you need expert regional eyes. You need people who can easily visualize how high the exit barriers of a project may become, or if those barriers can be expected to be brought down in a reasonable period of time. And you need to determine if future barriers are likely to arise out of the blue, which should not be surprising in emerging markets. Hire the locals and try to capture their knowledge quickly so that the knowledge-transfer process gets optimized and the risks diminished. However, be aware that while locals are important, they should not be regarded as genies in a lamp. Make sure you have their views and opinions duly cross-checked. Rogues and opportunists are everywhere, and here, again a CQO may earn his or her salary here alone.

3. *Political wisdom*

Your CPE lead and risk manager, if you have one, need to understand quite well the ongoing political system and environment, as well as the local tendency to make abrupt changes when circumstances require it in emerging markets. A typical example is a country whose public spending surpasses its income revenues, leading the politicians to look for alternative sources of revenue, or what is usually regarded as the easiest way, changing the rules. In other words, rising taxes, demanding anticipated revenue transfers, compelling developers to become connected with the state governments' appointed agency that wants to raise import fees for capital goods turn out to be good examples on the way politics may impact project development plans. Connecting the passage of laws targeted at certain infrastructure investments may help politicians rank better in the polls.

Any of these risks can well be anticipated, and therefore mitigated, provided that an expert eye has been appointed and utilized. Do not try to extrapolate experiences from country to country, but rather treat every project as unique while trying to learn from it. A CPE and political risk manager should, by all means, have a look at the ruling party's track record in terms of institutionalism. This is an issue most projects erroneously tend to leave for later. In the USA, studies show that for every 1 dollar spent, an organization benefits by 20 dollars when utilizing lobbyists. Before Hong Kong reverted to China, an organization we worked with hired a well-connected, individual to manage our affairs in the mainland. When the British left Hong Kong, guess who the first administrator was – yes our man. Politics is important.

4. *Procurement*

Procurement is a global activity that involves knowing who the primary suppliers are across the Northern Hemisphere and where to find reliable secondary suppliers across the emerging world. It also encompasses the ability to anticipate the outsourced countries where some parts of capital equipment will be manufactured under the guidelines of its main customer. Along with this is the way the entire logistic processes will be designed and carried out from the various origins up to the project site. In addition, frequently there will be so-called favorite son firms, or import/export banks that have a say in who is on the list of potential suppliers. One example was that an organization we worked with had the Bin Laden Group assigned as a *preferred* vendor.

All this cannot be undertaken in isolation but rather must be linked with the previous dimensions, be it stakeholder management, cross-cultural management, or knowledge sharing and transfer. Some recommendations follow. First, keep a broad view. PMs and their teams tend to classify logistic operators mostly on the basis of their geographical track record, existing facilities near the project, and a network of offices in the host country and globally. Even though this approach may have its merits, it is pretty much what the elementary manual on logistics says – zero innovation, zero differentiation. By limiting oneself to a given geographical area, various potentially valuable extraregional suppliers who could enrich the operations by bringing in best practices may not be included.

This is often the case on the grounds of a firm not counting on its own offices, not having a particular certification, or not owning the required facilities near the project site. Sometimes this happens to be a very convenient argument to get rid of potential contenders. Here executive management should keep their eyes on the procurement team. Moreover, tight financial restrictions that are supposed to filter those organizations having modest turnover compared to global firms may work as an insurmountable barrier which otherwise would enable other valuable operators to qualify.

Requisites and conditions to bid or qualify to integrate a tier one, two, or three type of supplier may turn out to be time consuming and excessively rigorous. Even though our experience indicates that extrapolations should be avoided, there are circumstances where exemptions become advisable on the grounds of seniority and expertise. Our recommendation is to keep an open mind when selecting logistic suppliers and try to get the right blend when it comes to culture, facilities, network, and expertise.

In our experience, segmentation based on expertise pays off by far more than if based on structure or global network. Procurement officers must be wise and try to bring value to the project, not just global networks with impressive brochures. At the end of the day, cost optimization and operational timing are what counts. Moreover, liabilities when contracting should be shared by various officers and departments as a way to avoid inducing officers to always contract for the most global and financially sound. If contractual liabilities are detailed and planned as we have suggested, you provide your procurement team with more freedom and less pressure to decide on potential suppliers. Not a single individual should be liable for a given supplier, but rather a team of professionals. Too often suppliers are selected based on the impressive structure and image they project. But mostly because should anything go wrong, it was one of the world's largest companies that failed and not the one that selected the company. We do suggest that procurement officers and executive management give procurement a second look if OPEX optimization is a target.

5. Look beyond the obvious

Contracting with an EPC organization is not an easy task, as it demands the evaluation of a rather long list of variables: engineering track record, corporate reputation, specialization degree on a given type of construction, CSR strategies, TBL approach, supply-chain strategies, environmental programs, and corporate governance. These are some of the variables that stand out. However, an increasing number of companies do prefer to rely on EPCM organizations with great contacts around the world, despite the fact that they may not deliver the best quality in a specific emerging location. Conflictive and unstable environments usually suggest considering a regionally focused EPCM, which may have a tight grip on the manpower, unions, supply-chain suppliers, and the like. It is often assumed, or believed, that a well-known global EPCM organization may impose stability and certainty during the construction stage of a project. This may be so in some countries, but it is not necessarily true in all. On the contrary, it may become a quality problem and also may alter relationships on the project.

Domestic-focused EPCM organizations tend not to improve the quality of its deliverables, given that most projects will sooner or later come to them for assistance. The PM should first have a look at the leadership style and the culture of a given EPCM organization, as well as the acceptance level or reputation the EPCM has with both suppliers and stakeholders. Having a Hernán Cortez leadership style, may render positive short-term outcomes, though it is likely to lead the project to face serious incidents long term. It may also ultimately affect the project's sustainability, shareholders, and corporate value. It is advisable for CPE leads not to simply accept the relative importance and influence a given EPCM organization may allege to possess. Most of the world is uncertain and unstable, and this is why one should become more discriminating at the time of awarding a contract. We suggest always keeping the long view and looking at the forest rather than the trees.

6. *Excessive bureaucracy*

Organizations that become obsessed with the selection process by adding more and more requisites to their tier 1 to 10 supplier classification program should give their systems a second thought. These systems too often become a burden for those who have to go through them to bid for a project. Such systems turn out to be confusing, time consuming, and discouraging, and may sometimes be regarded as close to ridiculous. This is bad news for both the EPCM and the supplier, as it makes room for discretional practices, and bad reputation; most importantly, it hinders both sides from optimizing their deliverables. Our recommendation here is to keep it as simple as possible and to be crystal clear on the selection criterion, while leaving room for special projects. A special or extreme project may be defined as the one taking place in a remote area lacking the elementary infrastructure or a place where financial or customs clearance restrictions demand either a local specialized organization, or a global corporation capable of financing the entire construction stage.

We have seen many cases where bidding practices such as this result in higher prices, risks, legal disputes, and loss of reputation. In domestic markets, informed organizations know their competition, and pricing structures. What every project should desire are bids that reasonably reflect the level of effort, quality, and risk required, along with a fair profit. An organization's reputation will determine the price paid for services. If it is perceived to be inequitable, arbitrary, or nontransparent, the prices quoted will be higher.

Whether you are an EPCM, offshore oil and gas operator, mining explorer, iron ore producer, wind farm developer, or nuclear power plant executive in charge of supply chain, we recommend that you keep an eye on the procedures and keep them as flexible and open as possible. The more complex and bureaucratic the system is, the more room for discretion and assumptions. Moreover, sometimes it is the procurement executive who builds an intricate system of suppliers' classification and selection ranging from tier one to, say, tier 10 as a way of gaining projection and relevance within the organization, as well as to hinder outsiders from interfering in the work he or she does. While it is a very human behavior, it can prove expensive and totally useless from an effectiveness standpoint. You should by all means avoid falling into this trap. Again, keep it simple, transparent, and efficient. This will encourage suppliers to come along and bring value to a project, instead of what normally happens when valuable suppliers grant priority to other projects with straightforward procedures and clearer guidelines.

7. Compliance

Last but not least, we recommend that organizations hire, train, and deploy Chief Compliance Officers to regularly visit and survey their projects across the emerging world. Lots of hidden agendas would become easily identified and could be dismantled earlier. In doing so, cultural gaps should be first worked out, and perhaps a more perfect understanding about the way a systemic project operates be achieved. This is essential to make it work and to optimize it. Depending on its size, a CCO could also be assisted and complemented by a CQO. Such a person is not easy to find, as this individual should not also be acquainted with both home and destination cultures and languages. This person should also understand the entire set of rules, regulations, uses and customs, written and unwritten rules that normally float around a project in an emerging context. We do recommend that the CPE lead have a background in COO and CQO, and that if the project budget will permit, hire a separate COO and CQO to support the CPE lead. This is the best way to keep surprises at the minimum and optimize both OPX and CAPEX figures.

E. How to establish leadership in extreme projects

1. Knowledge

A CPE lead that is appointed to work in an emerging market, which is usually remote, poor, harsh, and modest in facilities, must be knowledgeable in the technical fields associated with the project. He or she should also be knowledgeable about the cultures involved with the project and the political environments, including the job-site. He or she should have good self-knowledge, be curious, and be respectful. Whether this individual holds a MSc in Mining, Manufacturing Process, Oil Drilling, Metallurgy, Structural Engineering, or Business, he or she must get along with the local, operators, suppliers, and neighbor communities. Technical knowledge will help him or her gain respect in the short run, but the long run requires a wider spectrum of abilities that may come to be defined by all the cultural traits we have referred to earlier. Having technical knowledge in itself means little if it is not backed up by a general understanding of the context that surrounds one. And, most importantly, one must have the attitude and willingness to cope with the uncertain and change, without losing one's temper at the first opportunity. One will always find, for different reasons, people very interested in you biting the hook. This is leadership, and no room for improvisations please.

2. Good willingness

A CPE lead who pretends to successfully carry out a technical task in an emerging context should by all means avoid back and forth travel. He or she must remain at the job-site from the very outset until the job is finished or can be reasonably delegated to a third party. The CPE lead must share the facilities with the local employees and communities, share their food and drink, dress simply, and understand and respect local codes and values prior to wetting a foot on the ground, share cigarettes and drinks, exchange war stories and experiences from far away projects, and so on. In brief, a CPE lead should spend whatever time necessary to show empathy and most importantly to consolidate trust. Trust is the key element for success. This is leadership. However, in our experience, we seldom see CPE leads stay for long periods of time around the site. This is obviously a big mistake, which should, by all means, be avoided. Actually, whoever loves staying at the base camp might be the ideal candidate. A real CPE lead, and not a five-star cable TV-style hotel lover, is needed. Naturally, one needs training, which is a critical component for the corporation to undertake before the planning phase.

3. Resourcefulness

A CPE must fight to get the resources he or she needs in a way that is heard by subordinates and collaborators across the base camp. Let the rumor mill spread the word across the camp. One should not act like General MacArthur when he announced he was getting back to the Philippines. Always, act with compassion and tact, and ensure that your voice spreads out. Struggles or negotiations with headquarters and suppliers must encompass not only the delivery of pipes, generators, transformers, or tools, but most important those consumables that will be appreciated by all those who live at the base camp. The site personnel whose expectations are based on the day they leave should always be given priority, whereas the consumables should be ensured to be on hand at any time given the remoteness of the job-sites. Food and drinks as well as a good cook are the best ever known formula to avoid a mutiny aboard a ship. A base camp is not different, except for the water. Simple things like these are of great help in showing compassion and empathy and in building trust, cooperation, and successful results. This is also leadership, with the CPE lead a bit of a professor, confessor, friend, psychologist, and guide. Never forget this advice.

4. Teamwork

A CPE lead should not dictate what needs to be done when building a team. In practice, this is a concept that must be initiated, encouraged, fostered, tailor-made, and monitored to make it happen. It is not magic but the result of a process. To lead one must serve, and the Japanese idea of consensual decision making is a good way to start. The GLOBE survey found people everywhere want to be more empowered to make their own decisions. This sort of individualism can and should exist side by side with consensus, to build a team spirit. Leading by example is the way to begin building the desire to work as a team. This consideration is especially important when multiple organizations, with multiple goals and timeframes are involved.

Communicating effectively is essential, and teamwork will never be achieved if the previous concepts of knowledge, goodwill, and resourceful individuals are not in place. Teamwork works well to guard against bad behavior. It helps to avoid gradually falling into corrupt habits that may look harmless at an early stage but that later may become an unstoppable snowball. It helps identify visible and subtle risks in the process. It also helps in dealing with communities and negative stakeholders in a more positive manner. It forms part of the company's assets when trying to attract a joint-venture partner or ally to continue with the project development. This is leadership as well. It is not about yelling and giving orders as is done in the army, but working together and focusing on the planning stage as much as possible to avoid facing unpleasant surprises later. True leaders are not easy to find. It takes a long time to shape a true leader capable of successfully deploying his or her abilities across remote, unpredictable, and often dangerous emerging markets.

Global corporations, no matter the field in which they are active in, should consider the leaders they count on, if they are available, and where to find them, when assessing the financial and commodity fundamentals of a project. They should engage those present or future CPE leads in training programs in full accordance with the regions and countries they believe will be operating on in the months and years to come. They should also make certain that the CPE lead participates in the initial negotiations for the project, review of the contracts, planning with all the key stakeholders, execution while living at the job-site, commissioning, construction of infrastructure, community relations, and at least the start of operations. The PMBOK limits, projects having a distinct start and finish, for a CPE lead is not workable and is not advisable.

After all, planning is the most important phase of a project and deserves a delicate approach during its initiation phase. They should keep this in mind as a way to better face what the future may bring with respect to extreme projects across the emerging world.

Index

Africa or African 3, 41, 77, 81–82, 104–105, 108, 110, 117, 171, 174–175, 177; North Africa 116, 120; East Africa 163; West Africa 104, 163, 171, 174, 176; South Africa 32, 45–46, 104
aircraft 6–8, 10, 15, 90, 108
alliances 30, 54–55, 58, 59, 116–117, 146, 174
American Carriage of Goods by Sea Act 12
Australia or Australian 36, 45, 66, 77, 82, 86, 97, 104, 114, 133–134, 136, 140, 149, 151–152, 156, 159–161, 164, 171, 174, 176, 183

barges 3, 5–6, 9, 10–12, 16, 23, 51, 54–55, 57–58, 64, 83, 86–87, 90–91, 93, 135–138, 140–142, 145, 149, 155
berths 6, 12, 62, 67, 75, 145
BOD 7, 18, 32, 44, 61–62, 80, 82, 86, 89, 92–93, 95–96, 101, 103, 151, 155, 157, 159–160, 169, 176, 179, 184–185
BOT 94–95
breach 32, 47, 136, 159–160
breakwater 62, 66, 79
bridge or bridges 6, 66, 70, 77, 88, 101, 104, 107, 114, 117, 124, 164–168, 182; cultural bridge 140, 149, 151; land-bridge 22, 107, 115–116, 119, 124, 127; professional bridge 125
budget 3, 6, 11, 18, 23, 25, 38, 59, 86, 89–91, 95, 132, 142, 149, 156, 161, 168, 182, 188

Canada 1–3, 8, 20, 34, 36, 38, 40, 45–47, 50–51, 53–58, 60, 71, 76–77, 89, 92, 109, 128, 157, 176, 183
capacity 10, 25, 42, 61, 66, 71, 80, 81, 86, 93, 133, 140, 146, 153, 175
carrying capacity 14–15, 39, 62, 67, 73, 75, 136; lifting capacity 94, 138; load capacity 8; manufacturing capacity 72
CAPESIZE 66, 68, 70, 78–81, 124
CAPEX 21, 23, 30, 45–46, 62, 74, 76, 81, 84, 86, 88, 90, 92–93, 95, 101, 151, 154, 165, 167, 174–175, 182, 183, 188
CCO 2, 40, 82, 92, 96, 104, 109, 125, 169, 188
CEO 3, 22, 82, 103, 131, 143, 146, 181
Cameroon 104, 163, 171–174, 176

Central African Republic 171, 174
Central America 36, 46, 50, 108
challenges 1, 17, 23, 31–32, 40, 43–44, 48, 52, 59, 72, 76–77, 79, 92, 100–102, 155, 166, 171, 176, 179, 182; cultural challenges 5, 108; logistical challenges 86, 96, 164–165, 174; operational challenges 2, 4, 71, 81–82, 84, 164, 170; regional challenges 24
change 2, 17, 20, 34, 37, 43, 47, 50, 53, 85, 92, 96–97, 118, 126, 129, 135, 141, 149, 154, 161, 167, 176, 180, 184, 188
charter 11–13, 53, 55, 81, 137, 141, 164
child labor 26, 28, 32
collaborate 4, 145–146
commitment 5, 20, 33–34, 44, 49, 52, 57, 62, 67, 89, 92–93, 102, 104, 116, 120, 134–135, 137, 140, 143, 146, 151, 154, 159
communication 1, 4–6, 19, 23, 28, 30–31, 39, 42–44, 48, 56, 58, 93, 96, 103–104, 110, 112, 121, 148, 151–153, 155, 160, 176, 180–181, 184
compassion 151, 189
consortium 86, 89, 113
container 13, 39, 56, 60, 62, 74–75, 87, 92, 94, 107, 115–116, 123, 128–130, 164, 168
container terminal 67–68
containerized 54, 88, 90, 112
contingency 26, 41–42
contingency plan 27, 30–31, 85, 88–90, 97, 149, 151, 161, 170
contractor 19, 27, 32, 35, 40, 47, 55, 58, 84, 86, 88, 93, 94–95, 104, 114, 170, 175, 178, 183
corruption 7, 21, 25, 31–32, 43, 104, 110, 114, 161
CPE 3, 18–21, 34, 105–106, 112, 116, 121, 125, 131–132, 139, 146, 151–152, 155, 176–177
CPEL 3, 4, 27, 31–34, 104, 128, 155, 177
CPE lead (same as CPEL) 20, 43, 45, 49–50, 59, 72, 103, 114, 117, 126, 176–185, 187–190
CQ 126
CQO 149–150, 160, 184–185, 188
creativity 110, 153, 176
CSR 22, 25–26, 28–29, 31–34, 42, 45, 57, 97, 178, 186

culture 2, 4–5, 8, 19, 31, 41, 45, 46–47,
    50, 58–59, 98, 100, 102–104, 113–132,
    145, 149–153, 155, 157, 167, 179–180,
    182, 186, 187; Local customs 12, 20, 93;
    Organizational culture 131
customer 16, 21, 28, 42, 48, 51–55, 57, 67, 79,
    85, 90–91, 105–106, 135, 139, 174–175, 179,
    183–185
customs clearance 39–41, 77, 82, 86, 88, 91,
    93–94, 96, 108–112, 123, 149, 184

demurrage 10–11, 13, 39–41, 43, 89, 92
developed world 2, 5, 26, 77, 102, 104, 156,
    158, 180
dispute 23, 57, 85–86, 99, 105–106, 121, 152,
    159, 161, 177, 187
Democratic Republic of Congo (DRC)
    171–174
DSO 172–174

EIA 45, 62, 67
emerging markets 7, 179, 182, 185, 190
emerging world 5, 25, 41, 44, 77, 94, 96, 98,
    102, 156, 174, 183, 185, 188, 190
empathy 19, 41, 102–104, 112, 132, 146, 151,
    176, 179, 189
environment 17, 24, 33, 38, 42–43, 46, 51–53,
    55–59, 66–67, 70, 73, 82, 108, 116, 120,
    121–124, 131, 134, 137, 145, 151, 156, 161,
    177, 179, 181, 185; jungle environment 9,
    14, 18–19, 27–29
EPC 27, 175, 186
EPCM 37–39, 86, 89–93, 95–97, 101, 103,
    108–109, 135, 157, 170, 173, 175, 178, 183,
    186–187
EQ 125, 152
ETA 16
ethics 2, 20–22, 31, 36, 41, 43, 59, 72, 97,
    102, 131

federal 2, 26, 36, 38, 44, 53, 67, 71–72, 96–97,
    99, 103, 108–110, 151, 176
force majeure 12, 48, 80
foreign 5, 8, 14, 19–20, 22, 42, 47, 58, 86, 124,
    135–136, 149, 171, 174
foreign based executives 43–44, 58, 76
foreign based firm 5, 19, 41
foreign corrupt practices act 22
foreign organization 8, 14, 23, 29, 49, 55,
    98–99, 146, 151
foreign waters 59
freight 39, 54, 56, 78, 115, 128–129, 133–134,
    136, 144, 169
FS 45
FSTS 70, 78–81

GANTT 101
Gabon 104, 171–174

gestures 4, 104, 124, 149–151, 153, 182
GPS 16

Hague and Hamburg Rules 12
health 14, 29–31, 33, 47, 57–58, 87, 89–90, 108,
    112, 149, 158, 166
highways 108
HL 166, 169

indigenous communities 2, 8, 14–15, 19,
    22–23, 26, 28, 30–32, 34, 40, 56, 58, 64–65,
    71, 88, 91, 124–125, 148–149
infrastructure 2, 21, 37, 53, 56, 58, 61–84, 92,
    94, 100–111, 115–116, 121, 135, 137, 139,
    148–149, 163–164, 171–176, 179–180,
    184–185, 190; lack of infrastructure 1,
    22–23, 49, 89, 166
innovation 24, 26, 36, 52, 97, 104, 122, 140,
    146, 156, 158, 160–170, 176, 186
investment 24, 44, 51, 53, 56, 61, 71–72, 75–76,
    79, 82, 93, 99, 102, 110, 112–113, 135, 151,
    154, 170, 174–175, 185
invoices 20, 41, 120, 122, 126, 129–131, 168
IT 28–30, 93–94, 103, 110, 130, 152, 171, 179

JV 105

knowledge 5, 18–20, 23, 31, 34–35, 41–42, 44,
    53, 58–59, 81–83, 86, 89, 92, 95, 96–98, 100,
    109, 117, 126, 131, 143–146, 154–157, 164,
    170, 175, 177–178, 182, 184–186
knowledge acquiring 7, 38–39, 102
knowledge traditional 12–13, 55, 130, 136
knowledge tacit 137, 139, 152, 176
KPI 3, 13, 19, 52

language 31, 96, 102–105, 113–114, 153
language body 4, 9, 126, 152, 155, 157
LATAM 184
LAYDAY 13, 169
leader
leadership
legal 12, 23, 43, 45, 47, 99, 117, 142, 160, 187
listen 30, 42, 103, 125, 152–153, 181
loading 3, 13, 16, 57, 60–62, 64, 66, 69, 75, 78,
    80, 91, 93, 111, 123–124, 128, 133, 138, 144,
    163, 168–169, 172
logistics 3, 7, 22–23, 38–40, 46, 54, 56, 62, 73,
    76–77, 81, 91–92, 94, 97, 101, 104, 108,
    110, 127, 133, 137, 146, 156–157, 164, 169,
    174–175, 177, 186
lump-sum 12, 16, 24, 86, 91, 95

management 18, 20, 27, 30, 38–40, 42–44, 47,
    51–52, 54, 58, 61, 64, 75, 77, 88, 91–92, 94,
    96–97, 119, 129–131, 134–135, 140, 148, 158,
    160, 161, 165, 168, 172, 174–175, 180, 184;
    Cross-cultural management 1, 36, 102, 124,

183, 186; Environmental management 2, 29;
Operations management 95, 116, 128, 154,
164, 170; Procurement management 23;
Project management 5, 21, 26, 35, 49, 81,
153, 178, 182; Stakeholder management 32,
34, 46, 48, 76, 106, 128, 143–144, 150, 156
marine 50, 52–53, 55–58, 62–63, 76, 87, 91,
116, 160
marine terminals 61, 66, 70–71, 73–74, 77, 116,
119, 129, 171
metaphor 126, 177
micro culture 125, 182
mines 29, 37, 72, 77–80, 101, 112, 133, 146
modality 7, 89, 115
MTPA 60–61, 64, 66, 68, 72, 74, 172
multinational 29, 120, 132, 141, 144, 164

OD 166, 169
oil and gas 1–3, 6, 13–14, 29, 34, 44, 51–57, 71,
91, 109, 156, 158, 187
oil spill 26, 29, 32, 56–57, 184
OPEX 21, 30, 43–44, 73–76, 81, 86, 90, 92–93,
95, 97, 101, 110, 125, 154, 165–166, 169,
175, 186
owner 4, 10, 12–14, 28, 38, 77, 81, 94, 99, 120,
128–130, 134, 139, 143, 163, 169

PANAMAX 62, 64, 66, 70, 74, 76, 133
penalties 10–11, 16, 18, 22, 47, 136, 184
permit 93, 188
PMO 81, 156
PNG 149, 157–161
political 2, 19, 22, 35–36, 38, 45, 46–47, 49–50,
56, 71–72, 83, 85, 99, 108, 110, 118, 143,
156, 160, 174–175, 177, 184–185, 188
ports 1, 12, 37–38, 45–46, 60–61, 64, 72, 74,
77–79, 82, 85, 87–88, 90–91, 93–94, 104,
107–109, 115, 128, 133, 135, 171, 174, 184
PPP 4, 56, 105, 117, 164–165, 168, 170
procedures 18, 31–32, 74, 84, 87–88, 109, 119,
187–188
procurement 23, 27–29, 36, 41, 44–45, 92, 144,
149, 154–155, 168, 185–187
productivity 8, 11, 13, 15, 62–63, 69, 71, 111,
122, 133, 169, 176
program 1, 3, 11, 17–19, 21–22, 24, 32, 38, 40,
42, 45, 51, 57, 60, 62, 73, 75, 79, 96–98, 108,
116, 128, 133, 149, 151, 156–158, 165–166,
171, 179, 186–188

QHSE 58

rail 55, 115, 119
railway 51–52, 60–63, 67–68, 71–77, 83, 101,
104, 107–108, 123–125, 135, 143, 163,
171–174, 177, 184
relationship 4, 14, 20, 33, 39, 42, 51, 57, 59, 81,
94, 105, 123, 129, 137, 151, 161, 177, 187

remote 4, 7, 24, 26, 36, 44–45, 56, 71, 73, 77,
84, 88, 92, 108, 111–115, 148, 157, 175–176,
187–190
reputation 24, 26, 28–29, 47, 57, 80, 95–96,
134, 152, 157, 186–187
RFQ 37
risk 2, 4–5, 10–11, 16, 24–25, 28, 30, 32, 34,
37–38, 42, 46–48, 59, 62, 64, 72, 80–81, 83,
86, 89–90, 95–96, 99, 101, 108, 114–115,
133, 143–144, 146–147, 149, 151, 154,
156–161, 164–165, 169–170, 172, 174, 179,
182–185
rituals 126
rotorcraft 1
ROV 157

safety 10, 14, 30, 47, 51, 57–58, 87, 89–91, 108,
112, 149, 158, 166
SB 169
schedule 6, 21, 58, 81, 89, 93, 137, 141, 143,
153, 177, 181
scope 27, 42, 51, 90, 107–108, 130, 137, 179
servant leadership 112, 132
service provider 16, 18, 53–55, 91, 105–106
shipping 38, 40, 52–54, 66, 75, 79, 82, 84, 87,
92, 107, 115, 123, 133–135, 138–141, 148,
155, 161, 163, 165, 169, 173
shipping ocean 12, 21
shipping organizations 81, 116, 127–128
shipping operations 69, 172
SLO 34, 98–100, 153, 155, 158, 171
SMS 159
social 20
South America 3, 5, 7, 8–9, 18, 23–24, 26,
29, 37, 41, 77–78, 84, 104–105, 115–116,
120–121, 128–130, 149, 176
SP 169
stakeholder 24–26, 29–30, 37–38, 42–43, 45,
49–50, 53, 62, 64, 67, 72–77, 80, 82, 85, 90,
92–95, 101, 105–106, 112, 126, 131, 139,
141, 145–146, 149–151, 154–155, 157–158,
160, 175, 183, 187, 189, 190
stakeholder key or primary 144, 166, 180–181
storage 17, 70, 87, 91, 128, 165, 168–169
strategy 1, 3, 5, 7, 19, 23–24, 28, 29, 31, 33–34,
36, 38, 40–41, 44, 46, 49–52, 55, 59, 93,
100, 110, 112–116, 120, 122–124, 127, 131,
139–140, 151, 155, 159, 161, 167, 172
strategy cross-cultural management 102, 124
strategy long-term 129–130, 132, 177, 179
strategy operations 82–83, 96
strike 13, 40, 42–43, 47, 89, 99, 121, 123,
133–134
structures 4, 121, 128–129, 136, 187
subcontractors 114, 184
sullivan principles 20, 25, 32, 34
supplier 6, 7, 9–11, 13, 17–20, 28, 30, 32, 36,
39–41, 43–45, 47, 49, 66, 77, 85, 88–92, 101,

103, 109, 119, 130–131, 133–135, 140, 144, 148, 151, 173, 175, 178, 182, 185–189

supply-chain or value chain 40–41, 44, 62, 64, 100, 105, 117, 134, 137, 140, 175, 179, 187

survey 9, 64, 68, 73, 82, 87–89, 93, 117–118, 120, 122–123, 166, 176, 188–189

surveying 61–62, 68, 71, 78, 89, 92

sustainable 21, 23–26, 33, 35, 47, 72, 79–80, 108, 110, 128, 141, 146, 160–161, 169–170, 172, 175, 181

SWOT 65, 90

terminals 2, 61–62, 64, 66, 70–71, 73–77, 83, 87–88, 116, 119, 128–129, 133, 135, 144–145, 171

transfer 4, 16, 19, 44, 47, 49, 53, 58, 59, 61, 64, 67–68, 70, 73, 77, 79, 81–83, 87–88, 91, 93–94, 100, 102, 119, 123, 145–146, 157, 181, 183–186

transformation 19, 130–132, 143–145

transparency 13, 15, 17–20, 31, 34, 44–45, 47, 91, 175, 183

tribal 26, 28, 30, 99, 124, 150, 180

triple bottom line 20, 24, 35

trust 13, 18–20, 29–30, 34, 41–43, 48, 50, 87, 99, 103–104, 108, 112–114, 121, 131–132, 137, 142, 145–146, 151–154, 156, 175–176, 179–181, 183, 189

user 4, 15, 59, 74–76, 87, 105–106

virtual teams 3, 19

vision 20, 29–31, 34, 42, 49, 51–53, 56, 58, 82, 96, 104, 114, 130–131, 146, 148–149, 156, 174, 182

warehouse 16–17, 72–73, 93–94, 112–113, 116, 119, 130, 163

weather 16, 18, 22, 37, 40–41, 46, 81, 84, 86, 87–90, 93, 120, 123–124, 137, 161, 163, 166, 173

XLQ 126